Mordecai & Me
An Appreciation of a Kind

Joel Yanofsky

Red Deer PRESS

The Concordia University Chair
in Canadian Jewish Studies

Copyright © 2003 Joel Yanofsky
Published in the United States in 2004

All rights reserved. No part of this publication may be reproduced, stored in a retrieval system or transmitted, in any form or by any means, without the prior written permission of Red Deer Press or, in case of photocopying or other reprographic copying, a licence from Access Copyright (Canadian Copyright Licensing Agency), 1 Yonge Street, Suite 1900, Toronto, ON M5E 1E5, fax (416) 868-1621.

The Publishers
Red Deer Press
813 MacKimmie Library Tower
2500 University Drive N.W.
Calgary Alberta Canada T2N 1N4
www.reddeerpress.com

Credits
Edited for the Press by Norman Ravvin
Cover and text design by Erin Woodward
Cover photos courtesy of Canadian Jewish Congress National Archives
Back cover photo courtesy David Bier
Special thanks to Janice Rosen, Archives Director, Canadian Jewish Congress National Archives
Printed and bound in Canada by Friesens for Red Deer Press
Author photo courtesy of Cynthia Davis

Acknowledgements
Financial support provided by the Canada Council, the Department of Canadian Heritage, the Alberta Foundation for the Arts, a beneficiary of the Lottery Fund of the Government of Alberta, the University of Calgary and Concordia University.

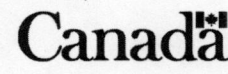

THE CANADA COUNCIL | LE CONSEIL DES ARTS
FOR THE ARTS | DU CANADA
SINCE 1957 | DEPUIS 1957

National Library of Canada Cataloguing in Publication Data
Yanofsky, Joel, 1955–
Mordecai & me : an appreciation of a kind / Joel Yanofsky.
ISBN 0-88995-266-3
1. Richler, Mordecai, 1931–2001. 2. Yanofsky, Joel, 1955– 3. Novelists, Canadian (English)—20th century—Biography.* I. Title. II. Title: Mordecai and me.
PS8535.I38Z97 2003   C813'.54   C2003-910928-3

5 4 3 2 1

For Cynthia and Jonah—love, requited.

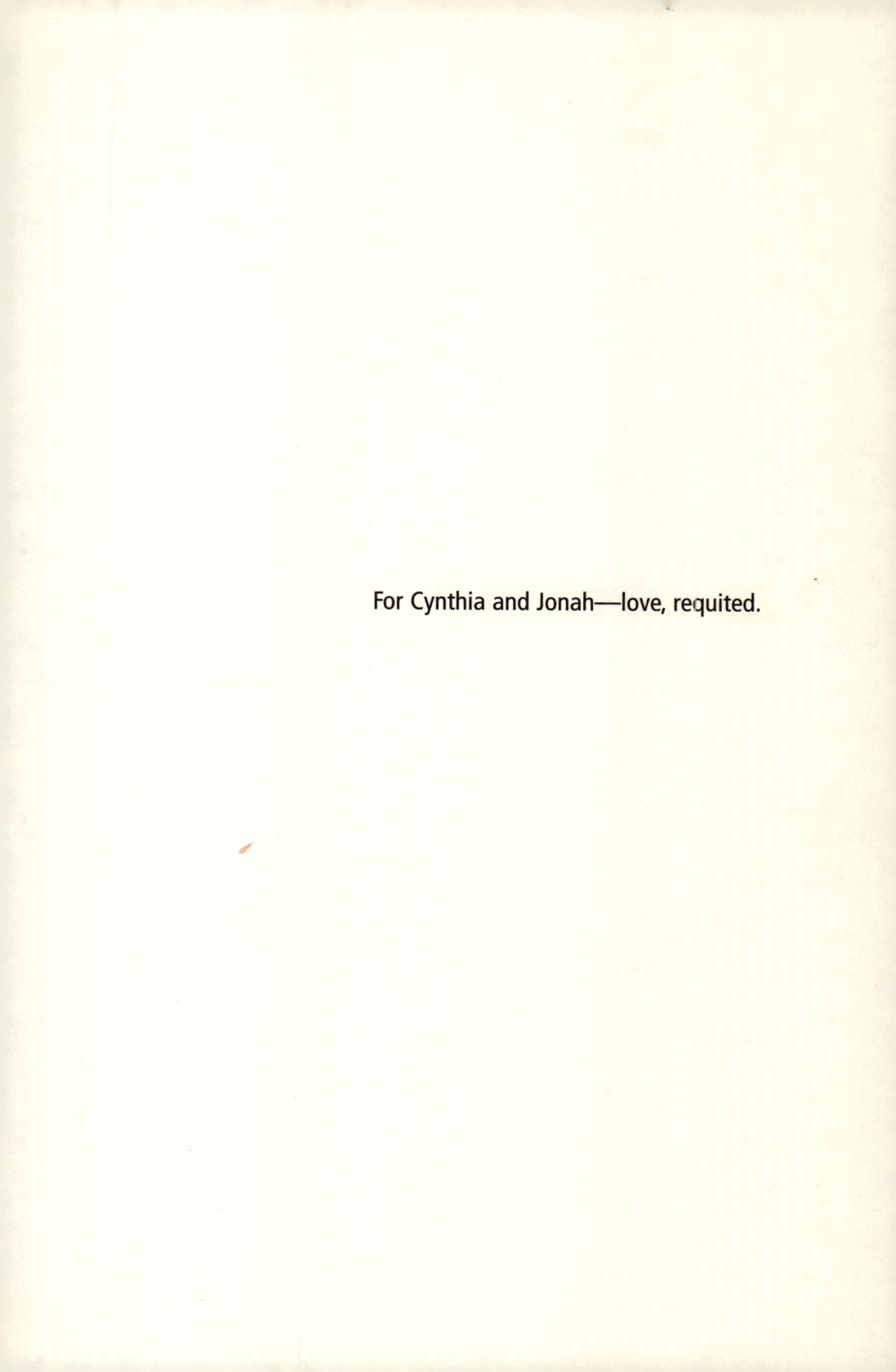

Acknowledgements

First, my thanks to Rachel Alkallay and the regulars at the Montefiore Book Club, which is where the idea for *Mordecai & Me* first occurred to me and where the book received an encouraging test run. My comrade in complaints, Dawn Rae Downton, was a rock, especially when I most wanted to give up. Thanks as well to William Weintraub, who was generous with both his time and resources, and to Elaine Kalman for the brainstorming session. Not expressed enough is my gratitude to my sisters, Renee and Marilyn, and to my mother- and father-in-law, Carole and Alex, for all their support, moral and otherwise.

Finally, I am grateful to Dennis Johnson at Red Deer Press for believing in this idea when others didn't, and, in particular, to my editor Norman Ravvin. From the start, he was encouraging and kind in both his suggestions and criticism, and he devoted himself to making this a better book. For his commas alone, he has earned my undying gratitude.

An excerpt from *Mordecai & Me* first appeared in *Maisonneuve* (Spring 2002).

All you read a novel for is to see what sort of person the writer is.
—Virginia Woolf

Don't make trouble. That's all I ask.
—Max Kravitz, to his son Duddy

Prologue
Spring 2002

When Mordecai Richler's first novel, *The Acrobats,* was published in 1954, his uncle calculated his nephew's writing income at an hourly rate and came to the conclusion that Richler should consider mowing lawns. It would be more lucrative and, at least, the *meshuggeneh* kid would get some fresh air. This is just a rough estimate, but I figure that over the last two decades, I've written well over a half-million words about writers and their work—book reviews, profiles, essays. I've also calculated my income against the time invested and realized that I, too, would have been better off in the backyard. Still, compiled, organized, edited, and, no doubt, self-published, all those words would fill a fairly long shelf dedicated to the literary life—to the variety of ways writers write and readers read.

Mordecai & Me

In the meantime, though, I've traded in all the writers I have written about for just one, Mordecai Richler, and it feels like an enormous risk. What I've discovered is that when it comes to Richler my mixed feelings have mixed feelings. Lost somewhere in a pile of thick file folders of clippings, notes, reviews, and transcripts of interviews with Richler, there is a copy of a fan letter I wrote to him twenty years ago, when I began my freelance career. What does it say? Who remembers? I could try to find it, but I'm guessing it's a plea for advice, for pointers. *Dear Mr. Richler, I want to be a writer, what should I do?* More of a Dear Abby letter than a fan letter, really. I had my reasons for writing it, I suppose. What matters is that I didn't send it. Somewhere in my Richler file, not quite so lost, there is also a copy of one of Richler's weekly columns for the *Gazette*, Montreal's English-language daily newspaper. The standard columnist photo—a head shot of Richler, in his sixties then—has been defaced, scrawled on, given horns, a thin moustache, and a goatee, transformed into a kind of dishevelled demon. I did this just a few years ago, and, once again, I must have had my reasons.

My dream analyst says my problem—the reason I've been having recurring dreams in which I pester famous and quite dead authors—is that I don't feel deserving enough to be writing a book about Mordecai Richler. She suspects this feeling of inadequacy goes back to my childhood. More than likely to an absent father or a father I perceived to be absent. Still, she says, she'd need to see me again to be sure. Layne Dalfen is a member of the Association for the Study of Dreams (ASD) and the author of *Dreams Do Come True: Decoding Your Dreams to Discover Your Full Potential*. A chubby, self-assured woman, she's a frequent guest on radio and television shows, and she has, I'm guessing, dreams of her own. I'm also guessing she sees syndication in her future and herself as a kind of Oprah of the Unconscious. Still, for now, she's doing fine. She lives in a mansion high in upper Westmount and charges eighty dollars an hour, so I'm not inclined to disagree with her about anything.

Your unconscious doesn't screw you over is the gist of what she tells me. I nod, though I'd always assumed that is precisely the purpose of an unconscious—to screw you over.

Prologue

I should also add that I'm not one of those people who has always had a dream analyst. In fact, until recently, I didn't even know such a thing existed.

But that was before I started working on this book. That I have one now and am prepared to overpay her for her time is just one more thing about this project, about Mordecai, and about me that is open to interpretation.

Part One
*Apprenticeship
1931–1958*

Chapter 1
Confessions of a Book Reviewer

Resist the Urge to Criticize
–*Don't Sweat the Small Stuff,* Richard Carlson, Ph.D.

It is in the nature of what I do—reviewing books, particularly for newspapers—that what I write disappears as soon as it's read. Or, more likely, disappears without ever being read. In the houses of friends and even family, I've seen my byline lining a kitty litter box or stacked next to a basket of kindling set to go into the fireplace. Even I can't find most of my tear sheets. Whatever perceptive or witty opinions I must have offered up over the last two decades—and in all that time, in all those words, there must have been some—are curled up in the back of desk drawers or went out with the recycling long ago.

In a better world, a less pragmatic one that cared more about literature, I would also be quite the name-dropper. I would impress friends and acquaintances with gossip about all the writers I have met. Shouldn't someone want to hear, for example, about the time I got kicked out of the Ritz-Carlton bar with John Updike? (I was wearing jeans.) Or that Saul Bellow cut our interview short to chat up a pretty female journalist? Or that Martin Amis expressed concern about my mental health? (Interviewing Amis after his novel *The Information* came out, I appeared, to him, too morbidly preoccupied with his twin themes—literary failure and envy. I know this because the next day Amis inquired about me to a friend of mine, who was also interviewing him. Amis asked, "Is this Yanofsky fellow going to be all right?")

In a more literate, high-minded world, I would be dining out on all this. These stories would give me cachet, make me influential friends, and impress women I'd never dream of impressing. But, as it stands, writers, even famous ones, don't rate. Not on the movie star or professional athlete scale of things, not even compared to the local weatherperson. Who spots writers on the street? Who seeks their autographs? Whose head is turned? Mine, I suppose. Which is my first confession. With *Mordecai & Me*, I have become, heaven help me, a literary stalker. This is not what I envisioned for myself when I began my writing career, and there are times when I feel like a kid with his nose pressed up against the glass, missing some big book party or, more to the point, uninvited and undeserving.

Another confession: I expected to make a splash. When I was twenty-two my first short story was published in the literary magazine *Prism*. It was a special issue for promising Canadian writers under the age of thirty. (Future Governor General's Award winners David Adams Richards and Erin Mouré were featured in the issue. And while, now, I wouldn't think of reading anything either Richards or Mouré write, you still get the picture.) I like to think my story was about a lot of things—loss of faith and innocence, unrequited love, of course—but mostly it was about my mother's death from cancer a year earlier. Not long after I finished the story, my father died of cancer as well, and I wrote about that, too. It seems I don't have much of an imagination.

Still, this is often how it works with writers. You don't go looking for your subject matter; it comes looking for you—usually with a vengeance. It leaves you no alternative. I had none anyway. But I was proud of my early fiction, and together with some stories I was less proud of, I sent my manuscript off to Oberon, a small literary press in Ottawa. Then, like most young, aspiring writers, I began making plans. Grandiose ones. I conducted interviews with myself wherein I explained my imaginary writing routine—work through the night, then cocktails—to imaginary television interviewers and radio hosts. I went on make-believe book tours. I had never attended a wine and cheese party—I didn't even know what a *cinq à sept* was—but still I imagined myself leaning against a bookshelf, holding court, bantering, besieged by fetching young women, literary stalkers themselves, who were deeply interested in what I had to say about life and love. Night after night, you might say, I was launched.

I have no idea where this confidence came from. In every other imaginable way, I was not a self-assured young man. Still, I believed, down deep, that it was only a matter of time before I was discovered. That someone influential, someone like Mordecai Richler, let's say, would read my barely disguised autobiographical fiction and give it and me a resounding thumbs up. I was also convinced this would happen soon. I believed that somehow this writing thing would work out. A couple of months after my manuscript went out, it returned, sheepish in its self-addressed stamped manila envelope. Movies about writers always get this small but crucial detail of the literary life wrong. In the movies, aspiring authors receive their rejections in a thin letter-sized envelope. There is always that moment of anticipation when, in some Hollywood hack's distorted version of literary success, the writer on screen gets to think, "I'm in."

In reality, your big fat manuscript, in its bulky manila envelope, comes back to you like a self-addressed boomerang—as if you had predicted it, rejected yourself in advance. You can't *not* see it coming. When the mailman isn't able to squeeze the damn thing through the slot in your door, again, and rings your bell, again, so you have to take it from him, you know, without a doubt, that you are a failure. My first manuscript came back with an added bonus—what still stands as the longest, most detailed, and devastating rejection letter of my life. Loss of faith's been done to death, it said. Unrequited love, it is to yawn. Pack it in, it basically said. Get a real job.

If I knew then what I know now it would be this: not being published and being published by an obscure press like Oberon amounted to the same thing. But I was naive. I took it hard. Or I think I did. Hindsight isn't 20/20. Seen from a distance, we get the past wrong all the time. Maybe I wasn't devastated; maybe I was just looking for a way to let myself off the hook. Who wanted to write a novel anyway? Who had anything to say?

One thing about writing that most writers don't readily admit and most readers don't guess is that we do what we do for all the wrong reasons, all the worst ones, the same base, petty, ignoble, pathetic reasons that motivate our fellow, nonwriting human beings. Like self-aggrandizement or revenge or bitterness or envy or fame or the need to seem clever. To this partial list, George Orwell added "sheer egoism" in his essay "Why I Write." The desire, he said, "to be talked about, to get your own back on grown-ups who snubbed you in childhood." Writers only talk about things like art and advances for the record. Off the record, all they want is to make a splash. It's what they dream about. If nothing else, a splash will keep you writing. A big one is preferable, but a little one will do.

For the first decade of his career, Mordecai Richler was doing nothing but splashing. Before he stumbled onto the story of Duddy Kravitz, a kid also desperate to be noticed, he was, like most young writers, more preoccupied with the idea of being a writer—in the manner of Orwell or Ernest Hemingway or E.M. Forster—than with writing. That's why he left Montreal for Europe. He was, it's easy to forget now, very young. Asked once what his greatest embarrassment was, he recalled when he was twenty, having a meeting with Forster:

> I was invited to [his] rooms at King's College in Cambridge, England. I wouldn't have described myself as a writer then, but Forster was a man of enormous kindness who talked to me as if I were a colleague. He served . . . sherry, which I'd never had before and I knocked it back like whiskey. I sat there embarrassed at how gauche I was.

Mordecai & Me

There was nowhere to go from there but up, and if Richler had some measure of success at an early age and was more driven than most in obtaining it, it's probably because he knew how badly he needed it, because he knew he couldn't have continued without it. Even in his twenties, with three novels to his credit, he was just a kid from the wrong side of the tracks, from the wrong side of the world, come to think of it, trying to prove he belonged—in Paris, in London, in print. In the beginning, that's what got him going, and for a long time after, that's what kept him going.

When I began reviewing books two decades ago, I thought it would just be a small means to a larger end—the best way for someone like me, with my otherwise pointless education in literature, to become noticed as a writer. I assumed magazine articles would follow, then books. In the meantime, I was a newspaper hack who'd read James Joyce's *Ulysses*, twice. It wasn't, I confess now, an unhappy combination.

"The review is a charmless form in itself," according to the writer Wilfrid Sheed, an old pal of Richler's, "but an excellent pretext for writing about something else entirely." In my case, that something else was *me*. A book, good, bad or indifferent, can't be taken in whole. There are too many corners to see around, too many layers to peel. It can't be explained in one thousand words or, for that matter, one hundred thousand, so why try?

Somehow, I instinctively understood the futility of the task. I also understood that once I set out to review a book, it was mine. I could and would do with it what I wanted. So I read the books I was assigned to review the way I had read them before they were assignments—selfishly, idiosyncratically. Looking almost exclusively for what mattered to me.

"The only books that influence us are those for which we are ready, and which have gone a little farther down our particular path than we have yet gone ourselves," Forster said. I referred to this quote approvingly in a review once, and my editor at the time, a sensitive poet masquerading as a hard-nosed newspaperman, asked me if I thought Forster was right. Sure, I replied, a little startled that anyone imagined otherwise. My editor frowned.

"Yes, that's probably so, but I still want books to take me places I've never been," he said. "I want them to take me out of myself. I'm so bored with myself sometimes."

Confessions of a Book Reviewer

"Really? Are you? I'm endlessly fascinated with myself."

The words were said before I could gauge their out-loud effect—before I realized how they might be misinterpreted. I wasn't arguing just for myself or for how undeniably interesting I was; I was arguing for every single one of us. If I found myself fascinating—and not always, not often, in fact, in a complimentary way—then I just assumed everyone else did, too.

In his introduction to *Portrait of My Body*, the personal essayist Phillip Lopate asks himself, "What gives me the right to assume my life is worth taking so seriously? Is it arrogance? Self-centredness?" Yes, he concludes, that's a big part of it, but not all of it. "I want to record how the world comes at me," Lopate adds, "because I think it is indicative of the way it comes at everyone." There you have it, a personal writer's credo and rationalization all rolled into one: self-justification in fifty words or less.

Yet another confession: in the two decades I've been reviewing books, I can't remember ever worrying about simply being wrong. There have been times, though, when I have worried about being spectacularly wrong. Sometimes I ask myself, "What if I was assigned *Ulysses* today—deadline, two weeks; word count, six hundred; fee, two-fifty?" How would I respond? Simple. I'd say the damn thing is too long and pretentious. I'd say, "Do we need a remake of *The Odyssey*?"

In much the same way, I have quickly dismissed contemporary books that have gone on to earn widespread acclaim: Anne Michaels's novel *Fugitive Pieces* comes to mind. When it was published in 1995, I called it paper-thin. It's a three-hundred-page prose poem, I said in my review, and since no one could reasonably be expected to read a one-page prose poem, Michaels was asking an awful lot. Not long after, *Fugitive Pieces* went on to win prizes in this country and internationally with a regularity that left me scratching my scalp till it was raw.

A more recent example: I did an onstage interview with fellow Montrealer Yann Martel, just after his novel *Life of Pi* was published. I asked generic questions because I could hardly say out loud what I really thought—that I couldn't finish his story of a man stranded on a life raft with a Bengal tiger because it felt, like so many novels I'd read lately, trumped up, a high literary concept at the expense of a straightforward personal story. Another example of a writer's imagination, considerable in this case, getting in the way of him telling me something intimate, gossipy, something I really wanted to know. Put another way, tigers don't talk, at least Martel's doesn't, and after a couple of hundred pages in the big silent creature's company, I felt at sea, too. I longed for some banter, some flirting, someone to make a pass at someone else, some human interaction. "What did you expect—Tony the Tiger?" a friend, fed up with my griping, my jealousy, asked. *That would be G-r-r-r-eat,* I thought. As most everyone knows by now, *Life of Pi* went on to win the Booker Prize, an announcement that set me off on a private tantrum (just ask my wife) that still makes me shudder with embarrassment.

I have interviewed enough writers on book tours to know that they are tame as pussycats. Like most people involved in a lonely, esoteric occupation, writers are overjoyed when they are finally asked about what they do and how they do it. The fact is that they all have thought about this kind of question too much, even those who claim not to. Writers are like door-to-door salesmen or Jehovah's Witnesses: they believe in word-of-mouth. They believe in converting readers, one by one. Every book sold is a moral victory, a step on the road to salvation—theirs and yours.

Mordecai Richler was an exception to this rule. He had earned a reputation as a hard case, which he did as little as possible to discourage. It's not that he was impolite or uninteresting in person; he was just so good at being unsolicitous. He made no effort to impress you with his appearance. His hair and clothes were always dishevelled—asked once to list his bad habits, he said, "smoking too much" and "being personally sloppy"—and he made no effort to impress you with his personality. Richler's impatience with foolish questions was legendary. Veteran journalists still tremble, recalling decade-old interviews. At one Montreal radio station, the staff used a photograph of Richler as a dartboard after an especially uncomfortable on-air encounter. Interviewing him, I was always cautious, always afraid of asking a stupid question. Our meetings were, as a result, strained and not especially illuminating. Talking to Richler on a book tour always left me with the overwhelming feeling that I'd rather not talk to him ever again. With Richler, I was also always working against my natural inclination, which was to talk about myself, especially when I was in the company of a writer I admired. And while I recognize this is not a particularly good quality for a literary interviewer to possess, I can't always help myself.

"I don't know you very well, but you seem awfully self-absorbed, malignantly self-absorbed. You seem to spend a lot of time thinking about how you're feeling," the Toronto writer David Gilmour told me once over a long and rather drunken lunch-hour discussion of everything except his new novel. It was, with Gilmour, a clear example of it-takes-one-to-know-one. Still, I think he meant his comment as a compliment. If reviewing books has provided me with an opportunity to write about myself, interviewing authors has provided me with an opportunity to talk about myself.

Another problem with meeting famous writers is that it's impossible not to play connect the dots between their life and work, their person and persona. Face-to-face, Mordecai Richler resisted this impulse of mine, which only succeeded in convincing me that I knew more about him than I possibly could. John Updike, in person, is as polished as his prose, except for the occasional and famous stammer, a reassuring defect in a man so accomplished and solicitous. Saul Bellow is, well, Bellovian. A scowler like Richler, he's still more forthcoming—but then who isn't?—and more of a snob. Every dumb question you ask Bellow he takes as a sign that civilization is coming to an end. Norman Mailer is combative, but canny, an operator. Months after I wrote about him, he sent me a complimentary note and a photocopy of a demonic-looking caricature I assume he'd drawn himself. The caption read, "Why does everyone insist that I am a devil?" It was endearing—I've framed it—but I still wonder why he bothered. Meanwhile, Margaret Atwood is, like her novels, smart as a whip and bitter as aspirin. During a telephone interview, she warned me, in her famous nasal, schoolmarmish tone, about giving away the ending to her latest bestseller. "Now, we don't do that, do we?" she said. Allen Ginsberg was in a hurry when we met in his hotel room before an interview, so he dropped his trousers in front of me—he was wearing boxers—rather than step into the bathroom to change. What did I expect from the author of *Howl?* Reticence?

"The literary interview won't tell you what a writer is like," Martin Amis says in *Visiting Mrs. Nabokov,* his book of literary profiles. But it will tell you enough to jump to a few conclusions.

Mordecai & Me, then, is about connecting the dots. It's also about jumping to conclusions. Here's a leap: having spent more than a year immersed in the life and work of Mordecai Richler, I am in a pretty good position to speculate on what he might have thought of this book. My guess: not much. Who am I kidding? He would hate it and hate the presumptuous twerp writing it. "Don't think of it as an unauthorized biography," a writer friend from Halifax e-mailed me. "Think of it as really, really, really unauthorized. Think of yourself as the Geraldo Rivera of literary biographers. Make the most of being under the radar, alternative, oddball, not the tiniest bit definitive or reliable."

"Geraldo Rivera?" I e-mailed back.

Still, I can't help thinking Richler would have considered the idea of a memoir disguised as a biography or vice versa (*Mordecai & Me?* How about *Mordecai & Who?*) unseemly or just plain silly. The notion that the lives of writers are essentially uninteresting was an opinion from which he never wavered.

In a 1965 review of Mailer's novel, *An American Dream,* Richler criticized Mailer for "becoming another wowser on the scene, a personality, rather than a working writer." Some twenty-five years later, he was humming the same tune. In a review of *Home Before Dark,* Susan Cheever's memoir of her father's life, Richler takes the author to task for not maintaining "a curtain of dignified silence" over the "details of [her father's] private life." Incidentally, John Cheever's private life ended up as a gag on *Seinfeld.* When the cabin belonging to the father of George's fiancée is burnt to the ground, Cheever's passionately homosexual letters are all that is salvaged. So much for a "dignified silence."

As for his own life and its connection with his fiction, Richler was forever shooing readers away. In his personal life, he was a father and a taxpayer, and, he added, he worried about the same things everyone else did—the population explosion and report cards. It's not the life but the fiction that is "charged with incident and invention," Richler pronounced in a disapproving review of Ian Hamilton's biography, *In Search of J.D. Salinger*. But that was the thing about Richler: he could take the literary high road and be completely disingenuous at the same time. He could be full of moral outrage and just plain full of it. Can anyone seriously imagine Richler worrying about overpopulation, unless, that is, his favourite bar was crowded? Can anyone seriously doubt that Richler's work was fed as much as any writer's by his life? Richler wrote incessantly about himself and incessantly denied that he did. Writers are "paid liars," he insisted. But what are they lying about? In his case, he was lying about lying. Richler was always telling the truth; he just didn't choose to own up to it. He was always writing about himself, even when he claimed not to be.

Responding to a question about writers kissing and telling, Philip Roth once said, "I certainly wouldn't want to be living with a loud-mouthed novelist and I sympathize with those who do. The invasion of their privacy accounts for much of our interest in Emma Bovary, in Anna Karenina, in Raskolnikov and Lord Jim. The serious, merciless invasion of privacy is at the heart of the fiction we value most highly." This invasion is also at the heart of what is valuable in Richler's work. He may have felt entitled to keep his personal life to himself, but he couldn't honestly expect his readers to enter into such a bargain. To Orwell's "sheer egoism" as the motivation for being a writer, Richler adds a codicil in his essay, "Why I Write." Egoism is "informed by imagination, by a desire to be known, yes, but only on your own conditions," he adds. In that comment, by the way, you have Richler in a nutshell: stubborn desire coupled with a quick disclaimer.

But next to Orwell's candid self-appraisal, Richler's qualifications and rationalizations sound like so much literary grandstanding. Writers are no different than anyone else; they don't get to choose their conditions. If they are either lucky or good—and Mordecai Richler was certainly both—there will be readers to choose for them, whether they like it or not. With writers we value, writers who provoke us, writers we love and sometimes love to hate, we are greedy. We want to know everything we can about them, and what we don't know, we will happily guess at or invent.

More than a year ago, when the idea for this book was no more than a three-page proposal and an alliterative title, I spoke to one publisher who expressed some interest in a Richler book, but who also worried about the timing of such a project. Was it too soon after his death—just a few months then—to be writing about him? Was it in bad taste?

"Absolutely," I said with inappropriate enthusiasm. Caught off guard by the question, I forgot for a second that I was making a pitch, that tact, not candour, was required. Still, I had given this question some thought.

"No doubt about it," I went on. "There is a vulturish quality to this proposal. How could there not be? What is literature anyway but picking at the bones of the dead?" This turned out to be a rhetorical question. Instead of a reply, I heard a slight but audible gasp at the other end of the line. Publishers, I assumed, were made of sterner stuff. Apparently not. I had shocked this one. So, for the sake my pitch, I backtracked or attempted to. I talked about the importance of reassessing Richler's place, pre-eminent, I insisted, in Canadian Literature. But it was too late to be convincing. Perhaps because I'd said what I meant the first time: vulture was the *mot juste*, the right creature, too. There was no way around it—what I intended to do was exploit Mordecai Richler's life or, more to the point, his death for my own purposes. Literary purposes, true, but so what?

In "A Sense of the Ridiculous," Richler's essay about his early days in Paris, he recalls, with a sense of shame, the moment he considered himself a writer. It was the moment he "became cunning, somebody with a use for everything, even intimacies." I had a use for a dead man. Richler was barely cold, the tributes were still pouring in, with other, more elaborate ones still being planned, and here I was with my worried-over proposal letter, my jaunty title, *Mordecai & Me*, ampersand and all, trying to rush to the head of the line that would no doubt be forming around Richler and his reputation. What kind of person does that? What kind of person stalks the dead for the sake of a publisher's go-ahead, for a project, for a piddling advance?

Frankly, I didn't know. I also didn't know where I got the *chutzpah*. Insofar as I have qualifications to write about Mordecai Richler, here they are: I was born on the same streets he wrote about and though I didn't grow up there, my parents and grandparents did. Like Richler, I'm a Montrealer, which means I'm more that than Canadian. I'm also Jewish, though not at all observant. I freelance, write novels when I can find the time and courage to work on one, and, as a literary journalist and reviewer, I have followed Richler's career and written about his work for more than two decades. These are qualifications, I suppose, but for what? An infatuation? An obsession? *Mordecai & Me* is the story of that obsession and how it has taken over my life, keeping me up nights, making me doubt myself and what I've gotten myself into. Still, there is no doubting this: Mordecai Richler was the most infuriating, the most engaging, and complicated character that Mordecai Richler *never* wrote about. This book will prove Richler wrong on that important point: writers' lives are not boring. But then he knew that, the endearing S.O.B. He was keeping the A material for himself. In *St. Urbain's Horseman,* the beleaguered hero, Jake Hersh, pines for the company of an admired writer:

> You know what's important to me? Really, really important to me? Dr. Samuel Johnson. I keep wondering, if I had lived in his time, would he have liked me? Would Dr. Johnson have invited me to sit at his table?

I'm lucky, I guess. I know the answer to whether Mordecai Richler would have asked me to sit at his table. I know because he never did.

Chapter 2
A Perverse Kind of Love

> *Never apologize. Never explain.*
> –St. Urbain's Horseman

Writers should haunt us. That's what they are supposed to do. If it were only amusement or even insight we required from them, we'd be better off turning on our television sets to watch *The Simpsons* or Bill Moyers. Writers should take up a place in our hearts and reside there, impertinent as squatters. If they can't manage that, then what purpose do they serve? I've heard it said that when a major writer is slighted the loss is ours, not his or hers, but is that really true? Doesn't a major writer, by definition, have to demand our attention? The shyest writers—Emily Dickinson, say—do that, even if it is after the fact. Because isn't making yourself known, against all the odds writers face, the biggest part of the job description? Whatever else there is to say about Mordecai Richler, he understood this intuitively. He was pushy, and he pushed himself from the start. Look at the photos of him as a young man. They are nothing if not self-conscious: raw ambition and studied contempt combined in what would become a trademark scowl. If he didn't feel like a writer just yet, he was going to look like one and act like one until he did. "And look, I want two more prints of 'young author, with hand cupped on his chin, having a think,'" he wrote his friend William Weintraub, requesting additional copies of the photos taken of him in 1953 just before *The Acrobats* was published.

Late in 1950, not quite twenty, Richler left Montreal's St. Urbain Street—the teeming, Jewish working-class neighbourhood in the heart of Montreal that he would eventually put on the literary map—for Paris (and later Spain and London) to become a writer. An honest-to-God one, like Joyce or Hemingway or F. Scott Fitzgerald. Those were his role models. There were British models, too—Forster, Orwell, and Evelyn Waugh—and French writers like André Malraux, Albert Camus, and Louis Ferdinand Céline. His influences, the ones he alludes to in his essays and novels, are so eclectic, in fact, as to be unrevealing: from Nathanael West to Henry Green. He read widely and borrowed liberally. Perhaps the only definite conclusion about Richler's influences that can be reached is that he would not have dreamed of patterning himself after anyone in his own country.

From the start, Richler's goal was not simply to get published or make a living or impress girls or show his bewildered relatives back home that he was not the good-for-nothing smart-ass they were thoroughly convinced he was—though, I suspect, all of this entered into it. His goal was to be important, great even. That took courage. Or presumption. Where did it come from? For my own sake, I wish I knew. A kind of hunger is my best guess. A hunger that grows from being left out, insecure, unhappy. Richler was always hungrier than he was brave, hungry to be noticed, full of ambition and of something even rawer, more undeniable—call it *want*. He liked no word better than *charged*. It shows up everywhere in his work, as in "charged with significance" or "charged with anticipation" or "charged with contradictions" or "charged with resentment." Pressed, I think it's fair to describe him, especially as a young man, as "charged with want."

Mordecai & Me

Alfred Kazin once said of Saul Bellow that even when the future Nobel laureate was just a kid he had "the aura about him of a man destined for greatness." The young Richler, scraggly, pimple-faced, surly, more urchin than protégé, had no such aura. There was no stamp on him. What he had was no business believing he could be a writer, let alone becoming one. But he wanted it; he wanted it tenaciously, which is the best and perhaps the only explanation for why he succeeded. By the time he was twenty-eight, he'd written four novels, the first three of which he would later distance himself from. Still, everything he did was meant to say, "Here I am. Pay attention. Notice me." It could be a writer's credo. At the start, it was Richler's.

"You were such a grabber," Joshua Shapiro's wife says to her estranged husband in *Joshua Then and Now*. "Charging into any roomful of people, determined to make an impression. 'Look at me. See what I made of myself.'" Richler was determined to say just that to an entire country. It's no wonder people in this overly polite, unassuming-to-a-fault place never quite knew what to make of him. This was never more apparent than after he was gone. Not long after he died, I gave a speech about Richler and Philip Roth at a Montreal synagogue, and though the audience was more respectful than usual when it came to Richler, one woman did ask at the end, "But why did he always have to go so far?" Why, she was asking in a polite way, did he always have to be so uncompromising, so nasty?

Not a bad question.

Writers can be as unrealistic as children. They want to have it all—to be loved and to be left alone. Part of them wants to be admired and respected; part of them isn't really happy unless they are misunderstood. They want to be of their time and a little too good for it. They want to be fêted at ritzy launch parties and still be permitted the luxury of finding the whole business distasteful. It has nothing to do with the work, they will say. But who's foolish enough to believe that? "Writers' lives are all anxiety and ambition," Martin Amis says in *Visiting Mrs. Nabokov*. "No one begrudges them the anxiety, but the ambition is something they are

A Perverse Kind of Love

supposed to shut up about. The two strains are, of course, inseparable, and symbiotic."

With Mordecai Richler, you can add another strain, anger, to the anxiety and ambition. Everything bugged the guy; everything was a prod, a spur. He was "an injustice collector," "a grudgy-type," like Joshua in *Joshua Then and Now,* with a Ph.D. in being pissed off. He was, after all, a man who couldn't get along with his mother or grandfather, his community or country or God. If he was always going too far, pushing too hard, it was because it was the only direction, the only pace he knew. "I'm much more interested in criticizing, always, the things I believe in or I'm attached to," he said in a 1971 interview with Donald Cameron, "which may be a very perverse kind of love, but it's the only kind I'm capable of." In a television interview done in the 1950s, after he'd had some success, he told the interviewer, "I don't want to be respected, man, I just want to be accepted." He said it with a self-conscious sneer. He was trying so hard to be cool that the effort looks silly now. So does the word *man,* plunked down mid-sentence. Richler was the most unhip hipster. He was the opposite of cool; he was hot.

In *Barney's Version,* Barney Panofsky's old friend and mentor, Hymie Mintzbaum, says of Barney in his younger days, "You were such a bundle of nerves when we first met. . . . Sweating anger and resentment and aggression under that assumed hipster's carapace." Later, one of Barney's three ex-wives updates the characterization: "Some people collect stamps, or bookmatch covers . . . but with you, my darling, it's grievances." Richler never bothered to explain why this was so. If he had been asked, he undoubtedly would have shrugged the question off. The best you might have gotten out of him—as I did when I interviewed him and reluctantly asked a personal question—was it's "all in the books." The reply was a sure-fire conversation stopper; it was intended to be. The times I talked to Richler face-to-face I cut the interview short. A preemptive strike: do it before he did. After forty-five minutes we would both be looking for the door. I went away from the interviews always thinking the same thing: Never do that again. I also went away thinking: What did he mean by that "it's-all-in-the-books" business? Did he mean that that was all someone like me—a reader, a reviewer, a fan—was entitled to know? Was it a

Mordecai & Me

reminder that his life and his writing were separate? If so, the reminder was wasted on me. The more he insisted on drawing a line between the two, the less I believed there was one. Maybe "it's all in the books" meant something else entirely. Maybe it meant that his life and his writing were virtually indistinguishable, one from the other.

According to Yahoo's astrology Web page, Aquarians are "the humanitarians of the Zodiac." Which means, if you give credence to such things, Mordecai Richler, who was born an Aquarian on January 27th, 1931, spent his life misaligned with the stars. Actually, he spent his early years misaligned with everything—shoplifting, playing hooky, watching his parents' marriage implode, becoming an atheist, a scold, finally, a satirical writer, and a self-styled moralist.

Richler was born in Montreal, but as strongly associated as he is with this city and as important as it is in his work, it was just dumb luck he ended up being its chronicler. Richler's paternal grandfather, on his way to Canada from a Galician *shtetl* in 1904, had a train ticket to Chicago in his pocket, but because he met a man with relatives in the States, he swapped with him and ended up in Montreal. This was a curious decision. For Jews escaping poverty and pogroms in eastern Europe, America was the destination of choice. It was the *goldene medina,* the golden land. Canada, when it was thought of at all, wasn't thought to be much of a country. It was, as Richler writes in *Solomon Gursky Was Here,* "the next-door place." It meant being "this side of Jordan," stuck in a suburb of the Promised Land. This was a sentiment Richler would inherit. "Canada was not a choice," he writes in his 1969 collection of autobiographical stories *The Street,* "it was an accident." Then he adds, "America was Roosevelt, the Yeshiva College, Max Baer, Mickey Katz records, Danny Kaye, a Jew in the Supreme Court, the *Jewish Daily Forward* . . . and Gregory Peck looking so cute in *Gentleman's Agreement.* Why, in the United States, a Jew even wrote speeches for the president."

The writers he first admired were also American: Hemingway, Fitzgerald, Faulkner, Algren, Mailer. In Paris, friends like Terry Southern and Mason Hoffenberg, future authors of the X-rated novel *Candy,* were

A Perverse Kind of Love

Americans. In his essay about Paris, "A Sense of the Ridiculous," he admits he considered himself and his contemporaries "real Americans hungering for recognition and its rewards, terrified of failure." Later on he would defy Canadian literary nationalists by speaking out against institutions like the Canada Council for what he called in his 1968 introduction to *Canadian Writing Today*, "handing out toupees to all comers, so our culture plan is vulnerable to the charge of staking just about all the alienated kids to committing their inchoate, but modish complaints to paper or canvas." Three decades later, in his last novel *Barney's Version*, he was still getting a kick out of skewering the CanLit establishment, singling out "mediocrity's holy trinity: the Canada Council, the Ontario Arts Council, and the City of Toronto Arts Council." In the 1980s he also distinguished himself as being one of the few creative writers in the country speaking out in favour of free trade.

It's interesting to speculate about how literary history might have been reconfigured if two of North America's most important Jewish writers had switched places as they very nearly did. What if Richler's family had ended up in Chicago after all and Saul Bellow, who was born in Lachine, Quebec, but grew up in the St. Urbain Street ghetto, had remained here instead of going to Chicago? Would we have *Kravitz* instead of *Herzog*? Or *The Apprenticeship of Augie March*? As it is, Bellow is the most Canadian of American Jewish writers—not wholly assimilated, the indelible inflection of Yiddish distinguishing his prose—while Richler, rebellious, fiercely individualistic, is the most American of Canadian writers.

Raised in an orthodox Jewish home, Richler grew up keeping the Sabbath, eating kosher food, wearing a skullcap, and following the 613 *mitzvot*, or niggling rules, depending on your point of view, that every orthodox Jew is expected to adhere to. There are commandments for everything—from dietary laws to business practises to sexual relations, especially the forbidden variety. Viewed in retrospect, these kinds of prohibitions weren't going to be a comfortable fit with Richler's increasingly stubborn and independent personality. Still, his grandfather on his mother's side had been a rabbi and so had his uncle. Richler was not only expected to carry on the tradition; he was being groomed for it. He attended a parochial school, the Talmud Torah, but even that wasn't sufficient for someone with his spiritual obligation. He was also compelled to take extra classes at night at the local synagogue, studying the Talmud and modern Hebrew and bridling at every minute of it. In *The Errand Runner: Reflections of a Rabbi's Daughter,* a 1981 memoir by Richler's mother, Leah Rosenberg, Rosenberg talks about keeping Mordecai (as well as his older brother) in "what amounted to a Jewish isolation" and imbuing them "with a strong feeling for our faith."

The Errand Runner is a curious book, full of quaint Yiddish anecdotes and unrelenting self-justification. No writer, Rosenberg rides her son's famous coat-tails, while seeming to resent it. There's little about her son's literary accomplishments. Instead, when she's asked about her famous offspring, she replies that she has two famous sons. She also regrets that Moshe, as she called Mordecai, never got to know her learned, devout father better. The implication is clear: knowing him would have made her son a better writer and a better Jew. (He hardly could have been a worse Jew, in her eyes.) More like Sholem Aleichem, she seems to mean—more acceptable, less of a *shande,* a scandal.

Another curious aspect of *The Errand Runner* is that although it is clearly identified on the dust jacket as a memoir by the mother of Mordecai Richler, Rosenberg takes Wilensky as her fictional married name, as if it wasn't obvious who she was and who she was writing about. But then, come to think of it, her son does much the same thing in his novels. Except they *are* novels.

For all her complaining—about everything from her husband's fecklessness to her children's intermarriages—Rosenberg manages to sustain a kind of eerie cheerfulness in *The Errand Runner.* The memoir also offers up the unstartling news that as a kid Richler was a handful. (In his book *On Snooker,* Richler recalls how his mother used to pretend to dial Eaton's department store and ask if she could "exchange my bad little boy for a nice girl.") Rosenberg recalls a meeting with the principal of Mordecai's parochial school, who tells her, "You know, I can easier cope with one hundred students than with [Mordecai]. Never can I get the better of him and win an argument."

From this "amusing incident," Rosenberg draws, as usual, all the wrong conclusions. She sees a boy with a Talmudic intellect and boundless religious curiosity. What she should have seen was a boy preparing to bolt. Like Duddy Kravitz, the young Richler seemed to have a gift for driving his teachers, not to mention his family, to distraction. At best, Richler, "a child of the new world," pitied "the old underpaid men" who instructed him in Hebrew at the Talmud Torah. At worst, as he recalls in *The Street*, he never forgave them: "[They] tended to be surly, impatient. . . . They didn't like children." As for the extra instruction he received at the synagogue at night, he spent most of that time having his knuckles rapped and his ear twisted for reading the sports pages or an *Ellery Queen* paperback. His mind was already elsewhere. In 1957, in an interview with *The Tamarack Review*, Richler told critic Nathan Cohen that he understood what was expected of him. "I should have been a rabbi," he said. Instead, he stopped observing the Sabbath and eating kosher food and wearing a skullcap.

"What are you rebelling against?" Marlon Brando is asked in the hopelessly dated 1953 movie *The Wild Ones*. Brando, who plays the leather-bound leader of a motorcycle gang terrorizing a small town, replies, "What have you got?" What didn't Richler have? For starters, there was his family and family expectations, his religious education, his small-minded community, his parochial country. He graduated from shoplifting (baseball bats from Eaton's) and skipping school to a high-minded contempt for everything around him. There was never any confusion about what he was at odds with—it was hypocrisy. That included his own disillusionment with being a Jew. After all, he had an informed and intimate knowledge of all those rules he was breaking and all the conventions he was rebelling against. He was also beginning to understand what would fill the vacuum. "I was only fourteen when I acquired a pipe and a lined notebook," he says in the essay, "Hemingway Set His Own Hours."

A year earlier, in 1944, a thirteen-year-old Richler finally broke free of religious instruction and began attending a secular high school, Baron Byng. In Richler's essay "St. Urbain Street Then and Now," from his 1984 collection, *Home Sweet Home: My Canadian Album*, Baron Byng is described as "a brick building as charming as a Victorian workhouse." In "the heart of Montreal's swirling Jewish quarter," Baron Byng, though officially part of the Protestant School Board of Montreal, was, according to Richler's reckoning, ninety-nine percent Jewish. "If the battle of Waterloo was won on the playing fields of Eton," Richler adds, "then the character of Montreal's . . . Jewish community was hammered into shape in the smelly classrooms of that big building."

A generation after Richler attended Baron Byng, the demographics at my high school in Chomedey, Laval, a North Shore suburb of Montreal, were almost identical, though we were not a particularly "scruffy bunch with an eye on the main chance," which is the way Richler described his classmates. But then we didn't have to hustle quite so hard. Our parents had ambitions for us, but they were subtler about foisting them on us and also less worried about us than their own parents had been about them. They had their own success, sometimes modest, sometimes extraordinary, as an example. Some also tried to learn from their own parents' bad example that you could push too hard, you could want too much and be disappointed.

We were overindulged by families that were either solidly middle-class or doing their best to cling to the illusion that they were. What was strange about us—and probably not that different from Richler and his "rough-and-ready lot"—was the feeling we had that, even in a place as undeniably Waspy as Canada or staunchly Catholic as Quebec, we could be Jewish and, in our little corner of the country, still be so overwhelmingly in the majority. What was even stranger was that until we got out of high school, that feeling was all most of us would ever know. We Jews were, for a brief, formative time, the only game in town.

At my school, Chomedey High—like Baron Byng it was Protestant in designation only—we were the offspring of the generation that had quite deliberately abandoned St. Urbain Street for the suburbs. By the time Richler left Montreal for Europe in 1950, he had already noted that the tiny, insular world he knew was relocating. Upwardly mobile Jewish families were heading west, mainly for big houses with manicured lawns in Outremont, then Cote St. Luc, and eventually Westmount. A decade later my parents had the same impulse, though not the same wherewithal. They left a cold-water flat on Van Horne, corner of St. Urbain, for a small bungalow and a modest but coveted spot on the bottom rung of the middle-class. Meanwhile, the small number of gentiles who attended

A Perverse Kind of Love

Chomedey High—later renamed Chomedey Polyvalent High, though there was no particular polyvalence to it—were the outsiders. They had to assimilate and they did. I knew gentile kids who knew as much about Jewish traditions and customs as I did. As for me, I went through five years of high school without making a non-Jewish friend.

On Jewish holidays the school all but shut down. Most of us weren't religious and neither were our parents—the kids from observant families went to Talmud Torah, the way Richler had—but we were top-notch chauvinists just the same, obnoxious about being Jews. On a day-by-day basis, the Jewish kids took their majority status for granted. We were safe, safer than Jews have ever been in their long, tragic history, and we took that for granted, too. We made jokes at our own expense. We assumed that the way we were, the way we thought and behaved, was the way everyone thought and behaved. We were our own microcosm. But unlike Baron Byng, Chomedey High produced no famous alumni. We did not lead the province in matriculation results, as Baron Byng had in Richler's day. There have been no well-attended reunions, at least none anyone bothered to tell me about. Most of our graduates are living in Toronto now, refugees from Quebec's uncertain politics of the 1970s and 1980s.

Baron Byng, which closed in 1980, the building now housing a charitable organization, was famous. Alumni include poets A.M. Klein and Irving Layton, actors Marilyn Lightstone and Captain Kirk himself, William Shatner, sociologist Lionel Tiger, and New Democratic Party leader David Lewis. And that list doesn't even take into account the doctors, lawyers, and successful business leaders that came out of the school.

It doesn't include Richler either, who was not only the school's most famous graduate, but the one who made the place famous by re-imagining it in his books. Baron Byng retains its real name in Richler's second and most transparently autobiographical novel, *Son of a Smaller Hero*, which was published in 1955. But by the time *The Apprenticeship of Duddy Kravitz* appeared four years later, Baron Byng had acquired a pseudonym and would be referred to from then on in Richler's fiction, as well as his nonfiction, as FFHS or Fletcher's Field High School.

"The first twenty years are the most important to a writer," Richler often said. "After that certain doors on experience close." A ludicrous generalization, this was nevertheless true for him, since outside his family life, nothing fed his fiction more than Baron Byng. It was *his* microcosm. Everything he needed was there: narrow-mindedness and single-mindedness, awkwardness and *chutzpah*, shame and pride, pettiness and righteous anger, bitter failure and hard-won, often extravagant success. Whether they liked it or not, whether they defined themselves that way or not, Richler and his classmates were New World kids determined to bury their Old World roots. They could do this by fulfilling their parents' expectations—invariably fulfilling them in ways their parents could never have imagined. Or they could do it Richler's way—by breaking free of those expectations. The past could dictate to them or be rejected by them, but they could not be indifferent to it. The classrooms of Baron Byng, Richler writes in his foreword to *The Street,* "reverberated with the ambition of 1,000 strivers."

It's no wonder Richler maintained a soft spot for the place, though with Richler the spot wasn't so much soft as raw. The last place most Baron Byng alumni expected to see Richler was at their frequent reunions, which went on being held long after the school closed. But Richler, against expectation, like a bad penny, kept turning up. In 1996, at his forty-eighth reunion, he was uncharacteristically inoffensive, telling a reporter for the *Canadian Jewish News* that "everyone seems to have done so well."

At an earlier reunion, though, he had, truer to form and expectation, been less diplomatic. The moment is captured in a clip from Alan Handel's 1986 National Film Board documentary *The Apprenticeship of Mordecai Richler,* and it is almost as painful to watch as it seems to have been to sit through. We see Richler at a table, which includes one of his oldest friends, Jack Rabinovitch, suffering through a rousing but curious (considering the occasion) rendition of the show tune *Oklahoma!* Richler buries his head in his hands and looks as if he isn't planning to remove it any time soon. When he finally does, he is scowling. He looks tired and like he's had a few drinks. His turn to speak comes and he is introduced as "St. Urbain's Horseman." This time he winces. At the podium, he keeps his remarks brief, but still can't resist a crack about "those appalling funny singers." He is heckled for the comment, but he goes back

A Perverse Kind of Love

to his seat and doesn't budge. He is not going to be forced out. The last part of the story is not in the documentary. It was filled in by Rabinovitch when he spoke at the CBC's televised tribute to Richler a year after his death. This was his place as much as theirs, he told Rabinovitch. But the truth was it was more his place and he knew it. Incidentally, his opening remarks to his old classmates that evening were characteristically blunt, inappropriate and accurate. "Baron Byng turned out to be more useful to me," he said, "than it was to most of you."

Chapter 3
Did I Wake You? #1

Our dreams present solutions to our problems or reveal strengths we can draw on.
—*Dreams Do Come True*, Layne Dalfen

Sometimes I will wake my wife in the middle of the night accidentally. I'll switch on the lamp or reach for a pen on my night table and knock over a book or a water glass. Lately, nature calls more often at three o'clock in the morning than it used to, a fact that worries my wife and has her insisting I see a doctor. More often than not, my tossing and turning is quite deliberate and, more often than not, it does the trick.

Usually, I wake her so I can tell her about a dream I just had about Mordecai Richler. This is not exactly alert-the-media news around my house. I have not been doing much lately besides thinking, talking, and complaining about Richler. I also don't usually dream, though my wife, who's an art therapist, insists everyone does, including me.

Did I Wake You? #1

"You just don't remember yours," my wife explains. Virginia Woolf had a room of her own; I have a shrink of my own.

"This one I remember," I say.

"All right, tell me."

"Now?"

"Well, I am up."

I've only been married four years, but I already know something about marital *quid pro quo*, about how turnabout is fair play. You watch the kid; I'll do the dishes. You do dinner with my family Saturday; I do brunch with yours Sunday. My wife routinely wakes me up to tell me her dreams, often around three in the morning. Her dreams tend to be about the world coming to an end in one apocalyptic scenario or another, and I tend not to listen. Not because her dreams are particularly boring, but because everyone's dreams are boring. For a moment, I think that's why she wants me to tell her mine. So she can be the one *not listening* for a change. But the truth is she's interested.

"So tell me," she says, propping herself up on one elbow. She is wearing a pink *Don't Sweat the Small Stuff* sweatshirt over her nightgown. I had one made for her, as a joke, after she picked up a copy of the book for me at a garage sale. She was also joking, she said, but now I'm not so sure. She gave me the book not long after I started working on *Mordecai & Me* and started demonstrating how things would be for the foreseeable future—with me doing nothing but "sweating the small stuff." Richard Carlson, Ph.D., designed his best-selling self-help manual to address the epidemic of stressed out and uptight men and women all over North America. With its simple-minded but intractable advice to just relax, it provides an antidote to obsessive behaviour as well as to literature. Can you imagine Anna Karenina not sweating the small stuff? Or Captain Ahab? Or Holden Caulfield? Or, for that matter, Duddy Kravitz?

My wife, incidentally, looks quite fetching in the near darkness, even in her sweatshirt, though there is still something disconcertingly clinical about the tone of her voice, about the encouragement she is offering and the now-tell-me-how-that-makes-you-feel manner in which she is offering it. She has also put her glasses on. What does she expect to see? Will she be taking notes?

Mordecai & Me

"Well, in the dream, we were at a party or something. A book launch, maybe. You were there. You were my witness, I guess. Richler told me he was working on a book, too. And I felt this chill. His book was commissioned by one of the publishers who turned me down."

"Which one?" my wife interrupts. She has a point. There were many.

"Probably that creepy guy, you remember the one, who took six months to reply and then wrote me to say that he thought that words like *haunted* and *obsessed* had negative connotations. Anyway, Richler started describing his book to me and the thing is it sounded a lot like mine. The flip side, almost—*Mordecai & You*.

"Then we were driving Richler home, and we ended up here, at our house, and he got out of the car, before it even stopped. I offered to take him the rest of the way, but he just lit a cigar, one of those thin, expensive ones—I never know what they are called. Shouldn't I know that? Anyway, he waved goodbye and walked away. He was waddling, I remember, like a duck. Still, I had to run to catch up to him, and it took awhile. Then I asked him if, under the circumstances, it might be okay if I called him some time about my book. In case I had a question I couldn't answer. He looked at me and sort of giggled, then said, 'No, oh heavens, no.'"

"He giggled?"

"I know, it doesn't sound like him, does it?"

"It sounds more like you. And that's it—the whole dream?"

"That's it. Not exactly a tough one to figure out, is it? You don't exactly have to be Sigmund Freud."

"Well, it is—"

"Don't say interesting."

"I was going to say transparent. You should put it in the book."

"What? The dream? I couldn't."

"Why not?"

"I don't like that sort of thing."

Actually, I hate it when writers write about their dreams. "Tell a dream, lose a reader," Henry James said. A couple of years ago, I taught a creative nonfiction course at Concordia University in Montreal, and all my students kept dream journals and then transferred their unconscious thoughts directly into their assignments. Stop that, was my advice. Stop that Ingmar Bergman crap. Since a dream could mean anything you want it to, I told them, it ends up meaning nothing. But they were kids—aspiring performance poets mostly and spoken word types—and they didn't listen. They weren't really into meaning anyway. Meaning didn't mean anything anymore, as one of them explained to me during class. They'd read Foucault and Derrida, and they sensed, correctly, that I hadn't.

"If I wrote down this dream, no one would believe it," I say to my wife, who is suppressing a yawn now, her elbow starting to slip.

"Did he really call his version of the book *Mordecai & You*?"

"No, I made that up, but that's all. Still, you see, you caught me cheating already."

"It's your dream and your book, sweetheart. Did he waddle?"

"Yes. Why would I make something like that up?"

"All right, I'm sorry. Go back to sleep."

"I can't now."

"You can rub my back," my wife says, removing her glasses and turning away from me.

"How is that going to help me sleep?"

"Trust me."

She's right. I should trust her. It has worked before, more than once. So I push my hands up under the back of her pink sweatshirt and rub. I count to twenty, one Mississippi, two Mississippi. I count because otherwise there's no telling how long I'll have to keep at this. I start to snore, a joke, but the truth is I do suddenly feel drowsy. It's the repetitive motion, I suppose, the counting, the focus required, the gesture, even half-hearted, of taking my mind off myself for a brief time, but still the cause and effect of it not only doesn't make sense, it doesn't seem fair. She's getting all the pleasure and all the credit for solving my problem. Which is why I usually balk at rubbing her back. But tonight I decide I'd rather have my rest than my pride.

"Don't worry," she says, "I have faith in you. It will work out. Now, higher, to the left, harder, don't forget the shoulders."

I appreciate the vote of confidence, but, really, what's she going to say—she's my wife and she's tired. She's my therapist, too, by default, so she's doubly obliged to be supportive. Still, I want to believe her. And before I know it, I'm asleep again. Dreamless sleep it feels like, though I know I am wrong about this, too.

Chapter 4
Grist for the Mill

You've not heard of Mordecai Richler, yet, but look out, she's a name to watch for.
—A *Globe and Mail* columnist commenting on *The Acrobats*

Mordecai Richler did not distinguish himself during his high school years. Instead, he made his most enduring mark at Baron Byng by being conspicuously absent, a habitué of burlesque halls, movie theatres, and, most of all, the Rachel Pool Hall, which was around the corner from Baron Byng. The problem, as Richler described it in *On Snooker*, a book published shortly after his death, was beating the rush to get a table:

> It meant hurrying to the poolroom as soon as classes were out, the race to the swift, until my bunch and I hit on a solution. If we sneaked out of school before the last class of the day, there was seldom a problem. Cutting afternoon classes altogether was even better.

Mordecai & Me

The local pool hall became Richler's deliverance "from classes in geometry and intermediate algebra." It was also where he received what he considered his real education. When high school ended, it didn't appear that Richler would be one of "the anointed few" destined to continue his education at McGill University.

That there was a quota system at McGill is well known now, but it wasn't a big secret at the time, either. The university's admission standards simply and unashamedly made it harder for Jews to get in than gentiles. This system was very much in effect when Richler graduated from high school in 1948, and he referred to it often. What he has also mentioned, though less often, was that, quota or not, he still wasn't destined for McGill. (Gentiles required a sixty-five percent high school average to be admitted, according to Richler, while Jews required seventy-five percent. He had neither.) So Richler attended Sir George Williams College instead—a "sort of loser's finishing school," as he called it—and, once there, had a memorable appointment with a guidance counsellor. The counsellor glanced at Richler's high school records and asked him what he wanted to be. A writer, he said. There was no hope, he was told. "It was a crushing blow," Richler would say later, "but, with hindsight, a blessing, for no critical blow I have suffered since compares." It would also be one more grudge for him to nurse: "For years afterwards, many years afterwards, I managed, understandably, I think, to keep well clear of the academy and its pronouncements."

This is one of many stories that Richler—an inveterate recycler of anecdotes, even of turns-of-phrase—repeated so often it sounds just good enough to be untrue. Richler's stories were not so much apocryphal as touched up and improved upon over the years. Like Barney Panofsky, in *Barney's Version,* Richler fine-tuned reality. "To come clean," Barney says, "I'm a natural-born burnisher." Read Richler's work straight through and you can watch the anecdotes evolve with use and sometimes overuse. They will usually show up first in an essay or review and then be transformed into the stuff of fiction, properly tweaked and delivered by the appropriate character. Over the course of his career, Richler wrote as much nonfiction as fiction, but he was always a storyteller before he was a journalist. He never let the facts stand in the way of a good story. The fact, though, is the misguided guidance counsellor—made to look like a fool in retrospect—had a point. There really did appear to be no hope for Mordecai Richler, the writer. Richler had to be as aware of this as anyone.

So he did what young writers do. He pretended he couldn't be deterred. This kind of trumped up stubbornness in the face of reality may explain why there are no affectations as embarrassing as the affectations of writers. They are inevitably coloured by our desperation, our shaky faith in ourselves, our longing to be noticed. Ponytails, bow ties, initials in our names—there's no end to the silly things we will do to make ourselves seem important in a world that is, more often than not, indifferent to us.

The young Mordecai Richler wasn't immune to this kind of thing either. As a teenager, he grew a beard—or, like Duddy, tried unsuccessfully to—and, smoking his pipe and sporting his beret, he composed poems in lower case letters. In the beginning, he had, like most writers, a romantic and unrealistic notion of being a writer. When the young Joshua Shapiro is asked in *Joshua Then and Now* what he wants to be when he grows up, he replies, "Rich and famous and popular with girls."

Same here. I became a writer for the girls. Looking back, I have no idea what I was thinking, except that I needed something to make me irresistible to women and telling them I was going to be a writer was, for some reason, all I could think of. Mordecai Richler, it's reassuring to know, entertained similar delusions. In his 1990 essay, "Hemingway Set His Own Hours," he admits his main literary ambition was to be "on first name terms, if not with Ingrid Bergman, then at least with Ruth Roman."

At least Richler's fantasy, set as it was in the 1940s, had some basis in reality. Back then, writers like Camus, Fitzgerald, and Hemingway could still be viewed as romantic figures—crashing sportscars, dating flappers, big-game hunting in Africa. What Richler didn't know back then didn't hurt him. Specifically, that Camus was suicidal, Fitzgerald a hopeless drunk, and Hemingway both. "But once you've made it as a writer," the title character in Richler's short story, "Some Grist for Mervyn's Mill" says, "the glamour girls will come crawling."

Richler was not alone in his literary ambition. "Everybody I knew in high school who wasn't going to be another Hank Greenberg or . . .

Mordecai & Me

Maurice 'The Rocket' Richard was willing to settle for being a writer. As far as we could make out, Hemingway . . . seemed to go fishing whenever he felt like it," he writes in "Hemingway Set His Own Hours." But a generation later, in the 1970s, I should have had no delusions. Everybody I knew in high school was going to be a dentist or, failing that, a chartered accountant. I also should have realized that writing down my adolescent longings with the goal of attracting the opposite sex was plainly ridiculous. If I had any sense or physical dexterity, I would have grown my hair to my shoulders and learned to play the guitar. But I was just posing; I didn't really believe I could be a writer. How could I? I didn't believe I had a story to tell. I wouldn't believe it for a while. In the meantime, I was waiting for something like life to happen to me.

Richler's short story "Some Grist for Mervyn's Mill" was published in 1963 in the *Kenyon Review,* chosen for Martha Foley's anthology of *Best American Short Stories* that same year and later collected in *The Street.* I cringe reading it now and recognizing aspects of my younger self. The title character shows up looking to rent a room in the apartment where the young narrator, a streetwise Richler-like kid, lives with his squabbling family. Mervyn Kaplansky is twenty-three, short, fat, and a failure, a nervous young man with no aptitude for writing or lady-killing. But for all that, he is still an inspiration to Richler's young narrator, who also longs to be "a wordsmith." Mervyn is the first writer the young boy has ever met, and that alone is enough to make him an object of worship.

Mervyn may be short on talent, but he has the patter down. Responding to a question from his landlady about his conspicuous lack of luggage, he says, "When Oscar Wilde entered the United States and they asked him if he had anything to declare, he said, 'Only my genius.'" Sleeping till noon every day, Mervyn explains the indulgence with an inspired excuse: "I'm stocking the unconscious," he says. "To a creative writer, every experience is welcome." That includes the attention of Molly, a looker, who is led to believe that Mervyn is about to hit it big with a New York publisher. Like the youthful Richler, Mervyn will have nothing to do with Canadian publishers, those small-timers.

By the end of the story, Molly breaks off her engagement to Mervyn, who can no longer fool anyone except the narrator into thinking he has a future in the writing game. He can barely go on fooling himself. But by Richler's standards, Mervyn gets off easy. There is an authorial tone in the story that is uncharacteristically sympathetic if not forgiving. Richler has his fun at Mervyn's expense, but he also seems to be thinking, *There, but for the grace of God....*

A trace of Mervyn in Mordecai is evident in his earliest letters to his friend William Weintraub, which are included in Weintraub's *Getting Started: A Memoir of the 1950s*. There we see a young man who feels put upon and unjustly neglected. "Everyone tells me I'm one of the only boys with IT in Paris but nobody wants to print my stuff," he wrote Weintraub. In his correspondence, Richler was capable of being just as ludicrously self-righteous as Mervyn. "I don't have to point out that publication is just a social hurdle and has nothing whatsoever to do with being a writer," Richler lectured Weintraub.

In *The Apprenticeship of Duddy Kravitz*, Richler got the chance to poke fun at his own youthful self-importance through the character of Jake Hersh. Hersh, a member of Duddy's gang at FFHS, returns later in the novel as an aspiring writer. "Writing is not a career. It's a vocation," he tells Duddy. Hersh, like Mervyn, also has lots of excuses to explain why his big break has yet to come but why it's imminent:

> Hersh quickly told [Duddy] what he thought about editors. He said his writing wasn't commercial. He pointed out that he didn't get the usual printed rejection slips, but personal notes from editors, always asking if they could see more of his work.
>
> "Sure," Duddy said, "but have you published anything?"

The less writing became a dream and the more it became a reality, the better Richler became at downplaying how important his chosen vocation was to him and playing up how his professional life was too boring to discuss. But as was often the case with Richler, his premeditated and public pronouncements couldn't always be reconciled with what he genuinely felt. Or, for that matter, with what is revealed in his fiction. For all his complaints about the boring literary life, Richler would still write obsessively about characters, particularly main characters, who were writers to one degree or another. André Bennett, the protagonist in

Mordecai & Me

Richler's first novel, *The Acrobats,* is a painter who may as well be a writer for all he knows about painting. "I'm not really a painter at all. I came here to study life in its entirety," André says, expressing an inside joke on his author's behalf. "One day I hope to write a book about it. You know, like that *Who Do the Bells Toll For?*" Noah Adler, in *Son of a Smaller Hero,* hasn't chosen a career path when we meet him, but it's impossible to imagine him becoming anything other than a writer. Norman Price, in *A Choice of Enemies,* writes television plays. Atuk, in *The Incomparable Atuk,* is the Inuit Allen Ginsberg. Mortimer Griffin, in *Cocksure,* is a literary editor. Jake Hersh, a wannabe writer in *Duddy Kravitz,* resurfaces in *St. Urbain's Horseman* as a film director who seems to be a lot more conversant with literature than cinema. In *Joshua Then and Now,* Joshua is a journalist. In *Solomon Gursky Was Here,* Moses Berger is a biographer. In *Barney's Version,* Barney is a successful businessman turned memoirist. Even hyperactive Duddy Kravitz is more concerned with making myths than money.

There are also the writers-as-fools, like Meryvn, and later incarnations, like Terry McIver, Barney's nemesis in *Barney's Version,* whose career prompts Richler to put some of his own favourite words—recycled from essays and reviews—into Barney's mouth: "We have all read too much in literary journals about the unjustly neglected novelist, but seldom a word about the justly neglected, the scratch players, brandishing their little distinctions à la Terry McIver."

L.B. Berger, the poet and father of the drunken and demoralized Moses Berger in *Solomon Gursky Was Here,* may be the most cruelly gratuitous portrait Richler ever drew, which is saying something. Crueller still because L.B., right down to the initials, so closely resembles A.M. Klein, the Montreal poet and author of the novel *The Second Scroll.* Richler would have known all about Klein, a fellow Baron Bynger. For one thing, William Weintraub wrote Richler to tell him how good *The Second Scroll* was and promised to send him a copy. (Klein was, as Ruth Wisse writes in her book *The Modern Jewish Canon,* the first writer in this country to make Canadian critics realize they had to accommodate Jews in their literary judgements.) Richler also would have known that Klein was just the kind of Jewish writer he would never quite be—one widely

Grist for the Mill

admired and respected by his community. One who could take his place beside Sholem Aleichem and I.L. Peretz on Jewish bookshelves and in Jewish hearts. L.B. Berger is Richler's revenge on the more respectable and, as it turned out, much more fragile Klein.

Constipated and pompous, L.B. is a failure as a writer, a husband and a father. He even fails as an adulterer, carrying on a tepid affair with a gentile admirer. In one instance, L.B. is so jealous of the success of others that he sabotages his son's writing career, destroying an acceptance letter that the talented but clued-out young Moses receives from *The New Yorker.*

In the 1980s, the time Richler was writing *Solomon Gursky*, the story of Klein's extended writer's block and ultimate decline into mental illness was well known. But even Klein's sad end would not induce Richler to forget that the poet had sold out to the powerful Bronfman family. Like Klein with the Bronfmans, L.B. ends up in the Gursky pocket. He goes from literary hero—though it's clear in the novel that L.B., unlike Klein, has no real talent—to literary lackey. A "speechwriter and cultural advisor" to Gursky liquor baron Mr. Bernard, he pens puffed-up tributes to celebrate bar mitzvahs and wedding anniversaries. He is also given the task of choosing the books for the library in the Gursky's Westmount mansion. It's an impossible job. Mr. Bernard wants only the best first editions; meanwhile, his fastidious wife insists that there be "nothing secondhand." Germs, she says, "that's all I need."

Richler's effortless meanness feels more like mean-spiritedness here. Pretentious and self-deluding, L.B. is the personification of Richler's low opinion of writers who betray what he perceived to be literature's higher calling. "A poet they should never be able to afford," one of L.B.'s colleagues says in *Solomon Gursky.* "It has to do with what? Human dignity. The dead. The sanctity of the word." Eventually, Moses also sees his father for what he is. He tells the old man off, employing a familiar Richler pronouncement. Not all writers, Moses says addressing his father, "are unjustifiably neglected."

Starting out in Paris, Richler joked about selling out and even negotiated with a few buyers. He wrote television plays, doctored screenplays, and even contemplated doing a pornographic novel for the famous

47

Mordecai & Me

Olympia Press in Paris. (Olympia published Vladimir Nabokov's *Lolita* when no one else would.) But hypocrisy was a character flaw Richler was incapable of sustaining. His skill at making characters like Mervyn Kaplansky and L.B. Berger look foolish concealed doubts he had about himself, about his own fear of becoming the one thing he despised most—an impostor, a poseur. When it came to literature, Richler, the cynic and atheist, was an idealist and a true believer.

To the left of centre on most social issues, Richler was, on the subject of literature, uncompromisingly conservative. It seems you could take the boy out of the *yeshiva,* but you couldn't make him any less self-righteous or judgemental. All his life, he would maintain his own rigid standards (double standards sometimes) for people who were acceptable—his immediate family, his bar buddies, the writers he admired—and for those who were, in another favourite Richler expression, "beyond the pale." The fact is that Richler was constant. He was the grandson of a rabbi, after all. Never religious, he was unfailingly orthodox. The things he believed in and disapproved of at the start of his career, he would go on believing in and disapproving of right up to the end. He would always value the individual above all else, especially an individual with an appetite for life. He would never forgive pretension and hypocrisy.

Joseph Epstein, the American critic and essayist, once responded to Thomas Wolfe's famous pronouncement that you can't go home again with, "Who said you had to leave?" Mordecai Richler would manage to have it both ways. He would leave St. Urbain Street repeatedly, and he would repeatedly come back. As a young man, Richler was the perpetual prodigal son—always on the verge of departure or, once departed, always contemplating his return.

In a tribute he wrote to his father in the *National Post,* Richler's youngest son, Jacob, recalled accompanying his father to Concordia University, where Richler was giving a speech on writing. During the question-and-answer period, a young woman identified herself as "a writer, too" and then asked Richler for some advice. She'd written, "like, a novel," she said, which her parents both considered great—"They're, like, totally encouraging"—so what, she wanted to know, did he think she should do now? "Leave home," Richler said.

The first time Richler came back to Montreal and to his St. Urbain Street neighbourhood was in 1952. He'd been in Europe for a year, and he was broke. In Paris he'd had his first short stories published—three "mood pieces" in *Points,* an obscure magazine. He also had many more stories turned down, receiving encouraging rejections—"the same fuckingold runaround," he wrote Weintraub—from popular magazines like *Atlantic, Harper's,* and *Mademoiselle,* which only made him more impatient to be published. The rejections were also enough to convince him that he was no short story writer. As a matter of fact, his short fiction is very good, but he kept scrapping it and—here was an early sign of the inveterate recycler he would become—turning it into novels. *The Apprenticeship of Duddy Kravitz, Cocksure,* and *St. Urbain's Horseman* all started out as short stories. As did his first novel, *The Acrobats.*

Before Richler's first return to Montreal, he had, at a friend's encouragement, left the manuscript of *The Acrobats* with a London agent who liked it well enough to submit it to a publisher. Richler would say later that if it had been up to him he probably wouldn't have submitted the manuscript, but it's safe to say this is Richler's attempt at revisionist history. The truth is he already had been submitting it to publishers; he'd also referred to it as a great book in his letters. The manuscript was accepted by the English publisher André Deutsch and then a little later by an American publisher. Richler, who was back home and working as a news writer for the CBC, must have felt triumphant. He'd done what he had set out to do, and he was barely twenty-three. From that point on, setbacks would only be temporary. He had become a writer, or more accurately, he had willed himself to become one. Knowing that, he could return to Europe.

But Richler's unwillingness to decide where to settle persisted, a reflection of how unsure he was of where he belonged. His decision to leave Canada for Europe was both courageous and conventional. ("He who returns has never left," Pablo Neruda said.) In this country in the 1950s, there was no real precedent for Richler's kind of literary ambition. In Europe at the same time, there were precedents everywhere. Paris, in particular, was a North American writer's cliché. It was also *déjà vu* all over again. The lost generation of the 1920s, of Hemingway and Fitzgerald, updated to the 1950s. This time though, it was a generation not so much marked by loss as by missed opportunities. Two decades after his adventures in Paris, Jake Hersh, the hero of *St. Urbain's Horseman,* voicing an opinion Richler expressed in his essays, would sum up the predicament he and his crowd found themselves in:

> Wrong place, wrong time. Young too late, old too soon was, as Jake had come to understand it, the plaintive story of his American generation. Conceived in the depression, but never to taste its bitterness firsthand, they had actually contrived to sail through the Spanish Civil War, World War II, the holocaust, Hiroshima, the Israeli War of Independence, McCarthyism, Korea and, latterly, Vietnam and the drug culture, with impunity. Always the wrong age. Ever observers, never participants. The whirlwind elsewhere.

"All that can be claimed for us," Jake adds, "is that we took 'fuck' out of the oral tradition and wrote it plain."

In addition to Richler, the list of writers who gravitated to Paris in the 1950s was long and included James Baldwin, Richard Wright, William Styron, Alice Adams, Mavis Gallant, Alfred Chester, and Terry Southern. George Plimpton was there, and in a recent essay on Southern in *Harper's,* he recalls that "at that point, soon after the war, Paris was kind of a culture dish for writers beginning their careers. It was outlandishly inexpensive, possible to get by on thirty dollars or so a week."

In "A Sense of the Ridiculous," Richler refers to his first trip to Europe as his real education. Just as the pool hall had seen him through high school, Paris was his university. Richler was a grateful alumnus; his memories of those days got sweeter with time—despite the fact that he got scurvy when he was there. He would also write often about his days in Paris, drawn back one final time in his last novel, *Barney's Version.* "My two years [in Paris] are a sweetness I retain, as others do wistful memories of McGill or Oxford," Richler would say years later.

Grist for the Mill

William Weintraub, who first met Richler in Paris late in 1950, acknowledges in his memoir *Getting Started* that he didn't share the same literary ambition as friends like Richler, Mavis Gallant, and Brian Moore, but he remembers those days with a fondness he can barely express. "Why did I go to Paris? Oh, what the hell, it was the place to go. What was it like there? Oh, it was wonderful, wonderful!" he told me recently, memories kicking in, a big sly smile on his face. "You didn't need much money. That was one motivation to go, but it was also so romantic because of the previous generation. Because of Hemingway and Fitzgerald and all those people who had been there in the '20s."

Of his own time in Paris, Hemingway said, "If you are lucky enough to have lived in Paris as a young man, then wherever you go for the rest of your life, it stays with you, for Paris is a moveable feast."

Paris and, later, London literary societies weren't exactly a hard sell for Richler and his contemporaries, who were looking for reassurance and acceptance as serious writers, but who also weren't averse to spending most of their spare time carousing. In Richler's case, this included smoking hashish on the Sabbath, an accomplishment of which he seemed to be simultaneously proud and ashamed. Richler learned quickly to put on a front of "café cool," though he would later admit he wasn't cool at all. In *Joshua Then and Now,* Joshua Shapiro regrets not having talked to Samuel Beckett when he was living in Paris in the 1950s: "He would watch him pass and smile. Hey, there goes big Sam Beckett, a man who used to shoot the breeze with Jimmy Joyce."

Likewise, Richler gawked at the tables in restaurants where Hemingway and James Joyce were purported to have eaten. In "A Sense of the Ridiculous" he says, "I was out of my mind with joy to be living in Paris, actually living in Paris, France." It was a heady time. In *Barney's Version,* Barney, an outsider to the literary world, remembers his friends at the time as "a pride of impecunious, horny young writers awash in rejection slips, yet ostensibly confident that everything was possible—fame, adoring bimbos, and fortune lying in wait around the corner."

Camaraderie among writers exists alongside unsuppressible jealousy. Barney comments that the writers he befriended in Paris were "as fiercely competitive as any Organization Man or *Man in the Gray Flannel Suit.* . . .

Mordecai & Me

They were driven by the need to succeed as much as any St. Urbain Street urchin back home who had bet his bundle on a new autumn line of après-ski wear."

London was not as romantic as Paris in the 1950s, but it was more practical. It was there that Richler realized a man could make a living as a writer. In London, there was freelance work—writing reviews and, later, writing or doctoring film scripts, often without credit. Richler also worked on television plays with Toronto-born director Ted Kotcheff. The two would become close friends, rooming together for a while in the late 1950s, after Richler's divorce from his first wife, Cathy Boudreau, became final. The arrangement provided Richler with the opportunity to tell everyone that he and Kotcheff were lovers, the kind of sophomoric joke he never could seem to get enough of. Later, when Richler married again, this time for keeps to the recently divorced Florence Wood Mann, Kotcheff was his best man. After Florence, Kotcheff was the second person to read the manuscript of *The Apprenticeship of Duddy Kravitz*. He vowed at the time to return to Canada and make a movie of the novel. Richler just laughed.

Before London and after Paris, there was Spain, more particularly the island of Ibiza, which offered very cheap wine and fewer distractions than Paris or London. It was in Spain that Mordecai Richler did most of the work on *The Rotten People,* a novel that would never be published. Although the manuscript was supposed to have been destroyed, it turned up recently in the Mordecai Richler Papers in the library at the University of Calgary. The sledgehammer of a title reveals most of what you need to know about Richler's feelings at the time, about the world and its sorry inhabitants. He was neither a happy nor a diplomatic young man. "Being seventeen or eighteen is not something I'd like to go through again," he told an interviewer in 1980. His first novel to be published, *The Acrobats*, is also marred by youthful resentment. It could easily have been called *Even More Rotten People.*

Richler's decision to leave Paris for Spain was made reluctantly, a fact he acknowledges in his introduction to the 1977 photo book *Images of Spain*. But in the winter of 1951, he was "ridden with scurvy of all things"—which was, considering the life he was leading in Paris, probably the best disease he could have hoped for—and he needed "two weeks of sun on the cheap." He ended up on the island of Ibiza and stayed for a year, a self-imposed exile turned into a love affair. Ibiza had, he said, "captured my heart." Ibiza also provided the setting for *The Acrobats*, which was published three years later.

The Acrobats is a novel that shows all the signs of being produced by a young man eager to get going, a young man who realized in his short time at Sir George Williams College that he already knew more about good writing than the people teaching him. Speaking at York University in 1972, Richler described what it was like to take a Canadian Literature course, circa 1948:

> We did not, I must admit, have a text; in fact, it was our pioneering chore to develop a Canadian bibliography. We were supposed to scan the library for Canadiana, any Canadiana, listing the books' dimensions, number of pages, and whether or not there were any illustrations. I do hope this bibliography is still not in use anywhere, for, at the time, we found it easier and much more fun to invent titles and authors rather than actually hunt them down.

So Richler dropped out of college, cashed in an insurance policy his mother had kept up for him since his childhood at the rate of fifty cents a week, and sailed for Europe. There, he designed his own curriculum—brothels, booze, and books. He read everything he could and took it all to heart. *The Acrobats* is Richler's crash course in serious literature: introduction to Joyce's Stream-of-Consciousness, Hemingway's World Weariness, Lowry's Drunkenness, Miller's Licentiousness, and, most of all, Existentialism in the French novel. There are all those dots, like pretentious freckles in the novel, a nod to Céline and his odd predilection for the ellipsis. The dust jacket for the American edition of *The Acrobats* also featured this portentous comment from its young author: "It seems to me that there is only one thing for a serious writer to write about today. Man without God. Man embarrassed. Stripped." *The Acrobats* is, Richler allowed many years later, more political than any of his novels and more humourless.

Judging by some of the descriptions in *The Acrobats*, a reader could be forgiven for thinking that Spain was not the most pleasant place to end up. It was hot and smelly, though one hopes not as hot and smelly as depicted in Richler's prose. Here's a typically overripe passage from *The Acrobats*:

> The heat smelled of rancid food, children with soiled underwear, uncovered garbage, venereal diseases, sweat and boils, pimpled adolescents with one leg and a stump for another, remedies exchanged across washing lines, cheats, cross-eyed whores, dirty persons, and no privacy.

Once again, Richler's writing was at odds with his life. In Spain he was broke, but having a ball. In a letter to Richler in Ibiza in the summer of 1951, William Weintraub wrote that he couldn't wait to arrive at his friend's "little haven of luxuriance and lechery." Weintraub also wrote to Mavis Gallant that while he stayed with Richler he found it too "expensive not to drink." Meanwhile, Richler's reports are full of overindulgence and bawdy adventures: he's frequenting brothels; the government accuses him of being a communist and threatens to throw him out of the country; and a guy named Dave is gunning for him, though Richler is not sure why. If he slept with Dave's girl, the likeliest explanation, he can't remember who she was. He was, he told Weintraub, "fornicating somewhat earnestly."

Earnest is one way to describe Richler's first published novel. Considering his age and his aim to be "a serious writer," this was probably unavoidable. Young writers worry about significance. They overcompensate for all the things they're afraid they don't know with all the things they've read about and feel are important. As a consequence, young writers can be insufferably pretentious. It's practically a rite of initiation. Most of us have a file folder full of lovesick poems; most of us have written short stories about racial discrimination or social injustice (Richler's was about a Jew saving the life of an anti-Semite); not to mention the story about all the "rotten people" we know, which we'd happily burn if

Grist for the Mill

we could just remember where we hid it. Reading *The Acrobats* now, I find it overwhelmed by a young man's unearned despair. Cynicism, like good scotch, needs to age. There isn't much of a story in *The Acrobats*, but what there is is relentlessly bleak.

André Bennett, the young, sensitive protagonist, mopes a lot, drinks a lot, and falls in love with a prostitute. Unfortunately, the prostitute is also the object of affection of a former Nazi who is living with his Eva Braun-like sister in Ibiza. André and the Nazi clash, though not nearly soon enough. Tragedy, well, it ensues. André is an unconvincingly Christ-like figure and comes to an unconvincingly Christ-like end. But before he does, he and the other characters in the book hang out in bars and brothels (later Richler cited the brothel scenes as the reason the book sold at all) pining for lost loves and lost faith and concluding that because their lives are at a dead end, everyone else's is, too.

The story is pretty much what you'd expect from a writer discovering that the world can be an even more unsavoury place than he imagined growing up in his cold-water flat on St. Urbain Street. Accordingly, there is a lot of spewing of vomit and self-pity in the book. And there are a lot of rats along with existential angst. Mostly, though, André sulks and makes grim observations about strangers—"Crippled beggars . . . singing imbecile tunes . . . cackling idiotically." Meanwhile, acquaintances are "intellectual maggots crawling, sucking, impervious to their own horrid secretions." Rejecting the manuscript, the American publisher William Morrow summed up the book this way: "All women and wine but no song."

Still, in its own untutored or perhaps overly tutored way, *The Acrobats* sets the tone for many of Richler's career-long preoccupations: the loss of innocence, the absence of faith and values, the recognition that we are all ultimately alone. His first novel is—he allows in "Why I Write"—"lumbered with the characters and ideas, the social concerns" that would show up in all his work. "Every serious writer has one theme, many variations to play on it," he adds. In *The Acrobats*, Richler plays what would become one of his. "I guess more than anything else," his doomed protagonist says, "we believe in not believing."

In *The Acrobats*, there is also Richler's desire—more theoretical than practical—to show us that there is a sympathetic side to even the most unsympathetic characters. Here is one speech that takes a direct route from the author's head to his protagonist's mouth:

> It's pretty damn elementary to be aware of social injustice and poetic truth and beauty, but to be capable of empathy, to understand the failings of a man—any man—even as you condemn him, well. . . . Look, every human being is to be approached with a sense of wonder.

Novelists have a moral obligation to be the "loser's advocate," Richler liked to say, but, as it turned out, he seldom practised what he preached. Richler's losers usually end up being objects of ridicule, not compassion. Still, in his first novel, he demonstrates that he at least knew he would have to try to look for something to recommend in human nature. More often than not, though, the effort would be strained. It would always be, for Richler, the hardest thing to do.

In a way, *The Acrobats* has suffered most from its author's own uncompromisingly harsh opinion of it, an opinion Richler wasted little time expressing. In his 1957 interview with Nathan Cohen, Richler was remarkably candid for a young writer, candid to a fault. He admitted, unsolicited, that he had reread *The Acrobats* recently, and he didn't think it was very good. He went on, again unsolicited, to explain why. It's "too wild . . . undigested," he said. More than twenty years later, in a 1980 interview with the *New York Times*, after the release of *Joshua Then and Now*, his opinion of his debut novel hadn't changed nor had his willingness to express it. He referred to it as "a very young man's novel. . . . Hopelessly derivative. Like some unfortunate collision of Sartre and Hemingway and Céline."

Richler did his best to keep *The Acrobats* out of print during his lifetime, but it was reprinted not long after his death, with a new introduction by Richler's friend and movie collaborator Ted Kotcheff. Michael Levine, Richler's lawyer, had jokingly warned him this would happen, and apparently Richler expressed no strong objections. No matter how much he would publicly regret his quick, reckless start, he would always cherish it, too. In "Why I Write," the opening essay in his 1972 collection, *Shovelling Trouble*, Richler says,

> It was the one book I could write as a totally private act, with the deep inner assurance that nobody would be such a damn fool as to publish it. That any editor would boot it back to me, a condescending rejection enclosed, enabling me to quit Paris for Montreal, an honourable failure, and get down to the serious business of looking for a job.
>
> A real job.

Looking back on *The Acrobats*, there must have been some acknowledgement of how unexpectedly well that first book paid off, considering how much was riding on it: Richler's decision to leave home, school, his family. Not to mention the threat of a real job. The first time out, his confidence, or nerve, didn't fail him. But then it hardly ever would. Weintraub would later say of his young friend that. "Mordecai was in such a hurry. He was working fast, too fast, I thought. But he was just so anxious to get going."

For all its admitted shortcomings, *The Acrobats* would turn out, indirectly anyway, to be a more important and influential novel than Richler could have imagined. It didn't just start his career, it also started the career of novelist Brian Moore. Moore was living in Montreal after the war, an immigrant from Northern Ireland and working as a reporter for the *Gazette*. In his spare time, he was also writing thrillers under a pseudonym. Like Richler he was anxious to get going on a serious novel. But Moore was Irish and had the sort of ghosts haunting him that Richler, Canadian-born, didn't. Moore couldn't get past the fact that if he was going to write a novel, it would have to measure up to Joyce's *A Portrait of the Artist as a Young Man*. Richler had the advantage of believing, with some justification, that there was no Canadian writer he had to measure up to.

I interviewed Moore several times in the 1980s. He was the polar opposite of Richler as an interviewee, approachable, forthcoming, charming, helpful, dapper. Each time, he told me about how he had only found the nerve to start writing serious fiction after he had read a novel by a colleague and had seen how bad it was. "I was kept from writing a novel for many years because of writers like Joyce, whom I admired very much. I knew I could not write as well as him," Moore told me. "Ironically, what got me started working—my influence, I guess—was a fellow I knew in Montreal who published a book that was so bad that I couldn't believe it had been published. I remember turning to another friend and saying, 'I can do better than that.' I suspect more books are inspired by bad or mediocre books than by good ones."

With the bar lowered reassuringly, Moore sailed over it with his polished 1955 debut, *The Lonely Passion of Judith Hearne*. Weintraub, who introduced Moore to Richler, is convinced the "mediocre book" Moore referred to was *The Acrobats*. "Brian, who was older than Mordecai, felt that if that kid could do it, he could, too," Weintraub told me. "Mordecai wouldn't have been upset by me saying so. He didn't think much of *The Acrobats,* either."

"Is it about Jews or ordinary people?" This was the second question Mordecai Richler's father asked him (following close on the heels of "What do you know about the circus?") when his son returned to Montreal and announced that his first novel, *The Acrobats*, would soon be published. Moses Isaac Richler was a scrap dealer, a lifelong ne'er-do-well. He wasn't educated or particularly well read. His tastes ran to *Popular Mechanics* and pulp fiction. *Reader's Digest* when he was feeling high-minded. It's no wonder his precocious, rebellious son, home for the first time from his European adventure, found his father's question, with its parochial concerns, ludicrous. As it turned out, it could hardly have been more pertinent, though it would take awhile for his son to realize this. ("There are some things even a man of genius can never overcome," a character in *Solomon Gursky* says some forty years later, "and that's his origins.") In the meantime, Richler was determined, in *The Acrobats* as well as in the two novels that came after it, to write about Everyman, every single damn one of us. Happily, Richler would get over his Everyman fixation, but this, too, would take some time. His apprenticeship had just begun.

Chapter 5
Welcome to Jew-ville

If you want to bet on something then bet on me. I'm going to be a somebody and that's for sure.
—Duddy Kravitz

Where is the greater sin—in wanting too much or not wanting enough? Our reach should exceed our grasp, but by how much? And how much is too much?

By the age of nineteen, Mordecai Richler was what we'd call nowadays overextended, living what he'd envisioned as a writer's life in Europe. When I was nineteen I watched a lot of TV and daydreamed about women I was afraid to talk to. I was going to a community college twenty minutes from my parents' home, where I had grown up and was still living. I was also hiding everything I wrote at the back of my underwear drawer and putting off taking my first creative writing class for as long as I could. In a letter to William Weintraub, written in 1954, Richler admitted that before his first book was published and just as he'd started working on his second, he "wanted to be famous. Have position. Anecdotes told abt [him]. And the rest of it." This much I had in common with him. I wanted the same things. But the difference was significant: he did something about it.

Looking back, I could have used a bit more Richler in me, a lot more, in fact. More drive, more *chutzpah*. I could have even used a bit of Mervyn Kaplansky, come to think of it. What was I so afraid of anyway? Announcing to the world—even my little world—that I intended to be a writer, I suppose. Or announcing it to myself? At the time, I couldn't imagine anything more presumptuous. I finally did take that creative writing class—vowing to myself that if I flopped I'd start thinking of a real job I could do. The first question the professor asked us was to name our favourite author. I waited as my classmates topped one another with names like Thomas Pynchon and William Burroughs and Vladimir Nabokov. Even the few names I recognized I hadn't read.

I had read *The Apprenticeship of Duddy Kravitz*, so when my turn came, I said Mordecai Richler. There was an audible give-me-a-break sigh from the class, as well as the professor. This was 1975 and Richler's reputation was enduring one of its frequent downswings, especially among college-age kids. He was not hip and not sexy. He was dishevelled, true, but not in a cool way. He was, in other words, no Allen Ginsberg or Kurt Vonnegut. He was certainly no Leonard Cohen. In a college setting, he was viewed as a local grouch at best—a middle-aged and provincial writer, as even he sometimes admitted. Not experimental. Not radical. Not a CanLit nationalist. Talent, which Richler did have, gets taken for granted by the young. They think of it as something that is available to everyone, a given, like a driver's licence.

Still, I confess that at the time and for a long time after that, I wished I'd said someone else, someone more esoteric, more, well, psychedelic. I could have said Richard Brautigan. I'd read *In Watermelon Sugar*, and while even then I realized it was an incredibly dumb book, I still could have said it. It would have played better. Richler was a mistake, uncool. He impressed no one and surprised no one. He was, for starters, too obvious a choice for me, too on the nose. I was Jewish, an anglophone, a Montrealer. My grandparents and parents had lived in all the places

Welcome to Jew-ville

Richler chronicled in his books. I was born in that neighbourhood, too—just a few blocks from where Richler grew up, and I lived there until I was five and my family moved to the suburbs.

By any measure, Chomedey, a bedroom community, a half-hour drive north of Montreal, was not the ideal place to grow up if you wanted to be a writer. Nothing very interesting or exotic ever happened, or so I thought at the time. I felt stopped before I started: mired in suburban innocuousness with my happy, harmless family. We were content and secure, and we must have looked boring. It sure felt that way. It took me a long time to figure out that it wasn't my suburb that was short on interesting material; I was short on the ability to recognize it.

It took me even longer to realize that when it came to choosing my first favourite author I couldn't have done much better than Richler. When you're young, you don't always know what you're learning even while you're learning it. But I know now. Richler, more than any other writer, would teach me, through his example as much as his work, that a writer could focus on a small, even a provincial place, and if he wrote about it honestly and intimately enough, he could make it his own. More than that, he could make it matter. Who had ever heard of St. Urbain Street before Richler turned his grumpy gaze its way? No one. Even the big talkers in the neighbourhood—many of whom Richler would give a voice to, the self-made philosophers and poets, the autodidacts who poured over Kafka and Maimonides, Tolstoy and Dante, Marx, Karl and Groucho—would never have thought of their neighbourhood as the kind of place you could write about. Richler learned how to be a good writer when he realized that where he came from was not a weakness but a strength, his most enduring one.

"I'm stuck with my original notion, which is to be an honest witness to my time, my place," Richler told me when I first interviewed him in 1991. He was repeating an already often-repeated comment. But he could still make it sound fresh, like he genuinely meant it. Obviously, because he still did. "I do feel forever rooted in Montreal's St. Urbain Street," he adds in "Why I Write." "That was my time, my place, and I have elected myself to get it right."

First, though, he'd have to get it wrong.

Mordecai & Me

Published in 1955, a year after *The Acrobats*, *Son of a Smaller Hero* is a novel overloaded with grudges. The story is slight, but it serves Richler's purpose. It allows him to settle a variety of scores—against family, community, religion, Jewish parochialism, and gentile prejudice and hypocrisy. No one was going to get off easy. Richler's gloomy young protagonist, Noah Adler, makes that clear. "Although Noah believed that you could love one man or two men or ten men he did not believe that you could love man," Richler writes. "Not man, and not mankind. Such generalities, such loves, were the tormented inventions of those who loved with much facility and no truth."

Richler's opinion on the subject of love would, thankfully, change qualitatively over the years, though not quantitatively. He would never see the wisdom or the percentage in believing in people by the bunch. He was a natural-born pessimist. For Richler, the choice was never between the glass being half-full or half-empty, but half-empty or turned over on its side.

In *Son of a Smaller Hero*, even the neighbourhood around St. Urbain Street, which Richler would treat with some measure of affection and nostalgia in his later fiction and nonfiction, does not fare well. Montreal's Jewish district is called a ghetto in the novel, which feels, in retrospect, like an overstatement. This description, on the second page, is particularly unforgiving:

> The ghetto of Montreal has no real walls and no true dimensions. The walls are the habit of atavism and the dimensions are an illusion. But the ghetto exists all the same. The fathers say, "I work like this so it'll be better for the kids." A few of the fathers, the dissenters . . . drink instead. But in the end it amounts to the same thing: in the end, work, drink, or what have you, they are all trying to fill the void.

Compare this to the description of the same streets in the early pages of *The Apprenticeship of Duddy Kravitz*, published four years later, and it's clear that Richler's relationship with his place had changed:

> To a middle-class stranger, it's true, one street would have seemed as squalid as the next. . . . An endless repetition of pre-

cious peeling balconies and waste lots making the occasional gap here and there. But, as the boys knew, each street between St. Dominique and Park Avenue represented subtle differences in income. No two cold-water flats were alike.

A whole lot of literary maturity is contained in that last line. So while it doesn't sound like much of an artistic rallying cry, it is just about the most important lesson a writer, particularly a young writer, can learn: the recognition that even in the smallest things, the most seemingly insignificant incident, the most ordinary person, the most recognizable emotion, there is incalculable richness.

The most obvious difference between *Duddy Kravitz* and *Son of a Smaller Hero* is one of tone. *Duddy Kravitz* is essentially comic—though Richler didn't originally see it as a comic novel—and *Son of a Smaller Hero* is essentially melodramatic, with moments of tragedy. But there is also a difference of intent. By the time he'd completed the manuscript for *Duddy Kravitz*, Richler had realized this was the world he would be writing about, in one way or another, for the rest of his life. In the winter of 1959, even before *Duddy Kravitz* was accepted for publication, Richler had plans, as he wrote to Brian Moore, to complete a trilogy of novels about his hero. (He had a tentative title picked out for his next novel, *Dudley Kane's First Marriage*.) But more than that, *Duddy*, he said, would also be "the springboard for a whole clutch of novels, big and small, about St. Urbain Street alumni. . . . Briefly, I'm staking out a claim to Montreal Jew-ville in the tradition of H. de Balzac and Big Bill Faulkner." St. Urbain Street, he would repeat in a letter to his friend William Weintraub, was to be his Yoknapatawpha County.

Richler's plans for *Son of a Smaller Hero* could hardly have been more different. In fact, *Son of a Smaller Hero* is a novel about a young man, almost identical to Richler, fleeing from "Montreal Jew-ville." The point of the book was to say goodbye to all that. To purge it from his system. It's no wonder that Noah Adler, Richler's hero, is so hard to warm to. He doesn't have a good word to say about anyone, himself included. Throughout the novel, he is referred to as "sullen," "ruthless," "slightly pompous," "an opportunist," and "a miserable flop." Instead of *A*

Mordecai & Me

Portrait of the Artist as a Young Man, we get *A Portrait of the Artist as a Pain in the Ass.*

There is no plot to speak of in Richler's second novel—because of its autobiographical elements, many critics referred to *Son of a Smaller Hero* as Richler's second first novel—just a series of scenes in which Noah, like his biblical namesake, prepares himself for a voyage away from a society he perceives as irredeemably corrupt and hypocritical. Like Joyce's young artist, Stephen Dedalus, Noah is determined to fly above the conventional bonds of society. And so he does. Noah is set up to be morally superior to everyone else in the novel, not a hard task given the collection of ne'er-do-wells, hypocrites, and schemers in the book. "A bigshot," Noah's father, Wolf, calls his son. The sarcastic tone aside, there is no doubt that Noah is a sincere model for a young man of promise, in other words, for his slightly older, slightly wiser creator. I never doubted for a moment that Noah's insights were also Richler's. "It's too bad," Noah tells an old lover, "that there is no longer anything that one could wholly belong to. This is the time of buts and parentheses." Which is, incidentally, about as pretentious a line as Richler would write. In the end, Noah is allowed his escape, although to Richler's credit, he doesn't get away clean. His mother dies, calling out for him. His grandfather, Melech, puts a curse on him: "Melech's God, who was stern, sometimes just and always without mercy, would reward him and punish the boy. Melech could count on that."

The author's note at the beginning of *Son of a Smaller Hero* is not a typical disclaimer, the kind that routinely accompanies a work of fiction. It is not the usual wink to the reader who, if he even bothers to read it, takes it with a grain of salt. Instead, Richler isn't winking; he's waving both arms in the air like a man trying to prevent a train wreck. He's also issuing a warning. Make no easy assumptions, he's saying. Things are not as straightforward as they seem. But in his warning, he ends up saying much more than he needs to. His comments are revealing.

"Although all the streets described in this book are real streets, and the seasons, tempers, and moods are those of Montreal as I remember them, all the characters portrayed are works of the imagination and all the situations they find themselves in are fictional," Richler insists in his author's note. Then he adds that "Any reader approaching this book in a

Welcome to Jew-ville

search for 'real people' is completely on the wrong track and, what's more, has misunderstood my whole purpose. *Son of a Smaller Hero* is a novel, not an autobiography."

Why did he need to be so adamant and condescending, chastising readers beforehand for not understanding his "whole purpose?" Doesn't this sound like a young man protesting too much? What was he so worried about? Letting the autobiographical cat out of the bag, what else? Or, in the case of his second novel, stuffing it back in once it was out. Where Richler's first effort, *The Acrobats*, is a kind of paint-by-numbers literary exercise—all his influences rolled into one story—*Son of a Smaller Hero* comes directly out of Richler's own experience. Literary artifice is laid on after the fact.

Fiction writers may be "paid liars," as Richler always insisted, but readers don't read fiction for lies. We read it for the truth and not just the big truth either, but for all the little ones along the way. Who behaved like a prick? Who fucked whom? Who loved whom? Who betrayed whom? After he finished the first draft of *Son of a Smaller Hero*, Richler predicted, in a letter to William Weintraub, that the book would "get me in good trouble in Montreal." For all its rough edges, *Son of a Smaller Hero* is still a powerful piece of work, despite itself and its not entirely compatible mix of farce and tragedy. By the end of the novel, Noah Adler shows signs of growing up and so does the author who created him. Set to leave home for Europe, for freedom, maybe forever, Noah delivers this surprisingly tempered and self-aware speech to his grandfather:

> You said you wanted me to be a Somebody. A Something. I've come to tell you that I have rules now. I'll be a human being. . . .
> I am going and I'm not going. I can no more leave you, my mother, or my father's memory, than I can renounce myself. But I can refuse to take part in this. . . .

"This" refers to all the things Richler was also trying to pry himself loose from: a striving after material success and Jewish solidarity, family loyalty and respectability. Of course, it's technically true to say, as Richler does in his author's note, that *Son of a Smaller Hero* is a novel and not an autobiography, but only technically. That he believed he could get away with this kind of denial of the story's origins is also a reminder that Richler became a writer at a time when the distance between a writer's life and his work was respected, even protected beyond the point that we can now reasonably expect in a world hooked on reality TV and confessional writing.

Still, when Richler was starting out, invisible barriers were set up to keep a naturally curious reader from making embarrassing assumptions about what was invented in a literary work and what was true or even inspired by true events. When I was in university in the 1970s and reading modernist icons like T.S. Eliot and James Joyce, no one—no teacher or student—thought to question a writer's lofty and self-serving claims to objectivity and detachment.

Writers got away with murder, in other words. They could deal with the most personal subjects and still claim, with a straight face, as Joyce did, that the writer "like the God of creation, remains . . . above his handiwork, invisible, paring his fingernails." Or they could say, as Eliot did in the essay "Tradition and the Individual Talent," that poetry is "not the expression of personality, but an escape from personality." But Eliot's personality, the supercilious old fogey, was in everything he wrote. So in *The Waste Land*, his most famous poem, not to mention one of the most influential poems of the twentieth century, you weren't supposed to know it, but you were reading the words spoken by his wife as she was having a nervous breakdown.

Who do writers think they are kidding? I always wonder. All the warnings and admonitions, all the disclaimers, will never stop readers from gossiping about what really happened in a book or who's really who. Does this take away from the literary quality of a novel? Of course not. Can it add to the reader's pleasure? I'm convinced of it. In the case of *Son of a Smaller Hero*, gossip adds another layer of interest and curiosity to the story. How can you ignore the fact that the incident which kick-starts the novel has an identical counterpart in Richler's essay, "My Father's Life." In the novel, an eleven-year-old Noah witnesses his beloved and revered grandfather Melech cheating a customer. Melech Adler, an unyielding and pious man, runs the family and the family scrap yard, and is viewed by Noah up until this point as being incapable of doing wrong.

Welcome to Jew-ville

In fact, Melech is harsh and demanding with his own children, in particular Noah's put-upon father, Wolf, but he treats Noah, his first-born grandchild, with uncharacteristic kindness. Meanwhile, Noah trails after the old man "like a shadow, leaping dreamily before him down the street and allowing no other to carry his prayer shawl."

So when Noah sees his grandfather getting a vulnerable customer drunk with the obvious intention of underpaying him, Noah thinks there must be a mistake. He confronts his grandfather about what he's witnessed, thinking his grandfather will be grateful to have the oversight corrected, but he gets slapped for his trouble and hurried out of sight. The slap is all the incentive Noah needs to turn away from his family, his community, his faith.

The Richler family was in the scrap business, too, and, as a boy, Richler also saw his grandfather, whom he describes in *The Street* as "uncompromisingly orthodox," giving "short weight on his [scrap yard] scales to a drunk Irish pedlar." There is hardly a difference in the real scene as it is described in "My Father's Life" and the fictional one in *Son of a Smaller Hero*, except that Richler's real relationship with his grandfather was already troubled before the incident in the scrap yard. Richler was looking for a reason to hate the old man, and, "scornful, triumphant," he found it. This was a sign of things to come. Richler as a child and as a man had no tolerance for hypocrisy. His talent was for exposing it.

Neither the child nor the man would forgive easily. After another run-in with his grandfather, in which Richler was literally thrown out of the house, the relationship between the two ended for good. Richler vowed never to speak to his grandfather again, and he stuck to that vow. Even so, when his grandfather died not long after their estrangement, Richler, at his mother's urging, attended the funeral. It turned out he was not the only Richler who could hold a grudge. "You are not a good Jew," Richler was told by an uncle, "and you are not to touch his coffin. It says that in his will."

Tolstoy was wrong in the opening lines of *Anna Karenina* when he said that happy families are the same while unhappy ones are all different; they aren't that different from one another. There is a template for the unhappy scenarios: weak men and disappointed women. (In my parents' case, and I daresay my own, weak men and strong women make for a much more amenable combination.) In *Son of a Smaller Hero,* the marriage of Noah's mother and father is a predictable disaster. She nags; he tries, though not always very hard, to appease her. Perhaps the most heartbreaking moment in all of Richler's early fiction comes when Wolf Adler recounts for his impatient wife a conversation he had with his father about the possibility of him becoming a partner in the business. Even though he gets nowhere with Melech, he still tries to hold out some hope to his wife that things are going to change. But he can't convince her; he can barely convince himself: "Anyway, Leah, what I mean to say is he didn't say yes but he didn't say no. That's a start, you know."

Just a few paragraphs later, Leah reluctantly watches her husband undress for bed: "She had wanted not to look but the very revulsion she felt for his body had compelled her to.... She had watched him scratch his back and then slump down on the edge of his bed and pick his toes.... She had seen him scratch under his armpits and then smell his hand. That's when she had turned to the wall. Turned quickly, repudiating him."

This is a scene written by a kid—a kid with neither the patience nor the experience to understand the mistakes and the compromises married people make. There is very little compassion in this scene; there is barely a trace of sadness. All parties are condemned—the father for his crudeness, the mother for her disgust, and the son, the author, too, for his coldness, his detachment. Everything Richler knew about marriage is conveyed in the turning away at the end of the scene, the moment of repudiation. Can there by any doubt where he learned it?

The marriage of Richler's mother and father was an arranged one and, to hear Leah Rosenberg tell it in her memoir, *The Errand Runner,* it was also doomed from the start. "I was strong and spirited, and Aron was weak and passive," Rosenberg writes, changing her husband's first name from Moses to Aron. "I could not abide weakness. As a wife I was eager to give of myself so that my husband could achieve his goals faster through my assistance. In the end my strength would prove a weakness."

In "My Father's Life," Richler describes the relationship from his father's point of view—a man who was nagged, humiliated, betrayed, and frightened by his wife. Marriage was not a partnership for his parents; it

Welcome to Jew-ville

was a debit sheet of disappointments, most of them caused by his father and endured by his long-suffering mother. The same dynamic exists in Richler's novels. The best you can do if you're the mother of one of Richler's protagonists, is be dead and buried before the story begins, as the mother is in *The Apprenticeship of Duddy Kravitz*. Otherwise, chances are you will be portrayed as the Jewish mother from hell—manipulative, demanding, and suffocating. This character is played largely for laughs in later novels like *Joshua Then and Now*, where Joshua's mother does a striptease at her son's bar mitzvah, or *St. Urbain's Horseman*, where Jake Hersh's mother is first seen rummaging through her gentile daughter-in-law's lingerie drawer: "For Yankel's princess, silk panties yet. If she ever got a splinter in her ass, that one, only rosewood would do." In *Son of a Smaller Hero*, Leah Adler is less amusing and a lot more destructive. Noah Adler doesn't have the advantage Richler's later heroes would have—a supportive, loving wife.

The fathers in Richler's fiction are invariably losers, though occasionally colourful ones like Reuben Shapiro in *Joshua Then and Now* and Izzy Panofsky in *Barney's Version*. They are also harmless—with the exception of L.B. Berger, Moses' father in *Solomon Gursky Was Here*—to the point of being ineffectual. They are small-timers, henpecked, eventually cuckolded. Judged, they are always found wanting. Like Richler's own father, they have "the Midas touch in reverse." But if they are leading lives of quiet desperation, they don't necessarily keep quiet about it. They are chroniclers of slights, big and small, bards of unhappiness. In *Solomon Gursky Was Here*, a cuckolded husband discovers his wife has cheated on him with his best friend and chess partner. Weeping, he asks, "Who will I play chess with now that Simcha has dishonoured me?"

Richler mostly joked about or dismissed the effect on him of his parents' disastrous relationship and their eventual break up. (His mother secured an annulment in 1944, providing her pleased son with an opportunity to brag that, yes, he really was a bastard.) But he also knew the damage being done. He had a front row seat, after all. His essay "My Father's Life," which is included in *Home Sweet Home*, remains one of the most moving and intimate pieces, nonfiction or fiction, Richler ever wrote. In it, he describes, in unsparing detail, all that his father—"a short man, squat, with a shiny bald head and big floppy ears, Richler ears"—missed out on:

> My father never saw Paris. Never read Yeats. Never stayed out with the boys drinking too much. Never flew to New York on a whim. Nor turned over in bed and slept in, rather than report to work. Never knew a reckless love. What did he hope for? What did he want? Beyond peace and quiet, which he seldom achieved, I have no idea.

While literary ambition was compelling Richler to leave for Europe when he was nineteen, his home life wasn't providing much incentive to stay. He was, he admitted later, "a very unhappy young man," intent on "getting the hell out of Montreal." But if he could run, he could not hide. Like Noah in *Son of a Smaller Hero*, Richler was "going and he was not going." He would take the home he was so eager to leave with him everywhere. He would take his grudges, too. Leah Adler is hit with a double whammy. She is clinging and suffocating, and by the end of the story, she is dead, though in the context of the novel, her death could be seen as her final revenge on her ungrateful son. It's also curious that Richler, so determined to point out that his second novel was fiction and not autobiography, did not even bother to change his mother's first name. It's a telling choice and a pointed one. It reveals how unwilling Richler would always be to compromise. There would be consequences for his obstinacy, but he would learn to live with them.

In *Son of a Smaller Hero*, fate isn't any kinder to Noah's father, Wolf, but the author is. Wolf loses his life during a fire at his father's scrap yard, where he is as unappreciated as the rest of the hired help. He dies rescuing a safety deposit box from his father's office, which turns out to contain a Torah that Melech Adler crafted himself. In a community already sliding toward assimilation, Wolf is hailed as a Jewish hero, a keeper of the faith. But the truth is Wolf knew nothing about the Torah. He had always assumed, incorrectly, that the box his father locked every night was full of cash. He risked his life for what he believed was his rightful compensation for years of neglect and humiliation at the hands of the imperious old man. Richler plays a cruel joke on Wolf, all for the sake of

Welcome to Jew-ville

an ironic plot twist, but even so Wolf is the kind of unsympathetic character Richler was determined to make sympathetic. Hard as he tries, Richler only succeeds in making Wolf pathetic. After his father's death, Noah discovers Wolf's diary, a sad list of mundane events and banal commentaries. Wolf calculates that "every twenty years (approx.) I walk across the earth just going back and forth in Montreal." The diary also lists "memories—projects—inventions—and thoughts," and all of them in an arcane, heartbreakingly easy-to-decipher code. His secret life was no secret after all.

A similar diary was kept by Moses Richler and is referred to in "My Father's Life." It wasn't lost on the son that his father had been a "keeper of records," a kind of writer, too:

> His diary, wherein he catalogued injuries and insults, betrayals, family quarrels, bad debts, was written in a code of his own invention. His brothers and sisters used to tease him about it.
>
> "Boy, are we ever afraid! Look, I'm shaking." But as cancer began to consume him, they took notice, fluttering about, concerned. "What about Moishe's diary?"

After his father died in 1967, Richler did everything he could to get his hands on the diary—"I wanted it. Oh, how I wanted it. I felt the diary was my proper inheritance," he says in "My Father's Life"—but his father's second wife would not cooperate. Instead, Richler kept his own catalogue of "injuries and insults," remembered slights he would "finally [publish] in a code more accessible than my father's. Making them the stuff of fiction."

Come to think of it, Tolstoy was wrong about happy families, too. They aren't all alike, though I suppose someone as miserable as Tolstoy would have been inclined to feel that way. A sense of moral superiority goes hand in hand with being unhappy, and writers are particularly guilty of this sort of presumption. The value of a miserable childhood to a writer's career should not be underestimated. "They fuck you up, your Mum and Dad," the poet Philip Larkin wrote, and Richler's parents obliged. But

Mordecai & Me

what if they don't oblige—don't fuck you up, I mean. Not in any noticeable way. What then? What's a fellow supposed to write about? To aspire to be a writer, as I did when I was young, and not have an unhappy or, better yet, a traumatic childhood to overcome is like being a bullfighter without the bull, Ali without Frazier, Hillary without Everest, Bill without Hillary. Where are the obstacles, the drama, the wounds, and grudges to nurse?

My parents never fought. I don't mean I never heard them fight. I mean they never did. Whatever slights married people routinely hold onto and try, usually unsuccessfully, to conceal—well, with my parents, they never showed. One reasonable explanation is that they weren't there. What showed, instead, was how much they relied on each other, how grateful they were to each other. My mother fell in love with my father because he was stunningly handsome and desperately needy. He had contracted polio at thirteen and had grown into a shy, self-conscious man. A cripple is what everyone considered him at the time; it's what he considered himself. He wore an iron brace on his right leg and walked with a limp that became more and more pronounced as he got older. But with his thin moustache and wavy hair, he also looked like one of those pretty-boy movie stars of the 1930s. Like Robert Taylor or Don Ameche. What my father lacked was faith in himself. He was given to self-pity, which was more crippling than any physical handicap. What my mother gave him was a break from all his negative thinking, a thirty-year marriage, a kind of remission. If he wasn't entirely free from feeling sorry for himself, the impulse was under control. My mother saved him from himself, and he never forgot it. How could he? He was always grateful, even though gratitude didn't come naturally to him.

Together, my father and mother ran a business, based on his ability as a sign painter and her unwillingness to let him do what he often would have liked to do—give up on himself. Together, they raised a family, bought a house in the suburbs, both miracles of a kind, accomplished at my mother's insistence and over my father's heartfelt but ineffectual objections. They were good role models for my two sisters and me, and if there was a problem, that was it—they were too good. "Happiness not only cannot be recaptured, it can scarcely be described,

Welcome to Jew-ville

let alone analyzed. Unhappiness, on the other hand, analyzes beautifully," the essayist Joseph Epstein says. I could not be a writer if all I had to describe was this happiness—if all I had to analyze was how safe and secure I felt. I didn't hold grudges, not then. I wasn't driven by appetite or anger. I couldn't think of anyone to be angry at.

It's also true that the only example of a relationship I had was that of my parents, so how could I ever expect to find anything to match it, anything that would measure up? It was the same for my two older sisters. None of us were good at relationships. "They fuck you up, your Mum and Dad," Larkin wrote, followed by, "They don't mean to, but they do." My parents' happiness made it impossible for me to conceive of my own. It's no wonder that none of us, my sisters nor I, wanted to leave home. And no wonder we didn't. Home left us instead. When I was twenty-one my mother died of cancer. My father died a little over a year later. Cancer, too, though no one, no doctor, no official cause of death, will ever convince me that he didn't die of a broken heart, his unanticipated loneliness crippling him first, like infantile paralysis all over again.

And so when it came to unhappiness, I was, as with so many other things, an amateur, a late bloomer. Like Richler, thinking he could write St. Urbain Street out of his system with *Son of a Smaller Hero*, I thought I could write my parents' deaths out of mine. Like Richler, I would discover it wasn't so easy.

A few years ago I called a friend to offer my condolences after his father died. He'd just returned from the funeral. He'd gone home several weeks earlier to be with his dying father. Over the phone he described the experience. He also said that he and another friend, who had also lost his father recently, were planning to get together to talk about their respective old men. He asked if I'd like to join them. I was noncommittal, but I knew I wasn't going to show up. I understood the impulse on his part, but I no longer felt it myself. My father had been dead almost twenty years by then, and I had no need to talk him out of my system. Besides, I knew I couldn't. I had absorbed his life, his loss, the way the skin absorbs ultraviolet rays, the damage done before you know it.

Because he was crippled, my father was always at the mercy of other people, most often his family. This often made him impatient. Needy

Mordecai & Me

people don't like feeling needy, so they lose their temper. Gratitude gets old fast; they understand that. Better to be short-tempered, to make people jump than to make them resent you. My father was impatient with me, but then I gave him reason to be. I seldom did what he wanted when he wanted me to. I was forgetful and dreamy. I was resentful, too, for having a crippled father. Writing about him after he died—in a novella, a novel, and a number of essays—I wanted his life to have the meaning I never thought it had when he was working in the basement, shouting up at me to do some chore that had slipped my mind. The last laugh would be on me. There would be more chores and harder ones to take care of after he was gone, which wouldn't slip my mind so easily. I would try to make amends—not to him as much as for him. This is another reason why writers write, in any case—to repair the past or re-imagine it. That this is impossible to do is the best reason I can think of to keep doing it.

"In hindsight, one reason I became a writer is that my father wanted to be one," Phillip Lopate says in his essay, "The Story of My Father." In Philip Roth's memoir of his father's life, *Patrimony,* Roth recounts how in university he felt he was carrying his father around with him from class to class. Roth describes the feeling of having the "impassioned if crazy conviction that I was somehow inhabited by him and quickening his intellect right along with mine." In "My Father's Life," Richler says, "So far as I know [my father] never took a risk or was disobedient.... Nobody was ever afraid of Moses Isaac Richler. He was far too gentle." For his father's sake, Roth would be the smart son; for his father's sake, Richler would take risks, be disobedient, and do his best never to be gentle.

Chapter 6
Richler Revisited

Maybe you should get some sleep.
—My wife

There are one hundred chapters in *Don't Sweat the Small Stuff*, so I'm reading one every night. The book is on my night table, and before I go to sleep, I make a show of thumbing through it, clearing my throat and announcing that night's topic for my wife's benefit. Chapter 29. "Become a Better Listener." She thinks I'm kidding around, teasing her for buying me the book in the first place, and maybe it started out that way, but it's becoming something of a bedtime ritual. Before I met my wife, I fell asleep with the television set on. It's what I'd been doing since I was a toddler. I was the youngest of three children, and my parents had become a lot more lenient by the time I showed up. I'd also been sick as a baby and had stopped breathing a couple of times in the middle of the night, so at bedtime they let me do whatever I wanted, which meant I fell asleep in

Mordecai & Me

the living room watching Jack Parr. But my wife, I discovered early in our relationship, will not watch television in bed. She also refuses to have a television in the bedroom, even one that's shut off. "I don't trust them," she says. You can't, I eventually realized, argue with logic like that.

But if *Don't Sweat the Small Stuff* is supposed to replace the television as a soporific for me, it's not working. If anything, it's keeping me awake, a reminder of all the books I should be reading instead—a growing pile of unmet literary obligations. For starters, there is the eclectic assortment of books that influenced Mordecai Richler: like Ivan Aleksandrovich Goncharov's *Oblomov*, the classic nineteenth-century Russian novel about a self-pitying, good-for-nothing serf owner. Richler speaks about it glowingly in his essays, and I've skimmed enough of it to know why. The title character is an ineffectual dolt, pushed around by everyone, including his unhappy servant. We should despise him, but somehow we don't. The point of the novel is to expose the evil of serfdom, but instead its author creates, in the title character, a man we can't help feeling sympathy for, despite everything he does and stands for. Goncharov, whether he intended to be or not, was "the loser's advocate."

I should also be reading Malraux and Céline and Sartre, but I've decided, quite arbitrarily, I'll admit, that no one over the age of forty should be obliged to ever read a twentieth-century French novel again. Richler loved part-time Canadian Malcom Lowry's *Under the Volcano*, too, but I read it in university and remember it most of all for being virtually unreadable. The same goes for Faulkner. Hemingway's *A Moveable Feast*, his posthumous memoir of his early days in Paris, is a must, of course, if only for all his nasty remarks about other writers.

I've decided not to read anything about Richler written by academics. A glance at *Perspectives on Mordecai Richler*, a 1986 anthology of critical essays, made up my mind for me. In the conclusion of an essay on the use of syntax in *Duddy Kravitz*, there's this indecipherable passage: "To the ends of the art of collocation Richler has fashioned a syntax unique in several aspects, most notably in its insistent use of nominal and paratactic devices." Life is short; scholarship is long-winded.

I want to read James Boswell's *Life of Johnson*, but I can probably save myself time by just looking up Dr. Johnson in a book of quotations. Or

Richler Revisited

cribbing from the quotes in *Barney's Version*. I'm also discovering a long list of books by writers who speculate, seldom kindly, on their fellow writers. These are the "Judas Biographers," according to John Updike. When he came up with the label, Updike was reviewing Joyce Maynard's memoir about her kinky nine-month relationship with J.D. Salinger, but he was also referring to any writer inclined to exploit his or her relationship, whatever it might be, with a more prominent colleague. Which is what Mark Harris does wonderfully in his chronicle of his unsuccessful attempt to get Saul Bellow to sit still for a biography in *Saul Bellow Drumlin Woodchuck*. There's also *Sir Vidia's Shadow*, Paul Theroux's irresistibly bitchy account of the deterioration of his thirty-year friendship with V.S. Naipaul. And Ian Hamilton's *In Search of J.D. Salinger*, a biography so unauthorized it caused Salinger to come out of seclusion to sue.

In *U and I*, Nicholson Baker is haunted by the book he should be reading but is deliberately avoiding—*The Anxiety of Influence*, Harold Bloom's elaborate theory on how poets invariably distort the work of the writers who have influenced them. I know I should read Bloom, too, but the copy I reserved from the Concordia University library has mysteriously disappeared. I'm taking this as a sign.

In the meantime, there is *Don't Sweat the Small Stuff*. "Chapter 30," I say aloud, for my wife's benefit, "'Choose Your Battles Wisely.'" She pulls her pillow over her head and groans. She's kidding, I think. My wife and I didn't get to know each other very well before we got married, and sometimes I feel the need to explain a running gag to her.

On a cold October Sunday morning, I am milling about with fifteen other curious Richler fans at the corner of Laurier Avenue and Boulevard St. Laurent—the renowned Main. We are gathered for a walking tour of Mordecai Richler's real and fictional neighbourhood. Stan Asher tells us the whole thing will last about an hour and forty minutes. The word *garrulous* was invented for Asher: he is chatty, even for a tour guide. He is, among other things, a college English teacher, a columnist for a community newspaper, and a volunteer radio host at a community station. But his specialty, walking tours of Montreal's literary landmarks, have taken a toll on Asher's legs. Getting around is an effort. Still, every now and then he guides people through Leonard Cohen's Montreal or David Fennario's or A.M. Klein's. Mordecai Richler's Montreal is more popular than ever these days.

Asher went to Baron Byng at the same time as Richler, but he doesn't remember him from those days. For that matter, he is not much of a fan or afficionado of the grown-up Richler. He prefers Richler's stories and some of his essays to his novels. But, like Richler, he is struck most by the differences between the neighbourhood of his memory and the one staring him in the face. In *Barney's Version,* Barney can't get used to the transformation:

> The shoeshine parlour where I used to take my father's fedora to be blocked has been displaced by a unisex hair stylist. . . . Mr. Katz's Supreme Kosher Meat Market has yielded to a video-rental outlet: ADULT MOVIES OUR SPECIALTY. My old neighbourhood now also boasts a New Age bookstore, a vegetarian restaurant . . . and a Buddhist temple of sorts.

Stan Asher carries a battered paperback copy of Richler's essay collection *Home Sweet Home* and stops every now and then to read a passage from the nostalgic piece "St. Urbain Street Then and Now." What he reads is supposed to connect with where we happen to be on the tour, but more often than not, the excerpt, barely audible because of the traffic, is just another example of Richler being deliberately provocative and spiteful. "Well, that's Richler for you," Asher likes to say.

When I showed up late, Asher introduced me to the small crowd with, "Ah, we're in luck—the biographer." I shrugged and shuffled my feet in the cold like everyone else. I wanted to tell everyone, individually, that I was not writing a biography. I had already told Asher as much when we spoke on the telephone. "Really, really, really unauthorized," I said when he asked me if I'd spoken to Florence or Richler's kids or Jack Rabinovitch. But it didn't register. I can't blame him for not understanding the distinction. I don't always understand it myself.

Asher leads us on a tour of the six blocks west and the two blocks east that make up most of Richler's literary landscape. (We don't make it as far south as Baron Byng.) The legend is that the first letters in the names of the streets in what was once Montreal's predominantly Jewish district—Jeanne Mance, Esplanade, Waverly, and St. Urbain—spell out the acronym J.E.W.S.. The implication of this is creepy: was someone trying to keep track of where we were? But this story is probably apocryphal, Asher adds, even though I have the feeling it's not the first time he's told it. Dramatic change is the theme of Asher's tour, so he makes a point of stopping at all the synagogues that have been converted to Ukrainian churches, pointing out the Hebrew writing on the buildings that has been erased. The Ten Commandments, routinely carved into the front of the buildings, have been sandblasted almost out of sight. Apparently, the Ten Commandments were considered too Jewish for the front of a church. There's also the house on St. Urbain Street where Richler grew up. Typical of the neighbourhood and reminiscent of Richler's descriptions are the three-storey apartments crammed together, the tiny balconies and the narrow, winding stairways on the outside, which are hell to navigate in winter. The front of Richler's childhood home is disappointing; it has been renovated and gentrified.

St. Urbain Street, as it's depicted in Richler's memory and imagination, is a rawer place, where life is lived out in the open, clothes flapping on lines, arguments, usually in Yiddish, carrying from one third-floor balcony to the next. The streets are dirtier and so are the kids roaming them. The people, in general, are hungrier and more vulnerable—a convergence of crooks, con men, and dreamers. Socialists are side-by-side with Zionists; atheists rub elbows with the pious. It's not much of a melting pot, and what comes out of it is indigestible. Disappointment, envy, and ambition are the main ingredients. It's a place to leave behind and a place you'll never leave behind no matter how hard you try. Richler could vouch for that; he tried very hard.

Of course, to me, the neighbourhood doesn't look all that different. To me, raised in the subdued suburbs, it is still a crazy, congested place to live. There's a new origami store next to the old twenty-four hour bagel place, a Sufi restaurant across the street from a bistro. There are still lots of Hassidic Jews, in big black hats and long black coats, coming out of kosher butcher shops, glaring at our small group like we're heathens. And in a way we are. Idolaters. Worshipping a blasphemous writer, retracing

Mordecai & Me

his steps like perverse pilgrims. A dapper middle-aged man in a cashmere coat and a red scarf comes out of an upscale café as we pass by. He looks at us with benign curiosity. In French, he asks what we are doing. Then, in the nature of this city these placid days, he switches to English.

"A walking tour of Mordecai Richler's Montreal," someone replies. The man's expression sours. Still, he looks like he's trying to think of something tactful to say. He settles for gentle sarcasm: "Oui, Mordecai Richler. *Our* friend."

After a while, we realize we are being tailed. An old man in a fedora with a frayed feather in the band and a mismatched plaid sports jacket and check pants double-parks his battered Pontiac Parisienne—the size of a stretch limo—on the street, ignores the honking this inspires, and approaches our little group with additional information about the old neighbourhood. He knows where everything is or was. Just ask. "This congregation moved to the West Island twenty years ago," he says pointing to one more synagogue converted to a church. "You want I should tell you the rabbi's name? Where he is now?" Asher nods and keeps moving. The old guy would keep talking if we let him; in fact, he still is talking as we move on. He can't keep up with us on foot so he gets back in his car and follows. The honking persists, now because he's driving so slowly. What Asher fails to point out is that the character in the Pontiac could have stepped straight out of a Richler novel—Duddy's fast-talking father or Joshua Shapiro's or Izzy, Barney Panofsky's dad, or one of the old men Richler always seemed to be running into when he made a public appearance, the guy who would line up at the microphone early for the question-and-answer period to make the inevitable speech: "So Mr. Big-Shot, what makes you so great? Stories? I could tell you stories."

Among my fellow walkers are some of the usual suspects. A couple of guys in their sixties, who didn't know each other before today but are now fast friends, reminiscing about the old days in the neighbourhood. But there's also a couple of women, not Jewish, out for a day of multicultural fun. They ask me what certain Yiddish words mean, but once I've explained that a *goy* is sort of a gentile—"Like us," they say—I'm no help. Asher's wife, who is along on the tour, helps out with *shnorrer* (a moocher or chiseller) and *nisht geferlech* (not so terrible). After the Richler tour and a quick lunch in the neighbourhood—a smoked meat sandwich with mayonnaise, I'm guessing—the gentile ladies intend to take in a lecture downtown on the impact of the Irish community on Montreal.

A young man wearing a *yarmulke* has brought a date on the tour—a pretty young woman from Boston, and even though it's early October, she's wishing she'd worn her winter coat. Both are students at McGill; the young man is from New Jersey. He discovered Richler by accident. In his school library back home, he was looking for something different to read and was struck that there was a writer with the name Mordecai. He was hooked—on *Duddy Kravitz*. From what I can gather, that's all he's read so far. We talk about the book, and his girlfriend perks up when she hears us mention Duddy's older brother, Lennie. "Lenny Kravitz?" she says, shivering but hopeful. "Not the musician," her boyfriend says, though maybe he's not her boyfriend yet. "I should have worn a hat," she says, putting her hands over her ears.

Jeff Barry, who drove in from the West Island for the tour, is a long-time Richler fan. His mother was born and raised on St. Urbain Street around the same time as Richler, and she is one hundred percent Irish, Barry tells me. But he still relates to Richler's writing and quizzes me on which book I like best. I'm noncommittal, so he tells me what he thinks. *Duddy Kravitz* doesn't hold up, he says. But *Barney's Version*, what a book that was! "That's the real loss. The guy was just getting better and better," Barry says.

The tour ends at Wilensky's, the tiny, hole-in-the-wall diner immortalized in *Duddy Kravitz*, novel and movie. In "St. Urbain Street Then and Now" Richler writes, "Nobody who was raised on St. Urbain Street ventures into the old neighbourhood without stopping for a special at Wilensky's, corner of Clark and Fairmount. A special, I should point out, is made up of cuts of different kinds of salami, grilled in a delicious roll." Richler was not above being nostalgic. The sandwich, one of our group says, is heartburn city.

As the crowd breaks up and we go our separate ways, the old man in the Parisienne honks and waves goodbye, rolling down his window to tell us that he'll lead the tour next time. Jeff Barry wants to keep talking about Richler. He wonders aloud, "Do you think he was a great writer?"

Mordecai & Me

I'm surprised that I don't know what to say. I shrug again. Shouldn't I have posed and answered this question for myself already? I'm noncommittal again; I talk about how I think Richler is the best writer this country has ever produced. But that is, as Richler himself would have recognized, a backhanded compliment. World-famous in Canada, as he would have put it. He was very good, I suggest; some of his novels should definitely last.

"But if we call Dostoyevsky or Dickens great, isn't it just because they lived a long time ago? If Richler's best novels measure up, and I say they do," Barry says, "then shouldn't we call Richler great, too? Or do we not say so just because he's from here, because he was one of us? And so what? So that disqualifies him? What does that say about us?"

I nod and duck the question. It's cold and I want to get home. Even so, I can't help thinking: what does that say about *us*?

In *Bellow,* James Atlas's biography of Saul Bellow, Atlas says, "Writers' images tend to become fixed in our mind at a late stage of their careers, the triumphant stage, when they've reached the pinnacle of fame." That's true of Mordecai Richler. The first task I set for myself when I started this book was to read or, in most cases, reread Richler's books with a fresh eye. With *The Acrobats,* his first novel, and *A Choice of Enemies,* his third, I assumed that would be easy because I'd never even heard of either of them before. But, despite that, reading these early novels, I couldn't clear my head of all the things I already knew about the author, about what he would go on to do and become.

For better or worse, our sense of Richler is fixed: the dishevelled curmudgeon; the man whose bad-hair day seemed to stretch into decades; who always looked as if he wanted a drink or a cigar, even if he had the one in his hand and the other sticking out of his mouth; who was making an effort, though not a particularly wholehearted one, not to act superior; who shunned the spotlight, but still seemed to believe he deserved it; who had, over the course of an almost fifty-year career, given us all what for. A thorn in the side was what he had been, a fly in the ointment, a satirist, a self-proclaimed moralist, a shit-disturber, a practical joker, a traitor, a judgemental, memorable, unrepentant, magnificent pain in the ass. He looked the way he looked and acted the way he acted because he wrote the way he wrote. "Mordecai's whole attitude was take it or leave it," his friend William Weintraub told me. "He was saying, 'I said that and I'm not ashamed of it and I'm not going to explain it to you. If you don't like it, too bad.'"

This is the challenge that reading—and rereading—Richler presents. It was foolish to think I could come to any of his work without bringing my mixed feelings about the author to bear. Forget the literary theorists. Books can't be deconstructed; they can't be detached from an author's biases or bad moods or, for that matter, a reader's. I can't help looking for Richler, the sourpuss, in everything he writes, in every novel and short story, every essay and every published interview and speech delivered. In *The Acrobats,* Richler hid, but he did not run—the protagonist André Bennett is a gentile and a painter, but his precociously gloomy outlook matches that of his creator. Young writers tend to be bleaker than they have to be, and Richler was no exception. The world sucks, *The Acrobats* tells us, and there is no hope. Whores aren't just whores; they are one-eyed. Adolescents aren't just pimply; they have a stump instead of a leg. "Nobody could quite believe again that he had grown up to find all Gods dead," Richler writes, "all wars fought, all faiths in men shaken."

A Choice of Enemies, published in 1957, is bleak, too. But where *The Acrobats* takes pleasure in its existential angst—it's charged with it, you could say—*A Choice of Enemies* is full of middle-class ennui. It feels like an intellectual exercise, like a book Richler shouldn't have been wasting his time on while on his way to *The Apprenticeship of Duddy Kravitz.* Early in their careers, it's common for writers to be out of control; in *A Choice of Enemies,* Richler exercises too much control. For a start, *A Choice of Enemies* has more plot than most of Richler's novels, though what plot there is tends to be hard to buy. It rests on the chance meeting and the unlikely bond between the protagonist, Norman Price, an expatriate Canadian teaching and writing in London, and the young German he befriends. Richler's literary influences are better integrated in *A Choice of Enemies* than they are in *The Acrobats.* The novel is also more mature than the autobiographical *Son of a Smaller Hero.* But what gets left out along the way is sorely missed. The novel does not play to Richler's strengths. He was at his best writing about characters who were scoundrels and schemers—like Duddy or Mr. Bernard in *Solomon Gursky Was Here*. A kind of impersonal scorn and apathy is the best he can muster for the cast of expatriates in *A Choice of Enemies*. In retrospect, *A Choice of Enemies* feels very much like a Canadian novel of its time: competent and predictable. Hugh MacLennan could have written it. MacLennan could have created Richler's earnest protagonist, Norman Price, too.

The creation of Norman Price may have been a case of literary wishful thinking on Richler's part, an attempt to do what he was not personally predisposed to do and what he would never do again—create a hero nothing at all like himself. It may have been one last attempt to write with the kind of detachment he always preached, but never practised. The strategy doesn't work, and the surest sign of that, reading the novel now, is how much you can't help missing Richler's sardonic, pushy presence. Norman Price's world-weariness may have fit the literary trend of the time, but it did not fit Richler. He never grew weary of the things and people he mocked and despised.

Placed between the novel it came after, *Son of a Smaller Hero,* and the one it preceded, *The Apprenticeship of Duddy Kravitz, A Choice of Enemies* feels like a misstep or, more precisely, a step back for a writer who had, in *Son of a Smaller Hero,* just stumbled onto his true material. *A Choice of Enemies* feels like a deliberate turning away from that material—another indication that *Son of a Smaller Hero* was intended to be Richler's goodbye to St. Urbain Street and all that it represented.

His intention was, as he confesses with some embarrassment in the essay "Home Is Where You Hang Yourself," to put his "picayune past" behind him and transcend the narrow-minded world he was born into. *A Choice of Enemies* is his valedictorian speech, and like such speeches it covers all the bases and is quickly forgotten.

Reading *The Apprenticeship of Duddy Kravitz* now—having read it for the first time more than thirty years ago—I have to agree with the fellow I met on the walking tour: not all of it holds up. Its comic scenes—like the avant-garde bar mitzvah documentary—are still wonderfully funny, classic in fact. But the narrative, driven by a kind of raw energy, appealed to me more as a young man than it does now. Whatever connection I felt to Duddy, whatever pity or even envy he inspired in me, has been replaced with middle-aged impatience. There is some of that same impatience with the writing. Now I wonder why the book isn't more polished. Why didn't Richler take more time with the simplest transitions from one scene to the next? Still, all that is quibbling. Reread *Duddy Kravitz* and you also can't help being struck, immediately, by how ideal the match between story and storyteller.

Richler was right—the first twenty years were the most important ones, for him anyway. After three more or less false starts, *Duddy Kravitz* would prove that point. There is no denying the importance of what Richler discovered writing *Duddy Kravitz*. It's what all writers eventually have to discover if they are going to succeed. You are who you are and you know what you know. And if you're going to be good, maybe even great, that should be enough. It would be for Richler. With *Duddy Kravitz*, Mordecai Richler's apprenticeship was over.

Part Two
Cocksure
1959–1971

Chapter 7
Dreaming of Yann Martel

Life is filled with opportunities to choose between making a big deal of something or simply letting it go.
—Don't Sweat the Small Stuff

"So how's that writing *thing* going?" a friend of my wife asks whenever she sees me. She doesn't ask the question immediately, but it comes eventually, and I have started to wait for it with more and more impatience. Maybe I'm oversensitive, but I always hear something like doubt in the inquiry, as if she can't quite believe writing is a real job. Or *my* real job anyway. Maybe that's because she's a physiotherapist by profession, and she can't get her head—or hands—around something she perceives as ephemeral or impractical. She always sounds as if she's asking me about a hobby, something I do in my spare time, like birdwatching or fantasy baseball.

My wife's friend is part of a couples book club, and when my wife and I were first married, we were eagerly recruited. We must have seemed like an obvious addition to the group. I declined. "Don't I read enough

Dreaming of Yann Martel

books?" I complained to my wife. "Is it too much to ask to spend an evening watching television?" But I did agree to show up if the couples book club ever decided they wanted to discuss my novel, which had been out less than a year at the time. So far they've declined.

This sort of thing shouldn't bother me. My wife, who is caught in the middle of my hypersensitivity and her friend's obliviousness, reminds me that her friend—"Our friend," she corrects herself—is a caring, compassionate person (she works with the Native community). She reminds me, too, that when our son was born four years ago, her friend could always be counted on for second-hand clothes and toys as well as advice. "Of course," I say, nodding. But my irritation only increases. Now, after my wife's friend asks me how the writing thing is going, she asks what I'm working on. No matter how often I tell her I'm doing a book about Mordecai Richler, she looks surprised, as if she were about to say, "You?"

"She doesn't mean anything by it," my wife says, giving her well-meaning friend the benefit of the doubt. "And, by the way, she'd also like to borrow *Life of Pi,* if you still have your copy."

"What does that mean?"

"Sweetheart, try not to make a big deal out of this. I know you're going to, but try not to. Lots of people are reading it. It did win the Booker prize. You said yourself it was amazing that a Montrealer, someone you actually knew—"

"She wants it for her book club, doesn't she?"

Several months before he won the Booker Prize, I dreamt about Yann Martel. I had just read a story in the newspaper about the gap in the Montreal literary scene since Mordecai Richler's death, and how, if there was going to be a logical successor to Richler in this town, Yann Martel was the guy. I also saw a brief but glowing mention of *Life of Pi* in a review in *Harper's,* which was, I'm ashamed to admit, enough to convince me not to renew my subscription to the magazine. If you want an idea of how petty writers can be—all right, this particular writer—there you have it. For a writer, jealousy is like solitude or carpal tunnel syndrome—an occupational hazard.

89

Mordecai & Me

Anyway, the Martel dream was brief, and I didn't bother waking my wife to recount it. But here's how it goes: I'm in a library or bookstore, I can't remember which and I don't suppose it matters, when Yann Martel shows up and begins to lecture me on all the things I'm doing wrong with the writing of *Mordecai & Me*. His main complaint is that the book is too subjective. This is puzzling. Or at least I am puzzled in the dream. *What else could it be?* I say. *What should it be:* Mordecai & Someone Else Entirely?

Later, Layne Dalfen, my dream analyst, targeted this subjective–objective business as worth exploring at our one and only meeting. We set up polarities in our dreams, she said, oppositional forces that are intended to make us view ourselves and our behaviour less subjectively. This fellow, Martel, who represents success for you, a kind of success you can only dream about, is not your nemesis, she went on, he's your sounding board. Maybe you do have to consider being less subjective; maybe that's the issue for you, not just in this book, but in your life.

How's that possible? I thought. But I said, "Makes sense." Ready to leave, I gave her a signed copy of my novel, my highly autobiographical, unrelentingly subjective novel, and then she said, "You do realize I am charging you for this session?"

"Sure," I said, though I realized nothing of the kind. I assumed she understood I was there to interview her, a journalist researching my book, discussing hers. She assumed I was there as a client. I turned away from her as I tried to calculate how much ninety minutes of my yammering about my rather transparent dreams was going to cost. If it did turn out to be more than I imagined, I didn't want her to see me wince or go pale. When she told me $120, I did both, but I did them out of her sight. As a consolation prize, she gave me a signed copy of her book, *Dreams Do Come True*. The inscription reads, "I hope this is the beginning of bigger dreams." What I wonder is whether I can afford them.

I first heard my dream analyst—she is mine now; I have the receipt to prove it—on a radio talk show interpreting a caller's dream. A woman on the line was wondering why she was dreaming about her late father from whom she had been estranged for years. My future dream analyst said, "A person doesn't have to be around for you to work out your issues with them."

"That's sort of what I'm doing with this book, don't you think?" I asked my wife that night.

"That depends."

"On?"

"What those issues are. Or, in this case, whether you really have any?"

"Obviously, I do. I must."

"Or you could be—"

"Imagining them? For the book?"

"Don't put words in my mouth. Or is it too late for that? It is, isn't it? Is this what you writers call creative nonfiction?"

"I have no idea what you're talking about."

Once I'd come up with the idea to write a personal book about Mordecai Richler, I needed something to show potential publishers and agents, so I wrote a six-thousand word essay entitled "Mordecai & Me" to accompany my proposal and outline. More of an overview than a sample chapter, it was really a preliminary attempt to sort out my mixed feelings. On the one hand this; on the other that. Long career. Short fuse. Good writer. Bad personality. Shy, arrogant. Fiercely individualistic, heavy drinker. Potatoes, patatoes. The essay was eventually published in the debut issue of a Montreal magazine called *Maisonneuve*, the title changed to "Me & Mordecai." Because *Maisonneuve* was a new literary magazine—a rarity in this country—it was written up in a few newspaper articles and in one of them, Robert Fulford's column in the *National Post*, "Me & Mordecai" was mentioned. Judging by his brief comments, Fulford, an old friend of Richler's and a much more experienced Richler observer than I, liked the tone of the piece—"breezy" and "skeptical," he called it, "covering a haunting sadness." As far as the content went, he said, "Yanofsky recalls how his identification with Richler grew into a desire that Richler recognize him. That never happened, leaving Yanofsky with a personal relationship existing in his own mind and nowhere else."

Mordecai & Me

"Look at this," I say to my wife, waving Fulford's column at her. This is just before she's at that getting-ready-for-bed zone women get into, so I'm taking my chances. As it is, she's in the bathroom; she's just finished brushing her teeth and my window of opportunity is closing. If I don't get her to read the passage about me, which I've highlighted, before she starts flossing, I know it will have to wait till morning, though maybe just three o'clock in the morning.

"At least he spelled your name right," she says. She reads the few lines quickly, so quickly it's clear she has no intention of reading between them. Then she congratulates me on attracting attention for the book even before it actually is a book. If I have taught her one thing about the writing business, it's that there is no such thing as bad publicity.

"But doesn't it make me sound, you know, a bit unhinged? All this stuff about a personal relationship existing in my mind and nowhere else. What does that sound like to you? Crazy? You're a therapist; you tell me."

"We don't use words like *crazy*, sweetheart. And, besides, you're always saying that's what readers do all the time—imagine a relationship with a writer."

"I guess, but this still makes me sound like some kind of a psychotic stalker."

"Not psychotic."

On the first page of J.D. Salinger's *The Catcher in the Rye*, Holden Caulfield says, "What really knocks me out is a book that, when you're all done reading it, you wish the author that wrote it was a terrific friend of yours and you could call him up on the phone whenever you felt like it." Ironically, Caulfield would never have had any luck getting in touch with Salinger. If he had, Salinger would have gotten himself a restraining order.

Mordecai Richler was another matter. In theory, he was accessible. A creature of habit, he could be found in one of a handful of downtown bars late in the afternoon, when he was still spending time in Montreal. When he was living in the Eastern Townships, you could find him at "an unassuming watering-hole" called the Owl's Nest after his working day, smoking, shooting pool, drinking scotch, and having his ear bent by the locals.

Around town, I heard him give lectures at libraries and universities, and I saw him at the occasional book launch, even for books that were

Dreaming of Yann Martel

not his own. When his own books came out, he did publicity, though always grudgingly. (After he had wandered away from a publicity tour one time too many, a publicist I know bought a pair of toy handcuffs in a dollar store and handcuffed herself to him as a joke. He was not amused.) He also showed up at high school reunions and at the bar mitzvahs and weddings of relatives who were not always happy to see him. He was no recluse. You could also look up *Richler, Mordecai* in the Montreal telephone book if you were a bit obsessed and felt compelled to call him. He might have preferred that his name not be listed, but his wife Florence insisted it would be "pretentious and snobbish" not to have it in the book. "My advantage is that most people don't know my number is there," he told me during an interview. "So they call all around asking other people if they can get them Richler's number."

In practise Richler was a closed book; at least as far as I was concerned, he was. Perhaps Fulford was right: whatever closeness I felt towards Richler I had manufactured. Our relationship was all in my mind. A year after his death, his phone number is still in the book, by the way. I looked it up the other day. Don't ask me why—who knows? All I can say is what good is an obsession if it's not an irrational one?

I first met Mordecai Richler in the fall of 1989 at the Ritz-Carlton Hotel in Montreal. The occasion was the gala for the second annual QSPELL Fiction Award, a literary prize presented to English-language writers living and working in Quebec. I was there because I was one of the jurors for the prize; Richler was attending because his novel *Solomon Gursky Was Here* was going to be declared the winner.

Officially, the jury was unanimous. *Solomon Gursky* had edged out Nino Ricci's *Lives of the Saints*, which would go on to win the Governor General's Award that same year, a prize *Solomon Gursky* wouldn't even be nominated for. Unofficially, I was the difference. Our jury meeting to decide the winner hadn't exactly been *Twelve Angry Men,* but I had behaved out of character: I had lobbied and cajoled my fellow jurors. One definitely wanted Ricci; the other was sitting on the fence and leaning toward Ricci. But I pushed in the other direction—for Richler. I had, also unusual for me, pushed hard.

My plan for my first anticipated encounter with Richler was to tell him all this. And maybe add a bit more about myself. I had been going over the meeting in my head for weeks. The only flaw in the plan went unforeseen—no one was around to introduce us. So I spied on him instead. I saw him in the crowded Ritz banquet hall and approached a bit like a secret agent—serpentine, ducking behind strangers and acquaintances. Richler was characteristically uncomfortable in the company of well-wishers—of readers, that is—and seemed eager to get his cheque for two thousand dollars and go home. He had shown up at the awards ceremony at the last minute—though he lived in the apartment building across the street from the Ritz—and only then because he had been assured that he had won. Nominees weren't supposed to know they had won beforehand, but an exception was made for Richler.

Finally, I approached him and introduced myself. In person and up close, he looked more like a caricature than he did from the distance of a speaker's podium or captured in a photograph or on a television screen. He was a small man with disproportionately large features—floppy ears, bulbous nose, unruly hair. It was a pleasure to finally meet him, I said to Richler at the Ritz, aware intuitively that this was my conversation to keep up. He seemed to grimace. But when I mentioned I was one of the jurors, he perked up a bit. We shook hands, but neither of us said anything more. He nodded, so I nodded back. He looked past me for a familiar face. I could think of nothing to say, and even if I had, I couldn't find the will to say it. I suppose I had used up all my courage introducing myself. And so I missed my opportunity.

But to do what? To slap him on the back and then, when he thanked me for standing up for him, for practically slipping the two grand into his pocket, I would say, "Don't mention it. Glad to do it. You can buy me a drink some time. How about Thursday? You pick the place, Mordy."

In *U and I: A True Story,* Nicholson Baker, the American novelist and essayist, imagines a friendship with his literary idol, John Updike. (The "U" in the title.) The book, which is half self-indulgent memoir and half self-indulgent literary criticism, is an alternately delightful and creepy meditation on the influence John Updike has exerted on Baker's literary aspirations. Mostly, Baker pines for a personal connection with Updike. So, early in his career, when Baker learns that a fellow young writer, Tim O'Brien, has been playing golf with Updike on a regular basis, Baker is stung:

Dreaming of Yann Martel

Out of all the youngish writers living in the Boston area, Updike had chosen Tim O'Brien and not me as his golfing partner. It didn't matter that I hadn't written a book that had won a National Book Award (as O'Brien had for *Going after Cacciato*), hadn't written a book of any kind, and didn't know how to golf: still, I felt strongly that Updike should have asked me.

Standing alone in the Ritz, with Richler already moving on to be congratulated with a slap on the back from a real pal or at least a real acquaintance, I understood exactly what Baker felt—unjustly neglected. True, I didn't hang around bars or drink scotch or shoot pool, but I was still waiting for some kind of invitation from Richler, waiting for him to beckon, and I guess I believed if the summons ever were going to come, it was going to come that night. But it gets worse. I didn't just want him to be my pal; I wanted him to discover me. I was writing a novel, after all. It was almost finished, or so I thought at the time. I could use a blurb, but even more than that, I could use a mentor, a sponsor, the literary equivalent of a sugar daddy. This writing business was tough, Richler knew that, and he could help me out. He helped other writers, according to the Saskatchewan novelist Guy Vanderhaeghe, who gave a tearful tribute to Richler's generosity at the televised Richler tribute marking the first anniversary of his death. Without you knowing it, Vanderhaeghe said, Mordecai would put a good word in the ear of an editor or publisher or agent.

Why not me?

But I also felt that Richler should sense what I wanted from him even if I didn't have the nerve to ask for it. What he probably sensed was that I wanted something entirely inappropriate and, sensing that, he moved on as quickly as he could.

An embarrassing truth: I couldn't think of anything to say to him that night at the Ritz because I was daydreaming. I was waiting for him to declare himself, to confide that he'd been reading my reviews or columns for years and found them droll and perceptive. That he particularly liked a review I'd written of Updike or Bellow or Roth, maybe. Or even the one on him I did for the *Village Voice*. That he was glad to hear I was working on something longer and sure he'd take a look at it. I wanted him to like me, really like me. Now, admitting this, out loud, in a manner of speaking, I feel as foolish as Sally Field accepting her Oscar, her you-like-me-you-really-like-me speech spinning out of control.

Of the invariably awkward encounters between writers and their readers, the British critic Cyril Connolly said, "It may be us they wish to meet, but it's themselves they want to talk about." That night I had missed my opportunity to tell *him* all about *me*. At the time, I wasn't sure I would get another chance. I certainly never dreamed that, given another chance, a few more in fact, I would miss them, too, or take a pass.

Chapter 8
Elected Squares

Writing about the Canadian scene some years back, I spoke of being raised in a country where there were only isolated voices of civilization, here a poet, there a professor, and between, thousands of miles of wheat and indifference.
—Mordecai Richler

It's impossible now to imagine a time when Mordecai Richler was not an integral part of this country's literary, cultural, and political landscape. But in the 1950s, his arrival on the scene was as unsettling as it was invigorating. It was, put plainly, stunning. This nation of "veritable masters of self-deprecation," and "elected squares," as Richler described his fellow Canadians, had never seen anything like him before.

He had that funny name, for starters, the rumpled appearance and an abrasive personality. He was, by his own admission, an arrogant young man, a smart-ass, cockier than he had any right to be. He was both quick to anger and slow to forget. The scowl on his face—judging by the photographs of him from the time—was a permanent fixture. A product of a broken home and some of Montreal's meaner streets, he had not been, also by his own admission, a happy teenager. He left Canada to escape the parochialism and the boredom. He also left to test himself on a bigger stage and he would, in the early days anyway, look "homeward only with scorn."

But here was Richler's "perverse kind of love" kicking in again. Richler would occasionally object to being called "a professional Canada-knocker," but in essays and articles as well as in his fiction, he kept writing about this country and those he left behind with the kind of trigger-happy animosity we reserve for the places and people we know we will never be able to detach ourselves from no matter how hard we try.

In *The Acrobats*, André Bennett is convinced he can't be a true artist until he leaves Canada; in *Son of a Smaller Hero*, Noah Adler believes he can't avoid mediocrity if he stays. In *A Choice of Enemies*, Norman Price sums up his own and Richler's predicament by saying that there was "no equivalent of the American dream to boost or knock. The Canadian dream, if there was such a puff, was how do I get out?"

Certainly, as far as literature went in the 1950s and into the 1960s, Canada was a place unsullied by accomplishment. Unlike our noisier, more flamboyant neighbours to the south, we weren't even interested in pursuing happiness. Happiness seemed too much to ask for; contentment would suffice. Richler liked to recycle the story of how his New York editor at Knopf, Robert Gottlieb, killed an afternoon once compiling a list of book titles with which to start a publishing house certain to fail. Topping the list was *Canada: Our Good Neighbour to the North*.

In 1965, Edmund Wilson, the legendary literary critic, appeared to be paying this country a compliment when he wrote in his book *O Canada: An American's Notes on Canadian Culture* that "it is possible, in English Canada, to have reasonable conversations in which people pretty well speak their minds—they listen . . . to one another instead of 'shooting off their faces' in competition as we are likely to do." No fan of reasonable conversation, Richler was the exception to the Canadian rule. He enjoyed shooting his face off. What's more, he was making a living and a reputation doing it. An anonymous Canadian editor put it bluntly at the time: "Mordecai has really built a thriving cottage industry out of knocking Canada."

Nathan Cohen was another critic who didn't appreciate Richler poking fun at the country he appeared to have abandoned for good. In his time Cohen was one of this country's best-known critics, a cross between Ed Sullivan and Edmund Wilson, according to William Weintraub. In 1958, just a year after Cohen had deemed Richler worthy of a lengthy interview in *The Tamarack Review,* Cohen also wrote a review, in the same journal, complaining about the flaws in Richler's writing: "the slovenly, undisciplined craftsmanship, the unsettling ambivalence of thought, the contrived violence and abundant bedwetting." He also called Richler's third novel, *A Choice of Enemies,* "a retrogressive step." Richler's work, Cohen said, capping the essay off, was showing "no sign of improvement." Curiously, he also complained that "Richler heroines have small breasts," a comment Richler made note of in a letter to William Weintraub. Not one to bow to critical pressure, Richler still managed to write a female character with ostentatiously big breasts into *Duddy Kravitz.*

But it's clear that what bothered Richler was the disproportionate nature of Cohen's attack. Richler complained to Weintraub of the way Cohen had gone out of his way to get him: "Cohen has butchered me in *Tamarack Review* . . . only in Canada would somebody attempt such a long [13 pages] and definitive piece on a young punk who has published a mere 3 bks. Makes me feel like I'm dead or something."

This was not the last time Richler would take it on the chin from outraged guardians of CanLit. Richler came to expect, even predict, that the criticism of his work would be tougher and more personal the closer it got to home. While *The Acrobats* had some encouraging reviews in England and the U.S.—the *New York Times* called it a story well-told but depressing—in Montreal the reviewer for the *Gazette* complained about Richler's "obsession with physical, moral, and verbal filth."

As Richler predicted, *Son of a Smaller Hero* was not appreciated in his old hometown either, while the *Times Literary Supplement,* in his new hometown of London, called it "one of the best books to have come out of Canada." The reviewer added, "Mr. Richler's next novel will be awaited with anxiety as well as with hope; but there is no doubt of his prodigal talent." Walter Allen, an influential British reviewer, also said that with *Son of a Smaller Hero,* "the Canadian novel emerges for the first time."

Mordecai & Me

But even when Richler was appreciated in Canada, it didn't amount to much. Initially, he had been encouraged to submit the manuscript of *Son of a Smaller Hero* to *Maclean's* magazine. The initial plan was to publish it in serial form and then later as a book. Just the kind of splash a young writer like Richler dreamed of. But the decision was made at the last minute to turn the book down. The magazine claimed to be backing off because of unspecified technical considerations. But it's likely that their decision was based on the uncompromising and often harsh content of the novel. Typically, Richler was, as he wrote William Weintraub, angrier than he was disappointed: "What business have they got pretending they are interested in promoting serious writing?" The explanation, when it did come, by way of a confidential letter from a *Maclean's* editor to Richler's agent, didn't help clear the matter up: "I think Richler has created an extraordinarily fine book and deserves every possible encouragement. He'll probably find my comments baffling. There's not much one can say when one is returning the most brilliant book we've ever rejected."

Son of a Smaller Hero, when it was published in 1955, also provided a preview of how good Richler was going to be at pushing the buttons of the Jewish community, particularly Montreal's traditionally close-knit and observant Jewish community. A hyperbolic though not entirely atypical example showed up in a review in a Jewish newspaper, comparing Richler's depiction of Jewish life to the kind of depiction found in the Nazi propaganda weekly, *Der Sturmer*. A review in the *Jewish Observer and Middle East Review* raised the self-hating issue for the first but not the last time in its appraisal of Richler's writing: "The core of the novel is self-contempt."

Richler, in his interview with Nathan Cohen, acknowledged that he wasn't surprised by the negative reviews for *Son of a Smaller Hero,* but that he was surprised by the personal nature of those reviews. "There was a violent reaction," he said, "and I expected that and I expected people to be hurt; but what I didn't expect was abuse. My book largely wasn't reviewed in Canada, it was abused." There was truth in this observation, a truth that would endure. Although most reviewers won't admit it, they are just readers, and like readers, they are just as prone to mix up an author with his characters. In Richler's case this was both easy and irresistible. For all his protests about his fiction not being autobiographical, you can't read more than a page or two in any of his novels without feeling as if you are getting an unobstructed glimpse into their author's feelings at the time.

It's not a coincidence that Richler's protagonists are all roughly the same age as he was at the moment he was bringing them to life; all of them are looking out the same window at the same usually disappointing view of human misconduct and miscalculation; all of them provide a time capsule of the current state of Richler's consciousness and conscience. The self-involved Noah Adler; the on-the-make Duddy Kravitz; the beleaguered Mortimer Griffin in *Cocksure;* the jealous Jake Hersh in *St. Urbain's Horseman;* the mischievous Joshua Shapiro in *Joshua Then and Now;* the perpetually intoxicated Moses Berger in *Solomon Gursky Was Here;* the vulnerable Barney Panofsky in *Barney's Version;* these are all disguised—and not very meticulously disguised—versions of Richler. So how else could a reader be expected to respond to these personal revelations other than on a personal level?

What was a reader's choice? To love Richler for making you laugh out loud or detest him for being such an incorrigible troublemaker. Provoking people, as Richler quickly learned and just as quickly and conveniently forgot, was the price you paid for being provocative. Later on, after he became a regular book reviewer himself—passing judgement on everyone from Norman Mailer to Maureen Reagan—Richler would adopt a surprisingly nonchalant attitude about his own reviews. In "Why I Write," he says,

> Each novel is a failure, or there would be no compulsion to begin afresh. Critics don't help. Speaking as someone who fills that office on occasion, I must say that the critic's essential relationship is with the reader, not the writer. It is his duty to celebrate good books, eviscerate bad ones, lying ones.

He would also state that reviews only interested him insofar as they helped promote his work. Will it move books? was his primary concern. Or so he said. Yet it is evident from his private papers at the University of Calgary that he kept many of his reviews, particularly the early, nastier

Mordecai & Me

ones. He was his father's son, after all: born to be an injustice collector. Slights he could use. "From my experience," he said in a speech at York University in 1972, "a writer can better endure, even luxuriate in, lack of appreciation than survive over-heated praise."

Even so, the praise was warming up, and he was not having a particularly hard time getting used to it. Robert Fulford was one of the first homegrown critics, aside from Nathan Cohen before his change of heart, to recognize and champion Richler's work, and he has recalled how important Richler's arrival was on an otherwise drab Canadian literary scene. Fulford was in his twenties and just beginning to review books when *Son of a Smaller Hero* was published in 1955. He remembers it as a novel "people my age had to read. At that time, we were just looking for anyone who was interesting and Mordecai was an intensely interesting guy." He had baggage, Fulford explained. And what's more, he was willing to unpack it in public: his Jewishness, his bitterness and contempt, his biting humour, his arrogance, his vulnerability—they were all out in the open.

Richler was also an inspiration to young writers like John Metcalf. Metcalf, who would in time become an even more unsparing critic of CanLit mediocrity than Richler, was happy to hear someone saying out loud the things he couldn't help thinking. "I thought Canada was pretty bloody dreadful in literary terms when I arrived here from England in 1962," Metcalf told me. "And, remember, Richler left in the early 1950s when it must have been indescribably awful in this country. What you have to put in context and understand is how illiterate this country was back then."

In the autobiographical first chapter of Margaret Atwood's book on writing, *Negotiating with the Dead*, Atwood also says she found the literary state of the nation demoralizing when she started out as a poet in the early 1960s: "It was as if the public role of the writer—a role taken for granted, it seemed, in other countries and at other times, had either never become established in Canada, or had existed once but had become extinct." You just have to look at who was winning the Governor General's Award, the country's top literary prize, to understand how discouraging it must have been for Richler as well as for writers like Atwood

Elected Squares

and Metcalf, who would come soon after him. "I mean Igor Gouzenko won the Governor General's Award for fiction," Metcalf said. "This man was not a writer. He was that anti-communist spy who used to appear on television with a paper bag on his head."

Gouzenko received the award in 1954 for a thoroughly forgotten novel with the portentous title *The Fall of a Titan*. That was the same year Richler's *The Acrobats* was published and presumably also eligible for the award. A year later, in 1955, the prize for fiction went to Lionel Shapiro for his novel *The Sixth of June*, a potboiler set during the D-Day landing, complete with nondescript one-dimensional characters and a relentlessly uplifting theme. To make matters worse, Shapiro won the award the same year Brian Moore's extraordinary literary debut, *The Lonely Passion of Judith Hearne*, was published and overlooked.

Although his novels have disappeared from bookstore shelves today and aren't much easier to find in libraries, Lionel Shapiro was hot stuff fifty years ago. A former war correspondent and New York columnist for *Maclean's*, Shapiro cut an undeniably dashing figure. His photograph on the dust jacket of *The Sixth of June* shows a handsome man with a pencil-thin moustache and a cocky grin. If he looked more like Lorne Greene than Errol Flynn, that was all the better. He was, like Lorne Greene, an unlikely combination: a dashing, debonair Canadian Jew. He was not the working class ruffian, "the striver" that Richler grew up with, that Richler was, in fact. (In a scene from *St. Urbain's Horseman*, Jake Hersh impresses his dying father by lying and saying that he's worked with Ben Cartwright, a.k.a. Lorne Greene, the Jewish cowboy.)

Sophisticated and assimilated, but not too assimilated, Shapiro was a B'nai Brith wet dream. Not a Jewy-Jew in other words. Not Duddy Kravitz. Not Duddy's father or grandfather, either. In his own admittedly perverse way, Richler was proud to be a Jew—at least as proud as he was disdainful. Even his most sympathetic characters, like Jake Hersh, are taken to task for their occasional moments of self-loathing. About to go on trial on a phoney charge of rape and aiding and abetting sodomy, Jake's "first embarrassed thought was he did not want a Jewish lawyer, no twisting, eloquent point scorer who would outwit judge and prosecutor, eat witnesses, alienate the jury, shine so foxily in court in fact as

Mordecai & Me

to ultimately lose him the case." As far as Richler's fiction was concerned, though, the foxier the better. He always preferred scoundrels to solid citizens. As Richler's friend Jack Rabinovitch told *Maclean's* after Richler's death, "The first thing you gotta understand about Mordecai is that he would rather deal with an entertaining rogue than an honest dullard. You had to earn your keep to be his friend: you couldn't be clichéd."

Raised orthodox, Richler would always resent assimilated Jews who tried too hard to conceal their roots. In Richler's 1994 memoir, *This Year in Jerusalem,* he meets a young journalist who is astounded to learn that Richler has managed to make a career for himself in North America with the first name of Mordecai. On the other hand, Richler also found Jewish parochialism immeasurably funny—"Special pleading . . . never fails to move me to mockery," he said in 1968, in the foreword to his first essay collection, *Hunting Tigers under Glass.* In his review of "Jews in Sport," which is included in that collection, he is practically gleeful at the notion that someone has decided to fill "a glaring void in the long record of Jewish achievement" by writing the *Encyclopedia of Jews in Sport*. The very existence of such a book provided Richler with a straight line he was incapable of passing up. So in his review Richler quotes one of the encyclopedia's more dubious entries—"Hertz, Steve Allan. Infielder. . . . Played for Houston in 1964. Total games: 5. Batting average: 000"—and then adds his own snide commentary:

> Is this the stuff the Jewish Hall of Fame is made of? Doesn't it suggest that in order to fill only 526 pages with Jewish athletic "Achievement" the authors were driven to scraping the bottom of the barrel, so to speak? Still worse. Put this volume in the hands of an anti-Semitic sportsman and can't you just hear him say . . . "Ho ho! Among them . . . nothing hitters count as athletes."

Richler also holds out hope that the authors of the *Encyclopedia,* having shattered the myth that Jews are "strangers to athletics," will go on to write *"Jewish Drunks, High School Dropouts and Thugs from Noah to Today,"* or a volume on *"Famous Jewish Homosexuals, Professional and Amateur, Throughout History."*

Elected Squares

To Richler, Lionel Shapiro was the literary equivalent of "a nothing hitter." He was this country's answer to American shlockmeisters like Herman Wouk and Leon Uris. Shapiro was the kind of writer who would not last, but who succeeded in making Canadian Jews excessively proud of him while he did. There's a Yiddish word *naches* that means an inordinate and vicarious pride in the accomplishments of others, particularly one's children. For Canadian Jews, Lionel Shapiro was a *naches* magnet.

Meanwhile, Richler repelled the stuff. He didn't ask for *naches* and none was sent his way. Or maybe it was the other way around. He didn't get it, and he'd be damned if he was going to ask for it. In any case, Richler was rightfully angry when Shapiro won the Governor General's Award for fiction over Brian Moore. But he seemed just as angry when *Maclean's*, the magazine that had rejected *Son of a Smaller Hero*, asked Shapiro to pronounce, in a 1956 article, on the state of Canadian writing and the dilemma of the Canadian writer.

Richler's grudge against *Maclean's* coupled with the snub of not being asked to pronounce on "Whither the Canadian Novel?" got under his skin. Just how much is evident in his interview with Nathan Cohen. Richler's personal disdain for Lionel Shapiro—Cohen didn't ask about Shapiro; Richler brought him up—as well as a fair-sized streak of literary snobbery comes through loud and clear:

> I mean this man Lionel Shapiro . . . if [he] had been American or English, he would be taken for granted. . . . I mean he wouldn't be considered on the literary level at all—just another guy turning out bestsellers very much like sausages. The very fact that he could be asked to write an article about Canadian writing . . . illustrates the dangers I see in Canada. I mean that Lionel Shapiro is not a serious writer.

In retrospect, Shapiro's essay in *Maclean's*—titled "The Myth That's Muffling Canada's Voice"—doesn't appear to be the kind of thing to provoke such a blistering response from Richler. True, Shapiro is shamelessly, even laughably self-serving: "Canada's voice" is clearly Shapiro's voice. He goes on at length about the praise his work has received and the movie deals he has signed. Even so, Shapiro's essay probably wouldn't have bothered Richler so much if he wasn't bearing such a personal grudge. What's more, Shapiro's point that Canadian writers shouldn't be afraid to test themselves on the world stage is a formula Richler was already following.

Schadenfreude—the pleasure derived from seeing your friends and colleagues fail, or, as Gore Vidal put it, "Whenever a friend succeeds, a little something in me dies"—is a staple of literary life. Someone is always getting a prize or a review or an interview you believe belongs to you. "Nobody is more embittered than the neglected writer," Richler says in "Why I Write." Still, why pick on Lionel Shapiro? Perhaps because every writer needs a nemesis, a spur in Richler's case, and Shapiro filled that role perfectly. Shapiro was a writer Richler could define himself against. In his review of Edmund Wilson's *O Canada,* Richler also dismissed Hugh MacLennan—"his characters seem to be fabricated of points-of-view rather than flesh and blood"—and Morley Callaghan's novels, though he was a fan of Callaghan's short stories. He didn't have much use for Irving Layton, either, which is clear from his correspondence with William Weintraub, though it's Weintraub who calls Layton "a versifying buffoon."

Shapiro was also a reminder to Richler of what he never would allow himself to become. The more recognition and praise Shapiro received—unjustly, according to Richler—the easier it was for Richler to believe in himself and what he was doing. Spite lubricated his career. Bitterness and envy kept it running smooth. Richler was not, it should be clear, always as cocksure about his ability as a writer as he pretended to be. Both publicly and privately, he expressed serious doubts about the quality of early novels like *The Acrobats* and *Son of a Smaller Hero.* He understood the odds were long on anyone writing anything worthwhile in this country, and he couldn't have known, until he wrote *The Apprenticeship of Duddy Kravitz,* whether he had any hope of beating those odds.

Chapter 9
What Makes Duddy Run?

Mothers warned their children not to play with that Kravitz boy.
But boys and girls alike were drawn to dark, skinny Duddy.
—The Apprenticeship of Duddy Kravitz

Here's one way to tell that a work of fiction has left a mark: it inspires two contradictory reactions in its audience. The feeling, on the one hand, that there's never been anything quite like it; on the other hand, the feeling that it's always been around. From the time it first appeared in 1959, *The Apprenticeship of Duddy Kravitz* has had that kind of dual effect. From the start, it was both fresh and familiar. The success of *Duddy Kravitz* is a testament to keeping things simple. Mordecai Richler's decision—after the stuffiness of *A Choice of Enemies*—to return to his old neighbourhood for inspiration and for a pushy, exuberant wonder like Duddy seems, in retrospect, like a no-brainer. An idea so good you wonder why it took him so long to get around to it. But then it also took Mark Twain awhile to place Huckleberry Finn on a raft on the Mississippi and

Mordecai & Me

J.D. Salinger to free Holden Caulfield from prep school. At its heart, *Duddy Kravitz* is, like *Huckleberry Finn* and *The Catcher in the Rye*, a story of initiation, and with that story come the inevitable questions. Will Duddy succeed? And if he does, will success ruin him? The answer to the first question is a qualified yes. The answer to the second is and will always be ambiguous—best left up to the individual reader.

Duddy Kravitz is also one of those rare, sure-fire literary works that seemed almost as can't-miss when it was published as it now seems in retrospect. It was highly anticipated, according to William Weintraub. "By the time *Duddy Kravitz* came out people were waiting to see what Mordecai was going to do next," Weintraub explained. "Waiting with trepidation but interest too. The kind of interest in a literary writer that was unprecedented in this country." But while there wasn't a precedent for *Duddy Kravitz* in this country, there was in the United States. "The America Canada is really like is the America of three decades before," the critic Leslie Fiedler wrote in a 1968 essay on Canadian literature in general and Mordecai Richler in particular. What Fiedler got wrong, it turned out, was the timing. There was just two decades lag time for *Duddy Kravitz*.

In 1941, Budd Schulberg, a young Hollywood screenwriter who would go on to write the script for *On the Waterfront*, wrote *What Makes Sammy Run?*, his first novel and a book that serves as a kind of blueprint for *The Apprenticeship of Duddy Kravitz*. The two novels are both traditional rags-to-riches tales, with a nasty twist. In each the title character's successful pursuit of wealth and status is undermined, though undeterred, by the fact that he is an unrepentant shit. Although *What Makes Sammy Run?* appeared almost twenty years before *The Apprenticeship of Duddy Kravitz*, Schulberg's anti-hero and Richler's have enough in common to make them literary brothers—with Sammy, the older and, when it comes to being a heel, the more accomplished sibling. Still, as much as these two precocious hustlers (both Sammy and Duddy are teenagers when we first meet them) are alike, the two books are as significantly different as the backgrounds and the intentions of their respective authors.

In *What Makes Sammy Run?* the unscrupulous behaviour of the pushy title character is a product of his squalid upbringing in New York's slums.

What Makes Duddy Run?

Sammy Glick has no redeeming features, but he has an overriding excuse for his behaviour. Sociology makes him do it. Here's Schulberg, through the novel's first-person narrator, Al Manheim, finally answering the question posed in the title:

> Sammy Glick rocking in his cradle of hate, malnutrition, prejudice, suspicions, amorality, the anarchy of the poor; I thought of him as a mangy little puppy in a dog-eat-dog world. I was modulating my hate for Sammy Glick from the personal to the societal.

Schulberg's debut is both entertaining and ham-fisted. Early in the novel, Sammy is referred to as "a smart little Yid," but the slur comes from Schulberg's narrator, Al Manheim, who is also Jewish, but who is more assimilated and intended to be more palatable. Manheim's presence in the story, his commentary, aims to make the point that Sammy is a one-off, the exception that proves the rule. Excused by his upbringing, he is still unlike most Jews, who are respectable, hard working, well educated, principled, and, if you want to know the truth, a bit harmless. In other words, nothing gentile America needs to worry about. *What Makes Sammy Run?* works as both a dark satire and an apology. It is Schulberg's nod to the American melting pot, his way of giving notice that pushy Sammy notwithstanding, the experiment has been a success. We, too, fit in.

After all, Schulberg did. He was a product of the American Jewish upper-middle-class: an accomplished, assimilated, left-of-centre Jew. The son of a successful Hollywood executive, Schulberg also had connections. Bennett Cerf, the legendary Random House editor and publisher, approached Schulberg about writing a novel when he was still an editor at his college paper. (The college was Ivy League Dartmouth.) Working in Hollywood, after graduating from Dartmouth, Schulberg got to call David O. Selznick "Dave." When *What Makes Sammy Run?* was published, it was accompanied by blurbs from John O'Hara and F. Scott Fitzgerald, no less. Fitzgerald called it "a grand book."

As for Sammy Glick himself, Schulberg had met types like him, but he had not grown up with them and he certainly didn't see himself as one of them. This is one of the persistent problems with Schulberg's novel:

Mordecai & Me

Sammy is always being judged from the outside. Schulberg, through his narrator, is always speculating on what makes Sammy tick instead of stepping inside his skin to find out. It's as if he's afraid of contamination. Writing about *What Makes Sammy Run?* many years later, Schulberg did try to muster up some sympathy for Sammy, but it's a sympathy that's absent in the reading of the novel. We never worry about Sammy Glick; we know he'll be just fine. Or at least he'll go on thinking he's fine even if he isn't. Sammy is as predictable and unflappable as a shark. He is appetite without conscience.

Duddy is a much more ambiguous figure for the reader, as well as for his author. Duddy has a conscience; it's just that it's crammed with loopholes. This makes him a harder character to dismiss. He keeps making us care about him, often despite him and ourselves. He is, as his Uncle Benjy calls him, "a little Jew on the make." But in Richler's novel, not to mention in his view of the world, that is both an insult and a compliment. "Having a conscience is like driving a car with the brakes on," Sammy Glick says, and while it's true for him, it's not for Duddy, who can only dream of being so conveniently callous. Duddy's behaviour, while as reprehensible as Sammy's, is propelled by a need for both material success and respectability. He doesn't just want to prosper, he wants to get even with all the people who have looked down on him. He also wants to make the people he loves—his grandfather, his father, his brother, his uncle, even the ghost of his dead mother—proud of him. He craves acceptance as much as wealth and influence.

Duddy Kravitz is not as obviously autobiographical a novel as *Son of a Smaller Hero*, with which it shares a setting and a similar coming-of-age theme, but it is autobiographical enough. What makes Duddy run also kick-started the man who created him. But this time out Richler is more relaxed, more prepared to let his readers think what they want about the personal aspects of his story. Compare the defensive tone of the disclaimer in *Son of a Smaller Hero* to the more mischievous tone in the one that precedes *Duddy Kravitz*: "All the characters and incidents described in this novel are fictional and any similarities to characters living or dead are, as they say, purely coincidental."

As they say?

What Makes Duddy Run?

Unlike Schulberg, Richler does not give his anti-hero sociological excuses, though Duddy does try to come up with one on his own behalf. "All I needed was to be born rich," Duddy says, near the end of the novel. "All I needed was money in the crib and I would have grown up such a fine, lovable guy. A kidder. A regular prince among men." Class may have a lot to answer for in *Duddy Kravitz*, but not enough to make readers think for a moment that Duddy could have ever grown up to be anything other than what he is. In *Barney's Version*, Duddy, all grown up, makes a cameo appearance. He is, not surprisingly, filthy rich and, as ever, on the make. He shows up to ask Barney's doctor, an old Fletcher's Field classmate, if there's a suitable and untaken ailment to which he can make a hefty charitable donation. Duddy needs to get his wife on the social A list. You get the feeling his sex life depends on it. Regrettably, all the good diseases are taken. The doctor suggests ulcerative colitis, the most conspicuous symptoms of which are gas and diarrhoea. Duddy is underwhelmed and typically blunt:

> Oh, great! Wonderful! I phone up Wayne Gretzky, I say, how would you like to be the patron for a charity for farters? Mr. Trudeau, this is D.K. speaking, and I've got just the thing to improve your image. How would you like to join the board of a charity my wife is organizing for people who shit day and night?

Richler, as always, revels in Duddy's pushiness and coarseness. How could he not? To be ashamed of Duddy would mean to be ashamed of who he could easily have been. Duddy is not Richler, but in upbringing, background, and temperament, he's in the ballpark. Besides, everyone Richler knew when he was growing up was on the make or at least appeared to be. Duddy wasn't the exception to the rule; he was the rule, dramatized. (Remember, Baron Byng and the "1,000 strivers.") Hate him or love him, Duddy was, for Richler, the kid next door, the kid at the next desk. Everyone in the old neighbourhood could have been a model for Duddy Kravitz, Richler included: everyone itching to get out and get ahead, everyone chasing after respectability and wealth. Uncle Benjy, before he dies, urges Duddy to become a *mensh*—a human being, a man with a conscience—but it's not advice Duddy is inclined to take. A *mensh* means a pushover where Duddy and Richler come from. Which was, of course, the same place.

In George Orwell's essay "Why I Write," Orwell described what made him—a lonely, unpopular, and disagreeable child—not just want to write, but want to succeed. He could be talking about Duddy Kravitz or Mordecai Richler:

> I think from the very start my literary ambitions were mixed up with the feeling of being isolated and undervalued. I knew that I had a facility with words and a power of facing unpleasant facts, and I felt that this created a sort of private world in which I could get my own back for my failure in everyday life.

A fetus, the Jewish joke goes, is viable when it is accepted into medical school. In his foreword to *The Street*, Richler recalls that, growing up on St. Urbain Street, "a head start was all." He adds, "School starting age was six, but fiercely competitive mothers would drag protesting four-year-olds to the registration desk and say, 'He's short for his age.'" Duddy is also short for his age and scrawny—"a small, narrow-chested boy of fifteen with a thin face" and "black eyes . . . ringed with dark circles." His cheeks are scratched from shaving twice a day, his futile effort to encourage a beard. Not much more physical description of him is provided. Duddy comes alive, instead, in dialogue—always Richler's strength—and action and, most of all, through the roller-coaster reactions of the reader. He is a running litmus test of our mixed feelings—about failure and success, betrayal and friendship, Jewishness as opposed to, well, Jewiness. Shortly after the novel came out, Richler wrote to William Weintraub, "The moral idea behind Duddy was to get inside, and show how sympathetic in many ways, the go-getter, the guy nobody has time for . . . really is."

But what Richler's intentions were and what he ends up with aren't exactly the same. Duddy is more sympathetic in theory than in practise. We may marvel at his defiance, his resilience, his shrewdness, even his pushiness, but none of that changes the fact that he is, most of the time, in most of his actions, conniving and unscrupulous. Then again, Richler wasn't writing *Death of a Salesman*. Duddy is no Everyman. No tragic case. That's evident, not just in the novel in which he is the hero, but also

What Makes Duddy Run?

in the cameo appearances he makes in both *St. Urbain's Horseman* and *Barney's Version*, where he is as oblivious as ever to both the harm he does and the impression he makes. Like any enduring comic character, he doesn't change or grow; instead he squirms free of our best efforts to pin him down.

On the subject of creating characters, authors either believe that their creations take on a life of their own, as E.M. Forster said, or that they are galley slaves, as Vladimir Nabokov insisted. Duddy is a bit of both—a whirlwind and a *fait accompli*. Some characters just click, and Duddy Kravitz is one of these. Richler could feel it, too. Even before *The Apprenticeship of Duddy Kravitz* was published, he knew that it would change his career and his life forever.

Whatever made young Mordecai run—the ambition, the grudges, the unhappy home life, the lost faith, the adopted European angst—was not as easy to draw on by the time *The Apprenticeship of Duddy Kravitz* came out. If success wasn't about to spoil Mordecai Richler, it was starting to put a crimp in the speed with which he wrote novels. After his first four novels, the production line started to slow down. Success brought other temptations—like freelance assignments that took Richler to Stockholm to cover the World Ice Hockey Championships, Jerusalem to report on the state of Israel, upstate New York to visit the resort hotels in the Catskills and Trois-Rivières to chronicle the exploits of professional wrestlers.

Richler was also in demand as a reviewer—particularly with respected London periodicals like *Encounter, The London Spectator*, and the *New Statesman*, the latter infamous for not paying its employees. In "Writing for the Mags," which serves as a foreword to Richler's 1998 essay collection, *Belling the Cat*, Richler recounts the story of *New Statesman* editor Kingsley Martin stopping at the desk of "a new young deputy editor" to tell him how pleased he was with his work. The young man sees the opportunity to hint at a raise, adding how hard it is to support his family on the salary he's being paid. To which a shocked Martin says, "Good God . . . haven't you got a private income?"

Mordecai & Me

Reviewing books was also an activity Jack McClelland, who would be Richler's Canadian publisher through most of 1960s into the early 1980s, considered lose-lose. In a letter to Richler, McClelland said,

> To begin with, the pay is hardly worth it. Secondly, I don't think it does one's prestige as a writer any good—unless one plans to become a professional critic. It's an open invitation to other critics and novelists to slander the hell out of your future books when they appear. And also I can't help feeling that people who are able to write creatively themselves can devote their time to much better ends than reviewing other people's books. So to hell with it.

Fortunately, Richler didn't take McClelland's silly advice. A true freelancer, Richler suffered from a common hazard of the profession—the inability to say no. Memories of the days when no one asked for anything make it hard to refuse a job on those occasions when you are asked. But it was also simpler than that: he liked writing reviews and he was very good at it. Reviewing also honed his skills as a satirist. He could test the limits of how much he could get away with. A good example is his parody of *The Jewish Community in Canada* by Rabbi Stuart Rosenberg, an innocuous but puffed up and parochial book, which served the sole purpose of illustrating how much Jews were contributing to contemporary society. Richler speculates on how Rosenberg might have described the Kennedy assassination:

> President John F. Kennedy (who was boosted in his campaign by such Jewish luminaries as Norman Mailer, of writing-fame, Senator Abe Ribicoff, and Danny Kaye, of film-fame) drove into Dallas on Nov. 22, 1963....
>
> As the car passed the Texas Public School Book Depository, with lots of titles by Jewish authors in stock, somebody called Oswald shot and killed Kennedy....
>
> Oswald, not a Jew himself, numbered among his acquaintances one Jack Ruby, who was to shoot him dead in turn, though not on the Sabbath.

What Makes Duddy Run?

In London, Richler was also graduating from television scripts to film scripts. And while he didn't always get a credit, as was the case with the work he did on the movie *Room at the Top*, his reputation, as he proudly explained to William Weintraub, was growing. The word is out, he wrote, "up and down Wardour Street, 'That bum Paterson couldn't have written *Room* (biz term for *Room at the Top*). So, dammit, chaps who was the script doctor and where is he?' Well, the word has leaked and my ever-sharp scalpel has been called in to serve once more."

Richler's new status as a writer in demand was also dovetailing with an increasingly happy personal life. In 1960, a year after *Duddy Kravitz* was published, Richler married Florence Mann and became stepfather to her young son, Daniel. It was and would remain, by all accounts, an improbably happy marriage for such a stubbornly unhappy man. In the summer of 1959, in a letter to William Weintraub, Richler informed his friend that the reason he was remaining in London and not returning to Montreal for a visit, as he had planned, was because of a woman. "It's Florence Mann that's keeping me here," he wrote. "I'm waiting for her divorce to come through so that we can return to Canada together. I don't know whether this surprises you—whether you've heard rumours from returning travellers—but anyway, that's the way things are. We are in love." In this letter, Richler also comes across as touchingly chivalrous:

> Just one thing for the record. My marriage was finished before I got involved with Florence—she's no "home-breaker," as they say—in fact both our marriages were done. I just don't want you or the Moores [Brian and his wife] to start off with any prejudices against Florence . . .

Richler's romance with Florence was love at first sight, at least for Richler. Also, despite his protests, it's hard not to speculate that the breakup of Richler's short-lived first marriage didn't have anything to do with his attraction to Florence. In *Barney's Version*, Richler describes Barney Panofsky's first meeting with Miriam Greenberg, his true love and eventual third wife, while he is celebrating his wedding to his second wife, a.k.a. The Second Mrs. Panofsky. A drunken Barney spots Miriam and can't take his eyes off her. Before long he is asking her out on a date, then declaring his love for her and finally running out on his wedding night to catch up with her as she leaves for Toronto on a train. In Ted Kotcheff's afterword to the recent reprint of *The Acrobats*, Kotcheff recalls Richler's first attempt to impress Florence—it wasn't on the day of his wedding to his first wife Cathy Boudreau; it was the day before—by asking her if she'd read *The Acrobats* and if she'd liked it. She had, she said, "but not enough to want to meet its author." Not long after that, Richler vowed to Kotcheff that he would win Florence. Kotcheff pointed out that both of them were married to other people, but Richler was smitten and undeterred. "I don't care," he told Kotcheff. "I want her and I'm going to take her."

Of course, in *Barney's Version*, for the sake of fiction, Richler throws a monkey wrench into Barney and Miriam's match-made-in-heaven, as he does into the essentially happy unions in *St. Urbain's Horseman* and *Joshua Then and Now*. In all three novels, the marriages either break up or are on the verge of doing so. This was never the case for Richler. "It was an amazing relationship," according to William Weintraub. "His devotion to Florence was astonishing. She's a remarkable woman, with great qualities and she became the pivot of his life." Away from Florence, Richler couldn't, by all accounts, go more than a couple of hours without calling her. Noah Richler's foreword to his father's posthumous essay collection, *Dispatches from the Sporting Life,* also reveals his father's doting side:

> Morning in the Richler house, before my father set to work . . . Pa prepares my mother's loving tray—hot black coffee with the froth still riding on it, a glass of orange juice freshly squeezed, and my mother's seaweed and garlic pills—and carries it to the bedroom at the back of the apartment. No one else goes there, unless summoned.

But personal happiness, for a writer whose view of the world was as jaundiced as Richler's, was also a kind of cross to bear. Some writers grow out of their cynicism; Richler grew into and more comfortable with his. *Duddy Kravitz,* beneath the scheming and the pranks, is the story of a man who sabotages every chance he has at happiness, who ends up absolutely alone. What Richler believed when he was a young existentialist, he still

What Makes Duddy Run?

believed when he was an established novelist. I interviewed him in 1997 after *Barney's Version* had come out, and as was my habit with other writers, I pressed him for connections between his fiction and his life. As was his custom with interviewers, he resisted any connections with a forbidding silence. Finally, I quoted the gloomy conviction attributed to Barney Panofsky—the belief that "life was absurd and nobody truly ever understands anybody else." This Barneyism he did not deny. "I started off long ago with the premise that if God was dead we had to work out a system of values and that is what most of us try to do," he said, his emphasis on the word *try*.

Chapter 10
Couldn't You Give Him an Italian Name?

There's a brute inside you, Duddel—a regular behemoth—and this being such a hard world it would be the easiest thing for you to let it overpower you. Don't Duddel. Be a gentleman. A mensh.
—Uncle Benjy to Duddy Kravitz

After he read the manuscript of *The Apprenticeship of Duddy Kravitz*, William Weintraub wrote to Mordecai Richler that with Duddy he had created his "first truly memorable character." What makes Duddy so truly memorable is how hard he is to get a fix on, how elusive Richler's own feelings are about the *"pusherke* . . . the little Jew-boy on the make." Duddy inspires ambivalence and a simple question: what are we supposed to make of this kid? Whether or not this was Richler's intention hardly matters; this is the triumph of the book and what endures about it, giving it an indisputable place in contemporary North American Jewish writing.

Well, almost indisputable.

A couple of years ago at Blue Metropolis, an annual Montreal literary festival, I did an onstage interview with Harvard Professor Ruth Wisse.

Couldn't You Give Him an Italian Name?

Among her many accomplishments, Professor Wisse introduced courses in Yiddish literature at McGill's Jewish Studies department in the late 1960s. She came to the festival to talk about her latest book, *The Modern Jewish Canon: A Journey Through Language and Culture.* As the title suggests, *The Modern Jewish Canon* is a proscriptive work, which makes sense given that Professor Wisse could safely be described as a proscriptive person. Deeply conservative in both politics and cultural matters, she bars as many writers from her book as she allows in. Professor Wisse is also a rare academic critic—she writes engagingly and she is not afraid to pass judgement. In *The Modern Jewish Canon,* the standard for inclusion in the Jewish literary tradition is based, both refreshingly and infuriatingly, on Professor Wisse's own arbitrary measure of a writer's Jewishness—on novels in which, she says, "the authors or characters know and let the reader know that they are Jews."

So on the professor's scale of Jewishness, Sholem Aleichem passes with flying colours as does Isaac Bashevis Singer and A.M. Klein. Franz Kafka, an assimilated Czech Jew who wrote in German makes the cut, but Marcel Proust, a half-Jew who wrote in French, doesn't and is dismissed with regret. Even half of Proust would have been a nice feather in our collective skullcap. There's a chapter for Isaac Babel, for Holocaust and Israeli literature. Saul Bellow and Cynthia Ozick are also shoe-ins, for their Jewishness as well as their conservative opinions. Philip Roth, meanwhile, backs in as "the rebellious Jewish son." Bernard Malamud is grudgingly admitted, though just about disqualified for being a "New York Intellectual." There is, however, no room for the likes of Nathanael West or E.L. Doctorow or Norman Mailer. For all their acknowledged energy as American writers, they exhibit no "Jewish energy," Professor Wisse says in her introduction. You'd be hard-pressed, she goes on, to guess that they were Jewish at all from reading their books. As for Stanley Elkin, along with Richler, the most Yiddish-sounding of English-speaking writers I can think of, he isn't even in the professor's index.

There are no special favours for a fellow Montrealer either. Mordecai Richler is mentioned only once and briefly, linked with Budd Schulberg. "When such novels as *What Makes Sammy Run?* and its Canadian parallel, Mordecai Richler's *The Apprenticeship of Duddy Kravitz* . . . criticize

Jewish success from the gentile rather than the Jewish perspective," Professor Wisse writes, "they turn ambition into a particularly Jewish form of corruption."

Richler gets left out, in other words, for not adequately supporting the home team. Which feels like less of a critical judgement than a deliberate snub. My mixed feelings about Richler may run deep, but not deep enough to try to support the unsupportable claim that he is not a Jewish writer. Even by *The Modern Jewish Canon's* own standards, he can hardly be called an author who does not identify himself or his characters as Jews. If Richler does not belong in the so-called modern Jewish canon, who does? Clearly, the issue for Professor Wisse is not whether he has "Jewish energy," but whether it's the right kind.

Still, I have to confess my indignation is retroactive and, mainly, a result of writing this book. Richler did not come up in my interview with Professor Wisse. As we spoke, I was forming my own personal—and, yes, subjective—question. Instead of listening to the professor's thoughtful answers, I was carrying on a distracting debate with myself, planning to do what an impartial interviewer should never do—ask a question that carried with it an agenda. My own. I was tactful or so I thought. I was also transparent. Professor Wisse is a smart woman, and she knows a self-serving argument when she's getting one. "What about ambivalence?" I asked. "What if you're as Jewish as you can be? What about that?"

"What about it?" she said.

"Well," I said, starting out on what I knew would be a ramble, "isn't ambivalence at the root of what makes most contemporary Jewish writers interesting, that and the feeling that they can't be Jewish in the way their fathers or grandfathers might have been, but that they and their work still can't help being influenced by the fact of their birth, the fact of their Jewishness, so aren't they, isn't their work, I mean, beholden to their being Jewish no matter how authentically Jewish they are?"

I took a breath. It was a very long question to which I received a very short answer.

"That's a sentimental notion," Professor Wisse said or words to that effect, looking at me as if I were one of those dumb students Harvard must let in now and again, one destined for a D. Clearly, my ambivalence

Couldn't You Give Him an Italian Name?

wasn't about to be admitted anywhere near the modern Jewish canon any time soon.

When we were first introduced, just prior to the interview, I gave Professor Wisse a signed copy of my novel, *Jacob's Ladder*. (I give the damn things out like flyers, like menus for two-for-one pizza.) Among other things, my novel is about a comic confrontation between a lapsed Jew and a rabbinical student. The lapsed Jew, the hero by default, would like to be more in touch with his faith and his tradition, but as far as he's concerned, that ship has sailed. A fact he can't help regretting. There is not a guiltless bone in his body. Meanwhile, the rabbinical student doesn't know the meaning of the word *ambivalent;* he is a nut—however, a nut secure in his faith and Jewish identity. Once the interview with Professor Wisse ended, on something of a sour note, it was my novel, trapped in her briefcase that I couldn't stop thinking about—that and how I could go about asking for it back. She had me pegged all right. I am not an authentic Jew; I am just a sentimental one.

There is a sentimental streak, albeit a thin one, in *The Apprenticeship of Duddy Kravitz*. You can detect it in such narrative threads as Duddy's longing to know if his deceased mother loved him or in the deathbed scene when Duddy's Uncle Benjy admits he may have misjudged his nephew. Unfortunately, by the time the novel appeared, Mordecai Richler's reputation as a troublemaker was firmly established. You couldn't blame anyone for not seeing his tender side; it was so completely overshadowed. Besides, *Duddy Kravitz* is much more intent on exposing hypocrisy than tugging on heartstrings. In this respect, it is more alike than different from his earlier work. What is different, this time, is that Richler is as interested in getting laughs, in being entertaining, as he is in expressing his moral outrage. Like the scene, early in *Duddy Kravitz*, where "the barechested bakers at Stein's across the street from Fletcher's Field High School" wink at Duddy and his classmates and then proceed to "wipe the sweat from under their armpits with an unbaked kimel bread before tossing it into the oven." Moments like this would become a Richler trademark—training an uncompromising eye on a tawdry, but

Mordecai & Me

invariably comic moment. In fact, Richler might just as well be standing in for the mischievous bakers here—exposing life's everyday ugliness and winking all the while.

This is also the kind of moment that would consistently get Richler into trouble with Jewish community leaders and spokespersons. It must have seemed gratuitous to them at the same time that it seemed absolutely essential to him. The story Richler recalls, with a perverse kind of pride, in the foreword to *Hunting Tigers under Glass,* is how after speaking at a suburban synagogue, he was asked, "Why is it that everybody loved Sholem Aleichem, but we all hate you?"

Late in the summer of 1994, I was asked to speak at a suburban synagogue by the woman in charge of the book review series. I'd done this kind of public speaking gig before, and I knew that while I was permitted to choose any book I wanted, there were constraints. It was incumbent upon me to pick something appropriate: in other words, something Jewish, the more so the better. This wasn't going to be a problem. I could hardly have come up with a more appropriate book than Mordecai Richler's *This Year in Jerusalem,* an account of two visits he'd made to Israel, one in 1962, the other thirty years later. I was going to be reviewing the book for the *Gazette* in the fall, and I'd just received my copy of the as yet unpublished manuscript. So, on top of everything else, this would be a scoop. *This Year in Jerusalem* wasn't just a brand new book by Richler; it was a book about Richler in the Holy Land. It was, *ipso facto,* as Jewish as a matzo ball. I told the woman on the other end of the line all this and awaited her enthusiastic reply. None was forthcoming. There was no reply at all for a while. Then she finally asked, "Have you read it yet?" I told her I hadn't. That no one had. It wasn't out yet.

"All right," she said. "Read it and let me know how *bad* it is."

It took me a moment to realize that what she meant by "how bad" was how offensive. *So Richler's in Jerusalem, so big deal,* she was thinking. *That will make him stop with the vulgar remarks, maybe? All of a sudden, you think butter melts in this guy's mouth? Not this piece-of-work. Not this shit-disturber.*

Couldn't You Give Him an Italian Name?

I asked the woman if she'd read much of Richler's work. "Enough," she said, by which she probably meant hardly any. But she likely assumed that you don't have to be a chicken to recognize a rotten egg. In the name of literature, I suppose I should have challenged her preconceived notions and the ease with which she arrived at them. But instead I said, "I'll let you know. How bad it is, I mean."

I didn't speak to her again until I showed up at her synagogue a couple of months later. I reassured her that the book was fine. And vetted, by me, it was. For my audience of mostly elderly women, I left out some of the more colourful things Richler had to say about the Holy Land. Like the remark he makes to a particularly zealous cabby who tries to lecture Richler on Israeli ingenuity: "Have you guys ever thought of bottling Israeli piss and marketing it abroad as perfume?" Or his comment about how Jerusalem, with its honourary plaques from rich North American Jews everywhere, is "a brilliantly organized panhandler's heaven. The ultimate *Schnorrerville*." Instead, I took the high and safe road. I gave them a Richler to be proud of. At least, I tried. There was, for example, the eager young man who had joined Habonim, a Zionist Youth Organization, in the 1940s, the young man who had even considered dropping out of high school to fight in Israel's War of Independence. There was Richler, the defender of the faith, boasting like a school kid about Israeli accomplishments, about blooming deserts, and Menachem Begin, "our Jimmy Cagney." But the audience was restless.

It turns out they *wanted* the bad stuff. They had come for it. And if I wasn't going to provide it, they would. After my lecture, the question-and-answer period consisted mainly of secondhand gossip about friends who knew friends who knew Richler and who knew what a no-goodnik he was. Or a lush. Or an anti-Semite. "He doesn't talk to his mother, you know," one woman said. "Or his brother," someone else added. "He's a dentist. He lives in New Brunswick, the brother, and he's changed his name." "Newfoundland," someone corrected, "the brother lives in Newfoundland." Meanwhile, I stood behind a lectern, trying to act literary and above it all. I also tried to interject a remark here and there about the art of writing, about Richler's career, but I was all but superfluous. I was also annoyed. How beside-the-point all this nattering was, all this

Mordecai & Me

gossip. How inappropriate and unbefitting a man of literature: by which I meant not just Richler, but me.

Now I wonder if I was wrong about how much this audience misunderstood Richler. Here was a room full of people, most of whom couldn't care less about the nuances of literature, most of whom hadn't read or, anyway, couldn't remember a word from *Duddy Kravitz* or *St. Urbain's Horseman*, and even so they recognized something about Richler that was unmistakably true. He didn't just make trouble; he liked making trouble. He enjoyed pissing people off, and here they were, the proof—the pissed-off people. Everyone was getting what they expected; everyone was happy.

In *This Year in Jerusalem*, Richler is regularly buttonholed by friends from the old St. Urbain Street neighbourhood. Myer, who now calls himself Woody because Myer is such a Jewy name, rings Richler up at his home in London and the two meet for a drink. Woody sums up his famous Baron Byng classmate's career this way: "Hey, there's nothing to compare to a Jewish childhood. Right? . . . But only you understood, you write it up, changing the names, telling a few lies, adding some *shmutz*, and there's big bucks in it. Don't look at me like that, I give you credit."

Credit (dirty look notwithstanding) Richler was happy to accept. By the time *Duddy Kravitz* was a hit, he couldn't have been prouder of his accomplishment—he'd succeeded in making an entire community detest him. This was worth boasting about and explained why he told the Sholem Aleichem story so often and with such glee, recycling it in essays, speeches, and interviews. He was also indebted to the woman in yet another suburban synagogue who had stood up and wistfully asked him, referring to *The Apprenticeship of Duddy Kravitz*, "Why couldn't you give him an Italian name?"

Of course, to hear Richler tell it, every time he stepped inside one of those generic and ubiquitous "suburban synagogues," where he always seemed to be reluctantly appearing, the collective IQ of the congregation plummeted. He'd take questions on one condition, he told an audience once, no stupid ones. The audience was predictably silent. That story may be apocryphal; it's also misleading. The truth is that while Richler may have appreciated and cultivated his reputation for not suffering fools, he

Couldn't You Give Him an Italian Name?

loved stupid questions and comments. He held onto them the way most people hold onto old family photos, taking them out of storage every once in a while to be reminded of where he was when he was asked, "Why do Jews and homosexuals write so much?" He was at Simon Fraser University, incidentally, in the early 1970s. "Am I expected to answer in my office as a Jew or a homosexual?" he replied.

The broadcaster Peter Gzowski, a friend of Richler's who periodically had the difficult chore of interviewing him, identified a phenomenon particular to Richler: "Wherever he goes people do stupid things. . . . There is a magnetic force about Richler which brings out the stupid in you and then he writes down what you say and makes a million dollars." It's clear from The Mordecai Richler Papers that Richler kept some of the more damning comments made about him and, I suspect, kept them happily. Like this one by Norbert Bernstein (a name Richler would have loved, by the way) who wrote in the *New York City Library Journal* that *The Apprenticeship of Duddy Kravitz* contains "sly tirades against Judaism and Christianity which may be regular fare in the gutters of Montreal but are not appropriate to the more restrained environment of New York's public libraries."

It's not hard to figure out why Richler didn't mind any of this very much, why he may have even been pleased by the various insults, the more preposterous the better; it was an indication that he was doing what he perceived to be his job—irritating people who deserved to be irritated. In this respect he was following in the footsteps of H.L. Mencken, a dreadful anti-Semite, but a writer Richler couldn't help delighting in. Apparently, Mencken not only kept his bad reviews and hate mail, he arranged to have the latter published in an anthology.

In Richler's case the reaction from disappointed and dismayed reviewers and readers must have also come as something of a relief. Even a natural-born troublemaker can't exist in a vacuum. He needs someone to rise to the bait. (Philip Roth also admitted to being secretly pleased with the Jewish community's immediate and negative reaction to his work. "I never felt neglected," he said.) Not until Richler started taking on the Quebec separatists could he have found or hoped for a more appealing and more easily provoked target than Montreal's Jews. On the one hand,

Mordecai & Me

the community was, when Richler began writing about it, well established—arguably the most prosperous and active ethnic, let alone Jewish, community, in Canada. On the other hand, the Jews Richler grew up with were still nervous about being singled out in a predominantly *goyishe* country. Richler's friends and acquaintances had made their peace, even if it was an uneasy one, with assimilation and ambivalence. You could be proud and ashamed of who you were at the same time. You could leave your parents' world, leave St. Urbain Street behind forever, and head for the less contentious suburbs, but if your parents spoke with a Yiddish accent you could still understand them. You were against intermarriage, Yassir Arafat, and the Parti Québécois. Despite all that, or perhaps because of it, it would have been nice to have somebody on your side, speaking for you. Somebody like Richler, say.

When he couldn't oblige or wouldn't, when it became clear that he wasn't going to make the people he grew up with feel or look good, that, in fact, he was going to go out of his way to do the opposite, that he was going to write about them wiping fresh baked bread under their arms, acting like *shnorrers,* like sex-crazed, hypocritical, greedy, pushy, flawed human beings, it was not surprising for them to feel hurt and betrayed. Readers are human beings, after all, a fact writers don't always take into account.

This desire to look good to others is not a uniquely Jewish one nor one that is hard to understand. Still, in Richler's case, it was more than just public relations his audience wanted. They were hungry, insatiable, for someone to be proud of. They wanted in their writers what they got, so uncomplicatedly, from their children who'd become doctors and lawyers and business leaders—*naches*. The success of *Duddy Kravitz* should have provided that. Here, after all, was the writer everyone in the country was talking about and who was he? Where was he from? St. Urbain Street—one of ours. They would have liked nothing better than to be able to brag about him. But how could they? Expecting *naches* from this guy was like expecting blood from a stone.

Richler recognized he was a disappointment. He just didn't mind that much. In a 1972 interview, he told novelist Graeme Gibson that Montreal's Jewish community thought they had a claim on him: "Here I am writing about their village and what in hell do I know about it that they don't know, and what right have I got to do this? Of course they never even read *my books,* they just know I say bad things about Jews in those books. Anyway it doesn't bother me."

Naches, according to the comedian Jackie Mason, transcends pride. It is "one of the greatest things a Jew can experience . . . a pride so deep that he feels it all the way into his *kishkes,* into the deepest recesses of his intestines." And while that definition conveys how much pleasure is wrapped up in the word, it doesn't convey how much pressure there is, too. Pressure, that is, for the person generating the *naches.*

In 1959, the year *Duddy Kravitz* appeared, Philip Roth published his novella *Goodbye Columbus.* Despite similarities in their backgrounds, aspirations, and age—Roth was born in 1933, two years after Richler—Roth and Richler were as different as cheese and chalk. Richler, raised in a strict, orthodox family, rebelled early and often. Roth, born in New Jersey, was the product of what he describes in his 1975 essay collection *Reading Myself and Others* as "a lower-middle-class neighbourhood." Hard as he tried, he could find nothing to rebel against:

> From the age of twelve, when I entered high school, to age sixteen, when I graduated, I was by and large a good, responsible, well-behaved boy. . . . I was probably a "good" adolescent partly because I understood that in our Jewish section of Newark, New Jersey, there was nothing much else to be, unless I wanted to steal cars or flunk courses, both of which proved to be beyond me.

So while you could hardly blame Richler's family for thinking he wouldn't amount to much, Roth was fulfilling his family's fondest dreams. He served in the army; he received an M.A. from the University of Chicago; he got a job teaching. He was the poster boy for *naches.* That was his burden.

As an adolescent and as a young man, Richler had a talent for embarrassing his family, his poor beleaguered father in particular. "Don't make trouble, that's all I ask," Max Kravitz says to Duddy. In Richler's essay "My Father's Life," Moses Richler made an almost identical request of his young son: "Don't embarrass me. Don't get into trouble." Richler did both: "I embarrassed him. I got into trouble." Philip Roth did neither.

Mordecai & Me

"My father had little aside from peccadilloes to quarrel with me about," Roth recalls, "and if anything weighed upon me, it was not dogmatism, unswervingness or the like, but his limitless pride in me." Of course, Roth would devote himself to subverting that pride, at least in his fiction. In real life—an admittedly tricky designation to make with regard to Roth's fiction—Roth's father, Herman, remained his son's biggest and most unequivocal fan, a fact confirmed in *Patrimony*, Roth's memoir of his father's final days.

Parental pride or expectations did not weigh heavily on Mordecai Richler. According to Richler, the only reason his father read his novels at all was so he would know what kind of mess his son was about to land him in. And in "My Father's Life," there's this confession: "Officious strangers would rebuke him in the synagogue for the novels I had written. Heaping calumny on the Jews, they said."

But being nice was not an option for Richler. He couldn't have been if he tried, so he seldom bothered. Still, in Duddy, for all his pushiness and his obsession with material success, there is a boy also obsessed with his family, who is driven as much by the desire to make his family proud of him as by the desire to succeed at any cost. When his grandfather imparts his Polonious-style wisdom that "a man without land is nobody," it's Duddy who takes the advice to heart. When his brother, Lennie, a medical student at McGill, drops out of school, it's Duddy who finds him and convinces him to go back. When his Uncle Benjy, who has always preferred Lennie, is dying, it's Duddy who heads to New York to bring back Benjy's estranged wife. Even after a bitter argument with a dying Benjy, Duddy makes a point of telling the doctor, "Don't let him die. He's my uncle." Family love of one kind or another—parents for children; husbands for wives; sons for fathers—figures prominently in Richler's later and his best work. And given all the institutions Richler happily ridiculed throughout his career, marriage and parenthood came out relatively unscathed. Philip Roth did his best work once he was free of his happy family; Richler did his best work once he'd found a happy family.

Couldn't You Give Him an Italian Name?

Although I gave my mother a copy of the first short story I published, she insisted on buying her own. The story appeared in a college literary magazine that was printed on coloured paper: green for prose, yellow for poetry, lavender for prose poems, of which there were, I seem to remember, an unsettling number. The magazine was called *More Than Apples,* which also seems, looking back, like a suitable title. What was printed *was* more than apples, just not a whole lot more.

My story was called "A City street mosaic Painted in After thought and Trivia . . ." The title appeared just like that, with the irregular capitals, with afterthought broken up into two words, and, I'm afraid, with the ellipsis, too. The title and ellipsis are all you really need to know about how pretentious the story was. I was eighteen at the time, and while I also can't recall what it was I was writing about—unrequited love is my guess and the usual hard-up autobiographical narrator—I vividly remember sitting in my mother's car in the college parking lot, cringing as she went into the bookstore. When she asked me if I wanted to wait in the car or come in with her, I just slumped lower in my seat. She returned with the remaining dozen copies and with an anecdote about how she had told the girl at the cash register why she was buying her out. "She asked which story you wrote and when I told her, well, do you want to know what she said?"

"No," I said and probably cringed again. Secretly, I was dying to know every word.

"Well, I'll tell you anyway. She said it was the best story in the magazine and that it wasn't only her who was saying that. Everyone was."

"Yeah, right," I said, acting indifferent. But the truth was that I was as happy as I had ever been. I didn't know it then, but my decision to become a writer was sealed. I didn't know either that I was in for a rough time and that the thing that would always hold me back, always make writing, at least the career aspects of it, so hard for me was in evidence that afternoon. I was too dependent on other people's expectations, too intent on ingratiating myself to others. (Ingratiating types rank even lower than the hypocritical and pompous as objects of scorn in Richler's fiction. In a piece he wrote for *Playboy* in 1991 on Woody Allen, Richler commended Allen for every aspect of his work except for sometimes being "too ingratiating, his appeal for love embarrassingly naked.")

Mordecai & Me

But then I had always been eager to please. A youngest child, an only son, a well-brought-up Jewish boy, I always cared too much about what other people thought. For all my teenage sullenness, I wanted to please my mother, make her proud. I wanted to do the same for the girl in the bookstore, who I would return to spy on the next day and who was not nearly as pretty as I imagined.

Chapter 11
Why So Much Shmutz?

Jews who register strong objections to what they see as damaging fictional portrayals of Jews are not necessarily philistine or paranoid. If their nerve endings are frayed, it is not without cause or justification. . . . In the aftermath of the horrors that have befallen millions of Jews . . . it isn't difficult to understand their concern.
–Philip Roth

Mordecai Richler had this thing for Eskimos. They just struck him as funny, in much the same way transvestites did. You can practically hear him snickering at his desk every time he puts one of his male characters in female lingerie, which he did surprisingly often. This is what professors of literature, bless their beside-the-point hearts, might call a motif. (I'd call it a running gag.) The plot of *Joshua Then and Now,* for example, turns on an incidence of cross-dressing, or presumed cross-dressing. But the first transvestite in Richler's fiction appears in his fourth novel, *The Incomparable Atuk.* He is a Mountie who ends up winning the Miss Canada contest and going on to challenge for Miss Universe. *The Incomparable Atuk* takes as its hero an Inuit poet, a kind of Kravitz of the North. Atuk is famous for penning lines like this *Howlesque* opening: "I have seen the best seal hunters of my / generation putrefy raving die from tuberculosis...." *The Incomparable Atuk* is a broad satire as well as a fish-out-of-water story—its title character stranded in Toronto and adopted by Canada's cultural and literary elite. Atuk, like Duddy, is a resilient rascal, an Inuit on the make, likeable, often in spite of himself.

The Incomparable Atuk, published in 1963, appears, at first glance, to be one long Inuit joke. Some twenty-six years later, Richler extended the joke in *Solomon Gursky Was Here.* Against the politically correct grain, he also continued to use the term *Eskimos,* even though, by then, Inuit, which means "The People," was preferred, and even though Richler knew the word *Eskimo,* which means "eaters of raw meat," was pejorative. He also came up with one of his most inventive gags at the expense of a tribe of Jewish Inuit. In telling the story of Ephraim Gursky, the patriarch of what would eventually become the Gursky liquor empire, Richler relates how Ephraim, the only survivor of the doomed Franklin expedition to the Canadian North, is rescued by an Inuit tribe. (In fact, there were no survivors of the Franklin expedition.) Out of gratitude and a new found colonial mindset, Ephraim subsequently converts his rescuers to Judaism. But one thing Ephraim doesn't account for is the Yom Kippur obligation to fast from sunset to sunset, a difficult ritual to follow anywhere. In the far north, though, it proves fatal:

> Once the sun went down [followers of Ephraim] were obliged to remain celibate and fast until it rose once more several months later.... As a consequence, some sinned against Ephraim, the men stealing out of camp to eat, their women seeking satisfaction among the unclean. But most stayed in place to starve, dying devout.

In *The Incomparable Atuk,* the Inuit identify themselves as "the chosen pagans," intent on reclaiming their Holy Land, Canada, promised to them by their gods. Making his case, Atuk sounds like a Jewish kid from St. Urbain Street or a refugee from *The Merchant of Venice:* "The white boys used to knock me over and beat me up and call me a dirty Eskimo.... I have feelings, too, you know. If you prick me, do I not bleed?" Perhaps even more than *The Acrobats* or *A Choice of Enemies, The Incomparable Atuk* is

Why So Much Shmutz?

the Richler novel most readers, even his most dedicated readers, have never heard of. That's unfortunate. Where *The Acrobats* and *A Choice of Enemies* feel like stunted, overambitious early efforts, *Atuk* is a self-assured lark. Entertaining and mischievous, it also spreads the ridicule around liberally—indeed, some of the best insults in the book are aimed at liberal sensibilities, like those voiced by the well-meaning Professor Gore:

> Indeed, the Professor adored Jews and Negroes so much that he felt put out when they exhibited human traits. If a Jew cheated on his income tax, for instance, or a Negro wore flashy clothes, Gore felt personally affronted. They ought not to do that to him and other liberals after they had tried so hard to be helpful.

But then who doesn't get it in the neck in this novel, which was titled *Stick Your Neck Out* in the U.S.? There is Seymour Bone, a theatre critic who eats nothing but bananas and, constipated, walks out on a play early one night, thereby earning himself a reputation as the country's "Rudest, Most Outspoken Entertainer." There is Bette Dolan, a pretty, pure-of-heart long distance swimmer and Canadian sweetheart who does everything—and I mean everything—she can to help the sexually frustrated men in her life. There is the aforementioned Mountie posing as a woman who falls in love with a journalist posing as a man. There are the capitalists and the socialists and the cultural nationalists to mock. There is no shortage of targets and no point, as far as Richler could see, in discriminating among them.

For all its scattershot charms, though, *The Incomparable Atuk* is a modest book—Richler referred to it as a spoof—and it may not have made much of an impression when it came out because it was being judged more as a follow-up to *Duddy Kravitz* than on its own merits. As much as Richler talked about how he'd found his voice with *Duddy Kravitz* and how writing got easier after it, the reality is that writing novels got harder. It certainly took him longer to write them. The reason may have been that with the success of *Duddy Kravitz,* he had raised the bar for himself. The four years between *Duddy Kravitz* and *Atuk* is not an inordinate amount of time between novels, unless you consider Richler's track record up to that time.

Mordecai & Me

In the 1950s, he'd published four novels in less than five years. If they were imperfect, rushed even, that hardly mattered. Richler was hungry to get going and establish himself. Once he was established, though, he would start feeling the pressure that comes with having to top yourself. *Atuk* wasn't a follow-up to *Duddy Kravitz,* after all; it was Richler ducking a follow-up. (He was already at work on *Cocksure,* adapting the short story it was based on. He was also starting to think seriously about a more ambitious novel, which would turn out to be *St. Urbain's Horseman.*) *The Incomparable Atuk* is lots of fun, but it is also the kind of book Richler could write in his sleep.

In 1996, I interviewed the British novelist Louis de Bernières. This was two years after the publication of his unexpected hit *Captain Corelli's Mandolin.* I'd expected de Bernières to be a more dashing, romantic fellow. His dust jacket bio listed stints in the army and work as a gaucho in South America. Instead, he resembled a chubby, British Woody Allen—balding, badly dressed and engagingly neurotic, going on about how he had quit smoking for his girlfriend and how she had broken up with him anyway. As a consequence, he was smoking again.

De Bernières came to writing novels late, but once he started he made up for lost time, writing three fat, rich books in three years. They are all set in South America and are part magic realism, part Rabelais. But while they earned him some recognition as a young writer to watch, they didn't sell particularly well. His fourth novel, *Captain Corelli's Mandolin,* wasn't expected to do well either and didn't receive the hype other novels, like Martin Amis's *The Information,* for instance, received (another thing de Bernières went on about). Still, the novel, a retelling of Homer's *Odyssey,* set on a Greek island during World War II, turned into a word-of-mouth phenomenon. Booksellers in particular championed *Captain Corelli.* In fact, it was the Chapters book chain, not de Bernières's publisher, who was sponsoring his Canadian tour when we met. All of which should have amounted to a dream come true for de Bernières, but he was candid about his anxieties when we talked. He couldn't get past his unexpected success. The idea that he had written a book so many people had loved spooked him. As did the thought that they weren't likely to love his next book anywhere near as much. "I'm blocked," he told me. "*Captain Corelli* did it." Six years later, he still hasn't written another novel.

But if there was an element of anxiety and stalling that went into the writing of *The Incomparable Atuk*, it wasn't because Richler was trying to break the mold. He was still dealing with his usual preoccupations. "Is it about Jews or ordinary people?" his father could have asked him again. Well, it's not about ordinary people or ordinary Jews either. In *The Incomparable Atuk*, Richler gleefully satirizes an enduring Jewish type— the Jew who thinks he is not just different from everyone else but infinitely better. Panofsky, a seemingly harmless elderly man, who has gone back to university to study sociology with Professor Gore, eventually reveals his findings that "the most boring, mediocre man in the world is the White Protestant *goy*, northern species, and in Canada he has found his true habitat."

This is probably as good a time as any to reveal a secret about Jews: we think we're better than everyone else. We aren't, of course; we just think we are. Most of us don't even want to think it, but we can't help ourselves. It's something passed down like an inheritance, as difficult to rid ourselves of as some ugly old family heirloom. In *Barney's Version*, Richler offers a Darwinian explanation by way of Barney's pontificating father, Izzy Panofsky. (The surname coincidentally was recycled from *The Incomparable Atuk*.) Asked by a pal, "How come Jews are smarter?" Izzy says,

> You're wrong. There's no such thing as a superhuman. But the only thing I got to tell you, if you take a dog and kick him around he's got to be alert, he's got to be more sharper than you. Well, we've been kicked around for two thousand years. We're not more smarter, we're more alert.

In *Joshua Then and Now*, Richler offers the view from the other side— the WASP's first encounter with the canny Jew. Joshua's ne'er-do-well brother-in-law recounts his experience in law school:

> What did we know about Jews? You have no idea how cocooned we were. What sheltered childhoods we led. We were the best. The

brightest. The chosen. . . . And suddenly, there were all those fierce, driving Jews, who didn't play by the rules, each one hollering "me, me, me." My God, they demanded space, lots of space.

The other Jewish type Richler pokes fun at in *Atuk* is encapsulated in the character of Rory Peel. Rory is the Jew who's graduated from the *shtetl* to the suburbs, but who still can't leave his past far enough behind. He's changed his name (from Panofsky to Peel), fixed his nose, named his son Garth. He cringes when he hears Yiddish spoken and overspends extravagantly to avoid being considered cheap. Rory won't even return a rotten piece of meat to the butcher because he's afraid to look like he cares about money.

Called a self-hating Jew once, Woody Allen responded by saying, "While it's true I am Jewish and don't like myself very much, it's not because of my persuasion. The reasons lie in totally different areas—like the way I look when I get up in the morning, or that I can never read a road map." The self-hating label stuck to Mordecai Richler his whole career, and it's likely there were times, lots of them, when it felt more like a badge of honour than a slur. What was the alternative, after all? Becoming a cheerleader for his community was not an option. Besides, there were plenty of literary cheerleaders around when Richler was starting out. Lionel Shapiro and Herman Wouk and Leon Uris were all examples of the kind of writer Richler despised. Even Budd Schulberg in *What Makes Sammy Run?* was sensitive to the idea that his portrait of Sammy Glick not be seen as a blanket condemnation of all Jews. He says as much in the novel, and he says it, too, in the afterword he wrote to a new edition of the book some fifty years later. Sammy didn't have to be Jewish, he argues. He could have had an Italian name. On this point, Schulberg was clear: Sammy Glick was and is the exception not the rule.

Other novels, like Laura Z. Hobson's *Gentleman's Agreement*, published in 1946, went to great lengths to prove that Jews could be an exceptional exception. In 1947, exactly two decades before Sidney Poitier, in *Guess Who's Coming to Dinner*, seemed like just the guy you'd want your daughter to marry—good looking and a doctor, too—Elia Kazan's movie version of Hobson's book came out. It's hard to believe, watching it now,

Why So Much Shmutz?

that it was ever considered controversial or groundbreaking. But it was. In the movie, Gregory Peck plays a well-meaning journalist determined to write an investigative article on anti-Semitism in America, but he can't come up with an angle. (It's two years after the Nazis systematically killed six million Jews and no one in this movie, ostensibly about anti-Semitism, even refers to that fact.) Then Gregory Peck has a forehead-smacking idea—the kind writers are always being visited with in Hollywood movies—why not pretend he's Jewish. His name, Phil Green, even sounds Jewish. He has, he tells his mother, dark hair, dark eyes like his Jewish best friend played by John Garfield. True, he doesn't have an accent or mannerisms—or a big nose, he all but says—but then neither does Garfield. "I'll be Jewish," he finally announces. "I've even got the title—'I Was Jewish for Six Months.'" His mother, already a candidate for Jewish motherhood, cheers him on enthusiastically. "If you're Jewish," she says, "I am, too."

From there, Kazan's kosher precursor to *Guess Who's Coming to Dinner* and *Black Like Me* (think *Jew Like Me*) just gets more earnest and sillier. Still, the message to gentile America is as unmistakable as a sledgehammer to the head: you know those Jews, well, they're not so bad.

Gwethalyn Graham's novel *Earth and High Heaven,* published in 1944, dealt with a similar theme in a similar way. Set in Montreal, it is the story of a star-crossed love affair between Marc Reiser, a Jewish lawyer, and Erica Drake, a plucky *shiksa* journalist, also "one of the Westmount Drakes." The novel exposes anti-Semitism among Montreal's WASP upper-class—Erica's father in particular—and then sets out to show that Jews, the good ones anyway, are just like gentiles. Maybe even a bit better. Before they end up living happily ever after, Marc, unnerved by the prejudice of Erica's father, decides to end the relationship. Erica's response to being unceremoniously dumped is to apologize for being who she is. "It's not my fault that I'm not Jewish and I can't do anything about it," she says, "but surely, surely the fact that I love you so much makes up for it!"

Earth and High Heaven was, according to *The Oxford Companion to Canadian Literature,* "an overnight sensation in Canada"—both a popular and critical success. (It won the Governor General's Award for fiction.) There was even a plan to make it into a film but that was cancelled when the film version of *Gentleman's Agreement* came out first.

I read *Earth and High Heaven* when I was in high school in a class called NAL or North American Literature, which, even in the early 1970s, the teachers were hard-pressed to make less American. As a consequence, we'd been subjected to the stultifying novels of Morley Callaghan with their heavy-handed Christian symbolism. Graham's novel should have been a relief, but after I read it, I remember thinking, Who are these people? I didn't know any Jews who talked or behaved like this. What's more, I didn't want to. I was a kid, but even then I knew that the sanitized characters and the uplifting message of tolerance and universal brotherhood in *Earth and High Heaven* wasn't literature; it was public relations. A few books down the line in NAL, *Duddy Kravitz* was waiting, and when I finally read it, it wasn't so much a revelation as an antidote. Mordecai Richler was not a credit to his race, and he didn't pretend to be. He was, compared to Gregory Peck and Gwethalyn Graham's hero, a traitor, a tattletale, a gossip. All good reasons to read him.

It wasn't in Richler's nature to say nice things about the Jews. But was he a self-hating Jew? It's the kind of question that should probably remain rhetorical. He was an ambivalent Jew, let's put it that way. This landed him in extraordinarily good company, which includes everyone from Isaac Babel to Philip Roth. At the start of the last century, Franz Kafka outlined the dilemma of the Jewish writer and not that much had changed by the time Richler came along. Of himself and the other writers who had made the decision to write in German instead of Yiddish, Kafka said, "To get away from Judaism is what most [Jewish writers] wanted. But with their little back legs they were glued to the Judaism of their fathers and their little front legs could find no new footing. Their despair over this was their inspiration." Writing in central Europe, almost two decades before the Holocaust, Kafka's anxiety about solid footing seems almost quaint. What a thing to worry about with Hitler on the horizon. There would be bigger problems than ambivalence and, to his everlasting credit, Kafka was eerily prescient on that count in his fiction, composing tales that foreshadowed though never matched the coming horror. Even Kafka, who died in 1924, wasn't Kafkaesque enough to imagine that future.

Why So Much Shmutz?

After the Holocaust, Jewish literary ambivalence persisted, transplanted in large part to the Diaspora, to North America in particular. But by then it was less a curse than a blessing, a last barrier against the dangers of the melting pot, against boring assimilation. So in the 1960s, Richler could afford to worry less about the anti-Semitism exposed a generation earlier in novels like *Gentleman's Agreement* and *Earth and High Heaven*, and more about being suddenly and uncomfortably in fashion. The critic Leslie Fiedler summed up the catch-22 at the time in his essay collection *Waiting for the End*. "We live at a moment," he explained, "when, everywhere in the realm of prose, Jewish writers have discovered their Jewishness to be an eminently marketable commodity, their much vaunted alienation to be their passport to the heart of gentile American culture." Richler might have put it more directly: do we really need to be loved? That was the question he was posing when he wrote about Jews. His answer was self-evident.

In his mocking review of *The Jewish Community in Canada,* Richler complains that by "washing our Jews whiter than the purest snow, sanitizing them, as it were . . . Rabbi Rosenberg has dehumanized a truly compelling bunch, whose colourful history has yet to be written." In novels like *Duddy Kravitz, St. Urbain's Horseman,* and *Solomon Gursky Was Here,* which rescues the Bronfman saga from publicity and puffery, he recorded that "colourful history." Like Moses Berger in *Solomon Gursky Was Here,* Richler was "the only one armed with flint among all the hagiographers in the woodpile."

Well, not the only one. Around the same time, Philip Roth was having the same problems with the American Jewish community. In his essay "Writing about Jews," Roth carries on an argument with readers who accuse him of making things harder for Jews by concentrating on the negative: "Why so much *shmutz?*" is how one of Roth's readers puts it. Roth's reply is what any serious writer or, for that matter, any serious reader of literature should understand intuitively: one person's *shmutz* is another's art. Responding to the charge, "Why must you be so critical?" Roth writes, "It is difficult, if not impossible, to explain to some people claiming to have felt my teeth sinking in that in many instances they haven't been bitten at all. . . . At times they see wickedness where I myself had seen energy or courage or spontaneity; they are ashamed of what I see no reason to be ashamed of."

It's harder to make the love-bite defence stand up in Richler's case. If his readers thought they were being attacked it's usually because they were. But like Roth, Richler would also claim that he really didn't believe the awful things he was saying about his characters were all that awful. "What I choose to celebrate," Richler told a *Time* reporter in 1971, "[Montreal's Jews] are ashamed of."

In fact, Richler envied the single-mindedness, the enduring faith of "the innocent and ordered world," he came from. A place "where everything fit" was a possibility he had stopped believing in long ago. Still, in *St. Urbain's Horseman,* he turns his envy and his rejection of this world into a grudging and nostalgic valentine:

> A scandal was when a first cousin was invited to the bar mitzvah kiddush, but not the dinner. Eloquence was the rabbi's sermon. They were ignorant of the arts, they were overdressed, they were overstuffed, and their taste was appallingly bad. But within their self-contained world, there was order. It worked.

The point missed by people, even communities, who have felt abused by Richler's fiction, is that his intention was never just to make them look bad, though that was often a side benefit. His intention was to make them look interesting. That's a literary impulse, and for all the politics and polemics he indulged in, Richler was first and foremost a man of literature. Let's face it, too, being Jewish can make things more interesting. Saul Bellow, for one, was quick to acknowledge his heritage as a lucky break. "It is a fact of your life," he said. "That's how I view my own Jewishness. That's where the great power of it comes from. It doesn't come from the fact that I studied the Talmud, or anything of that sort. I never belonged to an orthodox congregation. It simply comes from the fact that at a most susceptible time of my life I was wholly Jewish. That's a gift, a piece of good fortune with which one doesn't quarrel." Philip Roth also spoke of his "good fortune at being born a Jew." It's complicated, he said, "a morally demanding and very singular experience, and I like that. I find myself in the historic predicament of being Jewish, with all its implications. Who could ask for more?"

Why So Much Shmutz?

It's not the traditional comforts of Judaism that Bellow and Roth are referring to here. Instead, it's the complications, the *tsuris* they relish. "Don't you find it exhausting?" Solomon Gursky's would-be mistress asks Moses Berger, his would-be biographer, in *Solomon Gursky Was Here*. "I beg your pardon," he says. "Being Jewish . . . coloured Solomon's reactions to everything," she replies. "Like you, he always had his hackles raised."

Richler's hackles were never down, in any case, and being Jewish couldn't hurt. At times he could be fiercely protective of his heritage. In *Solomon Gursky Was Here,* Solomon defends his vulgar brother Mr. Bernard against the slander of outsiders, gentiles by definition. "You people. You people. Dig deep enough into the past of any noble family and there is a Bernard at the root," Solomon says. "The founder with the dirty fingernails. . . . No better, possibly a lot worse, than my brother." Perhaps the most refreshing aspect of Richler's Jewishness was his refusal to sanitize it. He understood there was a price to pay for candour. "Writing about Jews without condescension," he told an audience at the Montreal Jewish Public Library, "was to be a very reckless act." Reckless and essential: Richler's books are full of unapologetic Jews—the kind of Jews conspicuously absent from novels like *Earth and High Heaven* and movies like *Gentleman's Agreement*. And if they aren't treated with a great deal of respect, they aren't treated with any more contempt than his other characters.

After I got married, I moved out of the suburb I'd lived in since I was five and back into the heart of Richler territory. My wife's apartment was on Hutchison Street between St. Viateur and Fairmount, which is five blocks west of where Richler grew up. Hutchison was an adjustment even for a kid from Chomedey. Growing up, I was surrounded by Jews, but I wasn't surrounded by Jewishness, not the way I was on Hutchison Street. There, the flourishing Hassidic community is impossible to take for granted. Walking down the street is like walking into an Isaac Bashevis Singer story. Wherever you look there are men in beards and long black coats and fur-rimmed hats; women with wigs and triple strollers by the time they are twenty; children, well behaved but remote, taught, against a child's natural inclination, to be aloof. The women won't look at you if you're a man; the children won't smile at you no matter what you do. It isn't exactly that they think they are too good to talk to you; it is more like they think you aren't good enough to talk to them. Often I wanted to. Just to say something polite and innocuous—to see what kind of reaction I'd get. But I never did.

One morning, a sidelocked young man, wearing a fedora several sizes too big for him and a shiny black suit, came to our door, collecting for some charity or other. He rang the doorbell and stared at me in my writing clothes, sweatpants and T-shirt, and then looked at the *mezzuzah* on the door frame and did a double take. There I was—not studying or working as far as he could tell, nothing covering my head, no food cooking on the stove, no kids running through the long narrow halls. He could think of nothing to say, in English or Yiddish, but I knew what he was thinking. Faced with his scrutiny, I was thinking the same thing: what kind of Jew is this?

Self-hate isn't hard to summon up after all. And I would, I'm embarrassed to admit, feel uncomfortable and often resentful in the presence of my ultraorthodox neighbours, until one morning my wife and I were headed out for a walk and we stopped to say hello to another one of our neighbours, a pretty little Québécois girl of about six. My French isn't very good, and my wife was doing the talking. The girl was smiling and animated, and the only word I could make out from her rapid, rambling conversation was *juif.* The word Jew pronounced in the wrong tone will occasionally sound pejorative even though the evil intent will generally be in the mind of the person listening. *Juif* always sounds bad, I'm afraid. Generally, this is an unfair conclusion to draw. More often than not, it's being used innocently and correctly enough. But this time I watched as my wife ended the conversation and abruptly grabbed my elbow, moving me along. Her face was pale.

"What's wrong?" I asked.

"She was telling me that her family is moving—just a few blocks from here."

"So?"

"So she's very excited. She said there weren't going to be so many Jews there."

Why So Much Shmutz?

"What did you say?"

"What should I have said? She's only a child."

If she could have elaborated, the little girl would have made it clear that she didn't mean us. She liked us. I suspect her parents or schoolmates or whoever had explained the advantage of living in a place with fewer Jews, didn't mean us either. At least that's what they would have said. They probably just didn't think of us as Jews, not Jewy Jews, I mean. So how come that only made me feel worse? For the little girl and myself. You see, like her, I had spent the better part of the year on Hutchison Street thinking the same thing.

Alan Langner, rabbi emeritus of the Temple Beth-El, an orthodox synagogue in the Town of Mount Royal, one of Montreal's affluent suburban communities, has been watching Mordecai Richler's career since 1959. That was the year *The Apprenticeship of Duddy Kravitz* was published and Rabbi Langner, coincidentally, took his post at the synagogue.

"I came from a place in Canada, don't know if you've heard of it, called Toronto. My wife is from Montreal and she wanted to live here. I'm from Toronto and I wanted to live there. So we compromised and we live in Montreal," Rabbi Langner tells me when I arrive at his office. He has the deadpan countenance of a man who has spent his life contemplating spiritual matters. When he is asked a serious question, he looks like a serious man, who will give issues their proper weight and consideration. Still, he seems much happier telling jokes. Which he does as often as he can, undeterred by the possibility that they are old or unfunny or even a bit risqué. Asked how old he is, he invariably says twenty-five, Celsius.

His sense of humour is one of the reasons I asked if I could speak to him about Mordecai Richler. I met Rabbi Langner a few years ago at the Montefiore, a ritzy private Jewish club in downtown Montreal, one of the oldest private Jewish clubs in North America, in fact. Every other month at the Montefiore, I eat a meal I couldn't otherwise afford. All I have to do is sing for my supper by giving a literary talk.

Another reason I asked Rabbi Langner for his professional opinion on Richler is that he is a reader—interested in everyone from Sholem

Mordecai & Me

Aleichem to, yes, Yann Martel. Insofar as I have a rabbi or need one for the purposes of this book, he's mine. He wasn't sure what I wanted from him exactly, but once I turned the tape recorder on, a trooper, he had plenty to say about Richler. "I met him a few times here at the synagogue. We had a couple of scotches together and told jokes. He was here to attend a wedding or a bar mitzvah. We have quite a few Richlers in this congregation—cousins of his. How do they feel about him? By and large, they feel he is very talented, but they are quite observant and very much Jewish, and they find it hurtful to see some of the books he's written.

"I was also in attendance a few years ago when he delivered the Steinberg lecture, a very prestigious event, at the Shaar Hashomayim Synagogue in Westmount. It wasn't that long after the referendum in 1995, and people probably thought he was going to talk politics. They never had such a crowd; they were standing. They'd come to hear Richler. But he just started reading from the manuscript of his novel, *Barney's Version* it must have been. And with vulgar language, lurid passages, which was embarrassing. Especially in a *shul*. I think he showed very poor sense in sizing up the audience. People walked out. It was an unmitigated disaster. To this day, people still talk about it.

"But then I think he did a lot of these things deliberately. He was in your face. Somehow I have the feeling Richler set out to be negative; this is just my own feeling. In the beginning it may be he thought that he would establish himself as a writer if he wrote negatively about the Jews. Did it work? I don't know. He did become famous."

Like Ruth Wisse, Rabbi Langner doesn't consider Richler a Jewish writer, but he doesn't hold it against him as much. He also has his own informal ranking system for Jewish writers. So while Richler isn't as Jewish as Sholem Aleichem or Isaac Bashevis Singer, let's say, he is definitely more Jewish than Leonard Cohen. Saul Bellow isn't a Jewish writer either, according to Rabbi Langner, but he prefers him to Richler. "Bellow dazzles you with his vocabulary. He also has a much more positive approach."

Between Philip Roth and Mordecai Richler, it's a toss-up. "You know at the time that *Portnoy's Complaint*, came out I delivered a sermon on it. I gave my views of the book because people in the congregation were talking about it. That was a tricky sermon to give."

Why So Much Shmutz?

Rabbi Langner's feelings about Roth parallel his feelings about Richler; they're mixed in other words. "I remember I said about Roth that it's too bad such a *momzer* has so much talent. Too bad he couldn't use it in a more positive way."

Richler, too, causes him more disappointment for what might have been than bitterness over what was. "He was a complex figure. On the one hand, he didn't portray Jews in a pleasant light. I read *Duddy Kravitz* not long after it came out. It was a good book, but you know, it was painful to read about the Jewish characters in it. Not a single one sympathetic. Of course there are Jewish S.O.B.s, but there are also very nice people and they don't appear in Richler's work.

"On the other hand, I can remember reading a book review he wrote many years ago which contained a very strong condemnation of Ian Fleming for the anti-Semitic characters he portrayed in his James Bond books. I think as much as Richler wanted to detach himself from being Jewish, he couldn't. It remained with him." Which may be why Rabbi Langner felt compelled to deliver a eulogy for Richler to his congregation when he died. "I said that while we may not have liked the way he portrayed us, we have to give the devil his due."

After I turn off the tape recorder, the rabbi asks me if he should be reading Carol Shields's new novel *Unless*. He'd also just heard E.L. Doctorow speak at the Jewish Public Library and was considering getting a copy of *Billy Bathgate*. He wanted to know what I thought of it.

"Great book," I say. "One of his best. It has marvellous transitions from one scene to the next. I always admired that about it."

"And what about this *Life of Pi?*" he asks. "This Yann Martel fellow, is he Jewish?"

Chapter 12
On the Road to Dyspepsia

Generally speaking, I don't believe in kind humour—I don't think it exists.
–S.J. Perelman

On bad days, I make an inventory of my career accomplishments and wonder what I have been doing all this time. When I require consolation, I remind myself that I have managed for the last two decades not to have what anyone could conceivably call a real job. And while I've had to scramble to make a living, I've never really had to answer to anyone. Bosses, editors, I mean, are only a temporary annoyance. I've only been fired once; otherwise I've just been forgotten. I've also never had to sit in traffic to get to work—the commute from my bedroom to my office in the basement is an easy one—and I didn't own a suit until I got married four years ago. Generally, the dress code here is casual. Underwear, I reluctantly confess, is optional.

No, you can't beat the freelance life.

On the Road to Dyspepsia

Mordecai Richler avoided a real job for nearly half a century and still raised five kids and managed to indulge his taste for the best scotch and the best cigars. Even if he had done nothing else, I would consider this a remarkable achievement—one Richler was rightly proud of. In a letter William Weintraub wrote to Brian Moore, dated December 1960, Weintraub described how hard it was to take Richler out to a fancy restaurant in Toronto in those days: "Mort, depressed because it was me who was squandering on the cognac and not him, called for the plug-in telephone and made two long and hideously expensive calls to London, just to say hello." It was Richler's way of reminding himself that he was a success, that he had beat the odds and was making a living as a writer. "I enjoy these things," he told Weintraub about his extravagant behaviour. "You don't know what it's like to once have been poor."

But he also knew that there was writing and *writing*. He would always worry about his fiction selling, unable to shake the warning he had received early in his career. The problem, he was once told by a New York editor, is that "we are trying to market something nobody wants." Even *Duddy Kravitz,* Richler's breakthrough book, sold fewer than one thousand copies in Canada when it first came out.

So Richler survived, in his early days in London in particular, as a screenwriter and a journalist. Initially, the plan was to buy time with this work for whatever novel he happened to be writing. (Throughout the 1960s, it would be *St. Urbain's Horseman* that would consume him, first in the plan to write it and later in his inability to finish it.) And while he worked on some films he would be proud of—including his screenplay for *Duddy Kravitz,* which was nominated for an Academy Award—it was the journalism that took up most of his time, and outside of his fiction, it was the work to which he was most dedicated.

For a man with his misanthropic tendencies, Richler also admits in "Writing for the Mags" that he "almost always enjoyed the company of other journalists and found them to be a generous lot, good companions, who are willing to share sources and their knowledge of the most agreeable watering holes." Peter Gzowski, in his 1989 afterword to a new edition of *The Incomparable Atuk,* recalls hanging out in Toronto with Richler in the early 1960s. Back then he seemed to be just another happy-go-lucky hack, drinking, smoking, chasing down magazine assignments. Indeed, the four hundred dollars he received for a *Maclean's* piece about writing *The Acrobats,* titled "How I became an unknown with my first novel," was, according to Richler, more than he earned for the novel. But he was also, Gzowski realized, not just one of the guys. "All of us wore white shirts, loosened our ties and tried to hone our craft or, in [Richler's] case . . . art." Even so, his art often had to wait for his journalism to not only support it, but feed it. In retrospect Richler seemed to sincerely regret not having worked in the real world the way other writers had. Richler longed for adventure, too, or just more experience—for a spin in an ambulance during World War I, Hemingway-style, or a stint with the Resistance, like Camus put in during World War II. Journalism bought him some adventure, even if it was a tourist's version of it.

In *Negotiating with the Dead,* Margaret Atwood recalls how "in 1960, as a twenty-year-old poet," she was told "by an older poet, who was a man, that I would never come to anything . . . until I had been a truck driver, thus learning at first hand what real people actually did." Atwood saw through this advice for the macho bullshit it was, but Richler never did. In "Writing for the Mags" he says, "With hindsight however I wish I hadn't published so early but had been obliged to endure a number of unsatisfactory jobs first, either in offices or on the factory floor. Then, like other novelists I know, I would now be able to send a bucket down such immensely valuable wells of experience."

Journalism did get him out of the house—sending him off to Israel or the Catskills or, even more exotic for Richler, the gym. It also provided him with bits of scavenged material he could then bring home and shamelessly slip into his novels. For example, it was while he was working on a profile of Montreal bodybuilding entrepreneur Ben Weider that he stumbled across and filed away the silly slogan, "What You Dare to Dream, Dare To Do," which would later become the title for the first part of *The Incomparable Atuk.* And while he was doing an article on professional wrestling, Richler met characters like Killer Kowalski, the inspiration for the hapless villain in his first children's story *Jacob Two-Two Meets the Hooded Fang.* Like most freelancers, Richler also had no qualms about plagiarizing himself. Hunter S. Thompson said that there's a long-

On the Road to Dyspepsia

standing rule among journalists and writers that says, "When you start stealing from your own work you're in bad trouble." Which may be true for Thompson, but wasn't for Richler. He was always recycling a phrase first turned or an opinion first expressed in his nonfiction. His jibe that not all neglected writers are unjustly neglected shows up, in one variation or another, in the essays "Pages from a Western Journal" and "Hemingway Set his Own Hours," in his memoir *This Year in Jerusalem*, and in his novels *Solomon Gursky Was Here* and *Barney's Version*.

But then Richler was stuck with the experience he had, and stuck, fortunately, with a gift for exploiting it. In *The Incomparable Atuk*, he gleefully turns old grudges into satirical riffs. Seymour Bone, the banana-eating drama critic and host of the television program *Crossed Swords*, is a transparent swipe at the bloated Nathan Cohen, host of the 1950s panel show *Fighting Words* and the critic who wrote Richler off after his third novel. Novelists have long memories—it's a job requirement—and Richler's was longer than most.

These days I'll read an item in the newspaper or hear a story on the radio and think of Richler and cross my fingers that there's a heaven, comfy as an old couch, for curmudgeonly novelists. You want to believe Richler is somewhere keeping an eye on what's going on in this place he loved in his own perverse way. Like the news that Quebec Premier Bernard Landry's mother publicly—and correctly—wrote off her son's chances of winning an election a couple of years before he held one. Or Alexa McDonough, the former NDP leader, getting back at union leader and long-time nemesis Buzz Hargrove by calling him by his real first name—Basil. Or Joe Clark, a favourite Richler whipping boy, stepping down from the leadership of the Conservative party with the announcement that he was "more trusted and popular than ever." His only problem: the polls. They showed no one would vote for him.

In *Barney's Version*, Barney keeps an ongoing "ledger of ironies," a personal scrapbook of a world turned topsy-turvy. So did Richler. He was, he told John Metcalf during an interview, an avid reader of the newspaper, which on any given day yielded "a number of outlandish stories," and more often than not, those stories were put to good use, turning up in his fiction as "concrete examples of the absurd." Indeed, it was after coming across a notice announcing "a gathering of Jewish lesbian daughters of Holocaust survivors" that Richler said there is no longer any need to invent. The following item, which finds its way into *St. Urbain's Horseman,* is another example: "The headline in the first edition of *The Evening Standard* announced that Germany was to send Israel twenty thousand gas masks. Nowadays . . . everybody is a black humourist."

I also collect these outlandish tidbits now, on his behalf. For instance, there's the Canadian cruise company that enticed tourists to take a trip to the Arctic in the company of Margaret Atwood. In the brochure I sent away for they don't mention who came up with the idea. Who thought, Let's put two potentially unpleasant experiences together and see if they can be sold as a package? Then the other day I was mailed a thin pamphlet by the Writers' Union of Canada. It was a glossary, and, as an aid to its membership of working writers, it included definitions of words like "paperback" and "publisher." I wondered if other professional organizations, for firemen, let's say, were as helpful. Did they define "hose" or "blaze" for their membership? Richler also belonged to the Writers' Union, though this didn't prevent him from writing a column once poking fun at the appalling grammar in its monthly newsletter.

When I interviewed Richler in 1997, not long after *Barney's Version* came out, I ended our talk by telling him that I thought *Dykes on Mikes* was a great name for a lesbian radio show. (A lesbian interviewer shows up to ask Barney about his first wife, a self-destructive Sylvia Plath–type.) "You know, I didn't make that up," he said, more animated and engaged than he had been throughout the interview. Richler was usually not averse to leading journalists astray, but this time he felt compelled to acknowledge that there really was a *Dykes on Mikes* on McGill's university radio station. But I knew that. He didn't understand—I wasn't complimenting him on making the name up; I was complimenting him on finding it and putting it to such good use in his novel.

Perhaps it's because I am not gifted with much imagination or with the right kind that I comfort myself with the belief that the imagination is overrated, that it is not the be-all and end-all of storytelling. Experience

On the Road to Dyspepsia

and memory are still a creative writer's most important resources. What's more, the dividing line between imagination and memory is and always has been an arbitrary one. Even before memoirs became all the rage and terms like creative nonfiction were coined, the only difference between writing fiction and writing literary nonfiction (memoirs or personal essays) was one of degree, and that hasn't changed. Novelists still tell the truth and pretend they are lying; memoirists still lie and pretend they are telling the truth. As James Salter, a novelist and a memoirist, says, "I sometimes say that I don't make up anything—obviously that's not true. But I am usually uninterested in writers who say that everything comes out of the imagination. I would rather be in a room with someone who is telling me the story of his life, which may be exaggerated and even have lies in it, but I want to hear the true story, essentially."

Richler objected to being called an autobiographical writer, in part because he didn't want people speculating on all the true elements in his stories. But he also considered such a designation an insult. In this, he misunderstood what autobiographical writing does at the same time that he was doing it so well. Autobiographical writing is not about taking something that really happened, putting it down on paper, and then trying to disguise it. It's the opposite; it's about taking something that really happened, usually the kind of thing you could never make up in a million years, and trying to make it seem more real, more credible. Richler was always a much better embellisher than he was a flat out liar.

"If only I could invent as presumptuously as life," Nathan Zuckerman, Philip Roth's alter ego, says in Roth's 1979 novel *The Ghost Writer*. It is voiced more as a complaint than as an admission of defeat. But then Roth had thrown in the towel two decades earlier in a famous speech on the state of American literature and life, saying that no matter what he managed to dream as a novelist, it would never measure up to the sheer outlandishness of reality.

The 1960s were proving too outlandish for Mordecai Richler, as well. While some of the more outrageous scenes in *The Apprenticeship of Duddy Kravitz* contain a prescient element—would anyone be surprised

Mordecai & Me

today by an avant-garde bar mitzvah home movie?—*The Incomparable Atuk* veers off course in its final pages, from being a clever satire to an unbelievable farce. Then again, the ending, which has Atuk guillotined as a guest on a tasteless American game show, a martyr to the cause of Canadian cultural nationalism, isn't that far removed from *Survivor* or *Fear Factor* or the other reality TV programs popular today.

Indeed, Richler's next novel, *Cocksure*, published in 1968, shows signs of a writer at odds with the world. It manages to be a scathing and naive book at the same time, deliberately over the top and unintentionally silly. Like *The Acrobats, Son of a Smaller Hero, Duddy Kravitz,* and the yet to be completed *St. Urbain's Horseman, Cocksure* had its origins in a short story. The difference is the short story, in this case, was a pretty good one. "Mortimer Griffin, Shalinsky, and How They Settled the Jewish Question" is a delightfully irreverent piece, which begins with the premise: what if everyone thought you were Jewish, but you weren't? The story, while just far-fetched enough to be funny, never strays too far from reality. In this respect, it is more like the comic novels still to come—*St. Urbain's Horseman* and *Joshua Then and Now*—than it is like the satirical novel it inspired.

At any rate, the story goes like this: Mortimer Griffin, newly married and teaching a night course on Kafka, is a reasonably happy young man until Shalinsky, one of his keener and older students, asks him why he felt he had to change his name. Shalinsky is convinced that Mortimer, a smart, cultured young man, is Jewish. Mortimer, insisting that he isn't, only makes Shalinsky more sure he is right. Shalinsky is also convinced that what he is dealing with in Mortimer is a classic case of a self-hating Jew. As the story unfolds, Mortimer loses his best friends—a Jewish couple who interpret Mortimer's denials as a sign of his hitherto concealed anti-Semitism. He also loses his job—he is fired for being anti-Semitic—and finally his wife, who wishes he could just be proud of his Jewish identity. The story ends with Mortimer remarried to Gitel, a nice Jewish girl, and living an orthodox life, though dreaming from time to time of "a plate of bacon and eggs." He is having trouble finding work, but now, at least he understands why: "Last week my application for a teaching job with Western High School was turned down flatly—in spite of my excellent qualifications. It's hard to be a Jew, you see."

On the Road to Dyspepsia

There is something Kafkaesque in both Mortimer's unjust persecution and in his sudden transformation. This may explain why the story was the inspiration for *Cocksure*. But while the premise of "Mortimer Griffin, Shalinksy, and How They Settled the Jewish Question," does make it into *Cocksure*, it is a minor part of the book, a throwaway gag at best, an awkward inclusion at worst. Of the story upon which *St. Urbain's Horseman* was based, Richler said that it "just grew and grew . . . like Topsy." So did *Cocksure*. As a consequence, a polished, cleverly composed short story is sacrificed to a much wilder but more flawed novel. What's best about the story—its subtle wit, its absurdly logical outcome—is lost in the deliberately over-the-top *Cocksure*.

Cocksure, as the title suggests, is about sex—that is to say, it's Richler's idea of a sexy book. While he was working on it, he seemed to be shocking himself. He kidded his Canadian publisher, Jack McClelland, that his new book was "getting to be a very dirty novel and I'm wondering whether I should let you publish it, let alone read it. It could corrupt you."

After *Cocksure* was published, Richler would change his mind about the novel's relative dirtiness. At the University of Western Ontario in 1971, Richler, on hand to participate in a television program called *Under Attack*, was accused by a student in the audience of wallowing in sex, to which Richler replied to the poor kid, "If you think *Cocksure* wallows in sexual behaviour, possibly you excite too easily." Then he added, "It's not a titillating book by any means."

Mortimer Griffin, transplanted from Montreal to London, an expatriate Canadian and a book editor now instead of a teacher, is Richler's attempt to make the case, as he put it, "for that much abused man, the square." Squares like himself, that is, who when it came to the abundance of free love supposedly there for the taking, never missed an opportunity to miss an opportunity. But mocking poor beleaguered Mortimer proved too easy for Richler. The Mortimer from the short story, also a kind of square, does earn our sympathy; the Mortimer in *Cocksure* is a tougher sell. The case for him is never very convincing. Mortimer Griffin, in *Cocksure*, is not a protagonist Richler takes to, not the way he takes to Duddy Kravitz or even Atuk. His later heroes, too, like Jake Hersh, Joshua Shapiro, and Barney Panofsky all have their flaws, but Richler doesn't make it quite so hard for readers to sympathize with them. They are, for all the messes they get themselves into, for all their bumbling and self-pity, not *shlemiels*. Some writers have a fondness for the type, not Richler. He liked his heroes with a little more larceny, a little more mischief in their hearts. In a review of Mark Twain's *Innocents Abroad,* Richler points out that Twain was a writer "with an enduring affection for chicanery and for those who can get away with it." Richler had the same inclination. So Duddy and Atuk have their get-rich schemes, Jake his revenge fantasies, Joshua his housebreaking pranks, and Barney his politically incorrect patter. Even Moses Berger, the drunken, would-be Gursky biographer in *Solomon Gursky Was Here,* has his moments. He has spunk. In *Cocksure,* Mortimer Griffin is, finally, a man obsessed with the size of his penis.

For all that, Mortimer is still the only sane character in the increasingly insane world of the novel, a world in which prim, elderly schoolteachers administer blow jobs to young boys to inspire them to work harder. And where the villain of the piece, the Star Maker, an "ageless, undying" Hollywood mogul, is a self-designed hermaphrodite whose goal is to literally knock himself up. Like *The Incomparable Atuk, Cocksure* ends outlandishly, with Mortimer a martyr to squaredom.

Richler has this much in common with Mortimer Griffin: neither of them understood the kind of licence that passed for freedom in the late 1960s. The difference is Richler didn't have any interest in understanding it. "Wherever I travel I'm too late. The orgy has moved elsewhere," he writes in "A Sense of the Ridiculous." But the truth is he wasn't the orgy type. (Jake Hersh passes up his chance at one in *St. Urbain's Horseman.*) On principle, Richler disliked and distrusted the vast majority of people too much and too universally to be able to find a group he would be compatible with clothed, let alone naked. So *Cocksure,* Richler's hip, sexy novel, published in 1968, is, in the end, a broad and satirical warning about the danger of trying to be hip. "In many ways," he told John Metcalf in a 1974 interview, "I'm an old-fashioned man."

The novel was misinterpreted. It was both the bane and the great pleasure of Richler's career that most people at most times haven't known when he was kidding and when he wasn't. It would have saved everyone a lot of aggravation if they'd just assumed he was kidding all the time. But

On the Road to Dyspepsia

they didn't. When it came out, *Cocksure* was banned from the chain of W.H. Smith bookstores in Britain and banned entirely in Ireland, Australia, New Zealand, and South Africa. This was funny. Richler was no swinger, no counterculture revolutionary. In a 1970 review of Timothy Leary's *The Politics of Ecstasy*—the review was called "Not me, Leary, Not Me"—Richler writes:

> Leary's primary claim is that LSD is mind-expanding, more nourishing for our kids than porridge. Being a non-tripper, I can't say for sure. But what arouses my suspicions is that if Leary found LSD so incredibly mind-expanding, he had, on the evidence of the book to hand, the decidedly unfair advantage of there being so much room to begin with.

On the subject of the sexual revolution, he believed, with Woody Allen, that sex was only dirty if you were doing it right. He also liked to quote Hemingway's observation about Henry Miller that Miller, having once been fucked in the afternoon, came to the conclusion that he had invented the practise.

Besides, Richler was far too happily married to enter into the spirit of the swinging sixties. By the time *Cocksure* was published, he had been with his wife, Florence, for more than a decade, and he remained unfailingly romantic—calling her constantly when the two were apart or taking her out to dinner like they were on a date. The British novelist Bernice Rubens was a friend of Richler's while he was living in London, and she describes him as a man who was very attractive to women. She recalled how she and fellow novelist Beryl Bainbridge would meet him at literary events and would flirt with him. He would flirt back, but the moment things started to get interesting, Rubens said, Richler would get nervous and start looking around for Florence to rescue him. Always nearby, she would.

By the late 1960s, Richler had, whether he liked it or not (and mostly he liked it) graduated from rebellion to respectability, from working-class street urchin to bourgeois husband and father. Still, there was something unavoidable in the air at the time. Richler wasn't the only middle-aged North American male to try his hand at a so-called sexy book. The novels of the late 1960s had one thing in common: they were determined to let it all hang out, and it wasn't always a pretty sight. In *Couples,* published in 1968 like *Cocksure,* John Updike put fellatio on the literary map; a year later, in *Portnoy's Complaint,* Roth did the same for masturbation. Interviewed by Johnny Carson, Jacqueline Susann, author of sleazy novels like *The Love Machine,* said that while she wouldn't mind meeting this Philip Roth fellow, she'd just as soon not shake his hand. There was *Candy,* too, which sought to mix literature with pornography and which was dreamed up by two of Richler's old Paris pals—Terry Southern and Mason Hoffenberg. *Cocksure* was a departure for Richler, especially when it came to writing about sex. The typical sex scene in Richler's early novels consists largely of fade outs. This description of Duddy and Yvette's first sexual encounter in *The Apprenticeship of Duddy Kravitz* is typical: "Duddy made love quickly to Yvette. 'I feel good,' she said. 'Do you feel good?'"

Robert Fulford complimented *Cocksure* by calling it "the randiest novel ever written by a serious Canadian writer." Meanwhile, the blurb on the Bantam paperback edition of the novel describes it as an "outrageous new anti-establishment novel." The *New York Times* called it "saucy, dirty, abrasive, hilarious." The *San Francisco Chronicle* added, "shocking, disgusting, scatological . . . near-pornographic, funny, embarrassing, nauseating, bewildering . . . uninhibited, unruly, unabashed and very interesting." But in this long list of suggestive adjectives, the missing word is *moral. Cocksure* is judgemental as hell, a book full of its author's sense of righteous indignation and disapproval. Richler may have turned his back on religion, but he was still the grandson of a rabbi, after all. If he was no longer orthodox in observance, he remained orthodox in temperament. And, for all its outrageousness, *Cocksure* didn't take much imagination to write. To an eye as keen and jaded as Richler's, the excesses of the 1960s were apparent as they were happening. So, too, were the obvious hazards of free love and mind-altering drugs, the breakdown of the family and marriage and traditional values. Inside every fat satirist, Richler was fond of saying, there is a thin moralist. In this respect, at least, the angry and disappointed young man had stayed true to form—he had grown up to become an angry and disappointed middle-aged man.

On the Road to Dyspepsia

Richler had also become a comic novelist, and that was more of a surprise and less of a foregone conclusion than it appears in retrospect. In his first three novels, comic moments serve as a rare break from Richler's unrelenting angst and disillusionment. Reading *The Acrobats* and rereading *Son of a Smaller Hero*, I was struck by how irredeemably bleak they are and how Richler's disappointment with the world feels petulant rather than philosophical. Certainly, nothing about the restrained *A Choice of Enemies* prepares readers for the raucousness of the novel that followed it, *The Apprenticeship of Duddy Kravitz*. In *Duddy Kravitz* the comic moments are as in-your-face as Duddy is himself. They are impossible to overlook. In fact, they shoulder the more serious moments and concerns of Richler's story into the background. It may be that Duddy's fate was intended to serve as a cautionary tale, but he is a character who does not inspire caution. In *Duddy Kravitz* comic relief becomes comic tour de force. "It's not a comic novel, tho—I hope—there are 'comic' sections in it," Richler wrote to William Weintraub after he'd finished a first draft of *Duddy Kravitz*, "and it is a lot funnier than anything I've ever attempted before."

In his novels of the 1960s as well as his nonfiction, Richler would have to come to terms with his special talent. He wasn't just mildly amusing; he was damn funny. This would turn out to be both a blessing and a burden, especially for a Canadian writer. For starters, it meant Richler would have to get used to the fact that he wasn't going to be the kind of writer he had originally set out to be. For most writers, this is, incidentally, a more liberating than demoralizing realization. A playwright acquaintance of mine told me once that she never wrote anything worthwhile until her father informed her out of the blue one day, "You know, you're no Chekhov." Apparently, this hadn't occurred to her before, but once it did, she used it as a mantra whenever she lacked the confidence to see a work through. "I'm no Chekhov" is what kept her going.

Richler wasn't going to be Hemingway or Faulkner or Sartre, or, thank goodness, Malcolm Lowry. As a young writer, Richler had made his share of brash promises, promises he would no longer be able to fulfill, most notably his vow that it was his obligation as a writer to stick up for the disenfranchised and the dispossessed, to be the loser's advocate. But

Mordecai & Me

Richler didn't have it in him to be an effective advocate for the downtrodden. It was just too easy and too tempting to make fun of the people he was supposed to be championing and to make fun of them the way he made fun of everyone else—mercilessly.

There was also being funny and being Canadian to reconcile. We have a tradition in this country of overestimating novelists whose only real talent, as far as I can tell, is for bumming readers out. From Sinclair Ross to David Adams Richards, we take our serious literature seriously here. Some of us seem to like it bleak—the bleaker the better. The trouble is that this is a narrow vision, which leads to a narrow and dour literature. (Richards's work is a good, recent example.) "Useful though pessimism is, it can't cover it all," as the comic novelist Tibor Fischer said. At the start of a 1989 review of *Solomon Gursky Was Here*, which I wrote for the *Village Voice*, I introduced Richler to American readers unfamiliar with him in this way: "He's the funny one." The headline picked up on the theme and read: "Funny, You Don't Look Canadian." The point I was making was that literature in this country doesn't have a long tradition—or any tradition—of humour, certainly not the kind of uncompromising humour found in Richler's work. "It's much easier to write a sad book than a funny one. People are always on the verge of tears," the humourist Fran Lebowitz said, and while it's true most writers will admit that few things are harder than being funny in print, if you are Canadian and funny in print, you will, like a literary Rodney Dangerfield, get no respect.

Of course, if you really aren't funny, chances are good that you will be a front-runner for the Stephen Leacock Medal, which is given to the year's most humourous book. Richler finally did win the Leacock in 1997 for *Barney's Version*, though it was late enough in his career to make you wonder what the various Leacock judges had been thinking for almost forty years. During that time, Richler was writing some of the funniest books, novels as well as essay collections, in this country's history. Imagine, no Leacock for *Duddy Kravitz* or *Cocksure* or *The Street* or *Hunting Tigers under Glass* or *Shovelling Trouble* or *St. Urbain's Horseman* or *Solomon Gursky Was Here*. Even Richler's polemic about Quebec separatism, *Oh Canada! Oh Quebec!* is hilarious. Instead, the prize for the year's funniest book generally goes to the innocuous or the folksy or some combination of the two. More often than not, that means it goes to a CBC broadcaster for his latest collection of observations of small town life. Stuart McLean has won the Leacock Medal twice—for *Home from the Vinyl Cafe* and, get this, *Vinyl Cafe Unplugged*. Enough said.

Richler's dilemma was that he was a comic writer in a country that takes its literature far too seriously. It may well be a remnant of the WASP rectitude upon which this place was founded: if you're having too good a time, there must be something lacking in your work, something like *gravitas*. Richler struggled against this ingrained national bias his entire career. "To be funny here is to be frivolous, because I think people wear their culture very uneasily; to be funny in England is to be in the savage tradition of Waugh or Swift, and it's very serious indeed. And the same in America," he told Donald Cameron in a 1971 interview. In our first interview, almost twenty years later, he was still voicing the same complaint.

"Culture is supposed to be worthy," he told me, "a lot like health food, so there isn't as much appreciation for the comic novel here as there is in England or the U.S., where people are a lot less self-conscious about culture and where they realize how difficult it is to write a comic novel. Canadians still feel guilty about something that makes them laugh."

In the foreword to *The Best of Modern Humour*, a 1983 anthology Richler edited, he quotes Dorothy Parker's comment that in writing humour "there must be criticism, for humour, to my mind, is encapsulated in criticism." It is also, as Richler says, "bound to offend for, in the nature of things, it ridicules our prejudices and popular institutions." The two novels Richler wrote in the 1960s were also bound and determined to offend. The difference between the mischievously dark humour of *Duddy Kravitz* and the broad satire of *The Incomparable Atuk* and *Cocksure* is one of degree. It is the difference between being disappointed in human behaviour and having thrown in the towel. "The subject matter of *Cocksure* lent itself to savagery," Richler also told Donald Cameron. "I mean it was written out of, I guess, disgust."

Mordecai & Me

Misanthropy has its drawbacks, but it is a democratic way of looking at the world. The first rule of satire, as laid out by Jonathan Swift, the most uncompromising of all satirists, is simple: offend everyone. If no one is spared, no one is singled out. "I have ever hated all nations, professions and communities," Swift wrote to Alexander Pope, covering all his bases. He also wrote to Pope, "I propose in all my labours to vex the world rather than to divert it."

In Richler's essay on S.J. Perelman—"The Road to Dyspepsia," included in his 1991 collection *Broadsides*—he seconded Perelman's belief that humour is an angry business, "its office to deflate pretentiousness and expose man's follies." Richler took that office seriously—he had something nasty to say about everyone. A sample of his works reveals a man who could be both unmistakably Swiftian and unapologetically politically incorrect. Eskimos are greasy; blacks are thugs; Jews are pushy; French Canadians are low-class and consumed by self-pity; Scots are stingy; the Irish are drunks; women are superficial; children are an annoyance; politicians are stupid and on the take; the British are priggish; the Germans methodical and murderous; the Americans arrogant; and Canadians, the most pitiful of the bunch, are "the disgruntled progeny of defeated peoples." There is this summation of humanity, Canadian-style, in *Solomon Gursky*:

> Most of us are still huddled tight to the border, looking into the candy store window, scared by the Americans on one side and the bush on the other. And now that we are here, prospering, we do our damn best to exclude more ill-bred newcomers, because they remind us of our own mean origins in the draper's shop in Inverness or the shtetl or the bog.

A friend of T.S. Eliot's was asked once to comment on the famous poet's anti-Semitism. Bewildered by the question, the friend replied, "But, good Lord, he didn't like anybody." In the 1940s, Daniel Fuchs, a New York novelist working on screenplays in Hollywood, found himself paired with William Faulkner. Fuchs was thrilled at the idea of working with Faulkner. But when he finally did, he was less impressed: Faulkner was unfriendly and sloshed most of the time. Fuchs finally confronted

Faulkner, saying that their partnership wasn't working. "Furthermore," Fuchs added, "I don't think it's working because you don't like Jews." Faulkner admitted as much, then added, "But, you see, Mr. Fuchs, I don't like gentiles either." Richler always regretted not repeating that last anecdote whenever readers criticized him for being too hard on one particular group or another. "Asking a satirist to be in good taste," Philip Roth said, "is like asking a love poet to be less personal." If Richler found his voice in *Duddy Kravitz,* he found the tone to match his temperament in *The Incomparable Atuk* and *Cocksure.* His later work wouldn't be as broad, but, at its core, it would be satiric.

Roth has defined satire as "moral rage transformed into poetic art"—as "the imaginative flowering of the primitive urge to knock somebody's block off." Fuelled by moral rage, *The Incomparable Atuk* and *Cocksure* are roundhouse swings—impressive without earning a knockout. In *Cocksure,* for example, Richler comes up with a gruesome Holocaust gag about "the one-millionth Jew to be burned, not counting half or quarter Jews or babies who weighed under nine pounds before being flung into the ovens." The burning of the one-millionth Jew was, Richler goes on, running a bad joke into the ground, "one of the most ring-a-ding nights in the history of the Third Reich." This is designed to shock us, and it does, but it doesn't move us. In the end, *The Incomparable Atuk* and *Cocksure* are cartoons—clever ones, but cartoons nevertheless.

Richler was a better writer when he gave more weight to vivid reality and less to his vivid imagination. The essays he wrote in the 1960s managed to combine his instinct for rage with something else, something softer, something mitigating at least. Richler's trip to the Catskills for *Holiday* magazine in 1965 is a good example. It's safe to assume that the editor who assigned Richler to the Catskills was a sadist.

Richler must have seemed like a safe bet to savage the popular Jewish resort area in upstate New York. ("Disneyland with knishes," Richler dubs it.) But while he did have fun at the expense of his hosts and his fellow guests—he is the target for some enthusiastic matchmaking until it's discovered he's a writer and therefore not much of a catch—he also cut his real-life characters a surprising amount of slack. Was he going soft? Was he nostalgic after so long in London for his Jewish soul food, his *verenikas* and pickled herring? Whatever the reason, he is impressed by the Catskills crowd: they are tacky but at least they know it. In a contest between bad taste and pretension, Richler would always come down on the side of the former. ("I survived Hitler," the harried manager of one of the resorts tells Richler, "I'll outlast the Catskills.") At least, these people, like the old Baron Byng collection of strivers, know who and what they are. Richler notes:

> There is no deflating remark I could make about minks or matchmaking that has not already been made by visiting comedians or guests. Furthermore, for an innocent goy to even think some of the things said at Grossinger's would be to invite the wrath of the B'nai Brith Anti-Defamation league.

Observing the natives at Grossinger's (the largest resort in the area), Richler resists the urge to play the moralist for a change. Middle-class Jews were already "sitting ducks for satire," and for once, presented with an easy target, Richler holds his fire. He saves it for literary types like himself instead:

> The archetypal Grossinger's guest belongs to the most frequently fired at class of American Jews. . . . Saul Bellow is watching. Alfred Kazin is ruminating. Norman Mailer is ready with his flick-knife. . . . Was there ever a group so pursued by such an unsentimental platoon of chroniclers? So plagued by moralists? So blamed for making money? . . . This unlovely spiky bunch that climbed with the rest of middle-class America out of the depression into a pot of prosperity, is the least liked by literary Jews.

Still, this empathetic Richler—this sentimental defender of the Jews—was the exception to the rule. Satire came easy to him, and he always needed a powerful incentive to take the hard road when the easy one ran so smooth. In large part he wrote *The Incomparable Atuk* and *Cocksure* because he was getting nowhere with *St. Urbain's Horseman,* a novel as concerned with understanding human behaviour as it is with mocking it. Compassion would always come hard to Richler. He would have to work at it. And he would have to do his best to find it—for the sake of the characters he was planning to create and the big, bountiful, human novels he was planning to write.

Part Three
Home Sweet Home
1971–1991

Chapter 13
The New Vaudeville

> *If know-nothingness goes on much longer somebody will yet emerge from the commune having discovered the wheel.*
> –Mordecai Richler, at York University, 1972

In "Why I Write," Richler muses about the road not taken—in his case, life as an academic instead of a dropout. For Richler, the prospect of packing it in as "a perplexed freelancer with an unpredictable income, balancing this magazine assignment, that film job," and instead sipping an aperitif in the faculty club, salaried, even tenured, is appealing and ludicrous at the same time, though finally more the latter than the former:

> All of us tend to romanticize the world we nearly chose. In my case, academe, where instead of having to bring home the meat, I would only be obliged to stamp it, rejecting this shoulder of beef as Hank James derivative, or that side of pork as sub-Jimmy Joyce. . . .

The New Vaudeville

Alas, academe, like girls, whisky, and literature, promised better than it paid.

Still, academe paid well enough to be a temptation. In the late 1960s and early 1970s, the road not taken became the one flirted with for brief, barely tolerable periods—a year here (Sir George Williams) and there (Simon Fraser, Carleton, York). Teaching jobs were a necessary evil for Richler and abundant enough to be all but irresistible.

CanLit was a thriving industry. Small-time publishers and writers were receiving big-time government grants, and the chicken needed the egg as much as the egg needed the chicken. Creative writing programs were springing up, and brand name Canadian writers like Richler were in demand. Appointments like the writer-in-residence job at Sir George Williams College (later Concordia) in 1968 allowed Richler a luxury he had not been able to afford before—the chance, as he wrote to William Weintraub, to "look eighteen months ahead financially." As in demand as he was in London as a journalist and scriptwriter, he still had a hard time nailing down steady, reliable work in the 1960s. He was always on the lookout for some kind of retainer from magazines like *Maclean's*—proposing himself as a regular television reviewer or film critic. In 1988 he would land a monthly column—"Books and Things"—at *GQ*. He would also write a regular column throughout the 1990s for *Saturday Night*, and then, in the late 1990s, a weekly column for the *Gazette*, which would be syndicated in other Southam papers including the *National Post*. He would continue to write that column almost to the end of his life.

Throughout the 1960s there was the hope that the on-again, off-again interest in film options on *The Apprenticeship of Duddy Kravitz*, *The Incomparable Atuk*, and *Cocksure* would finally result in a big score. *Cocksure* enjoyed the most suitors, catching the eye of Norman Jewison and Alan J. Pakula. Even the novelist Joseph Heller expressed interest in turning it into a screenplay. Richler imagined the revised title—*Catch-23*. *Duddy Kravitz* would eventually make it to the screen, though not until the mid-1970s and then with a screenplay by Richler, directed, as predicted some twenty-five years earlier, by Richler's old friend, London roommate, and best man, Ted Kotcheff.

Mordecai & Me

University jobs, in contrast with the mostly unfulfilled promise of movie deals, provided Richler with the stability he needed, as well as the wherewithal to do what he'd already decided he had to do for the sake of his writing—leave London and return to Canada for good. Even so, he was not an enthusiastic teacher. He wasn't even conflicted. On the question of whether writing could be taught, Richler's feelings were definitely unmixed—it couldn't be. In a 1972 speech he delivered at York, called "Playing the Circuit," which was later published in the academic text book, *Creativity and the University*, Richler did what came naturally: he not only bit the hand feeding him (he'd just finished stints at Sir George Williams and Simon Fraser University and was on his way to Carleton for a two-year gig), but spit in the public face accompanying it. The title, "Playing the Circuit," refers to what Richler regarded as the dubious practise of hiring creative writers—himself included—to do their shtick for impressionable students, aspiring poets and fiction writers on university campuses across the country. In the 1960s, he said, "I suddenly found myself *persona grata* at universities as an act, another performer on the touring Canadian writer's circuit. And make no mistake, it is a circuit. A sort of higher cultural literary vaudeville belt."

Richler had a knack, an instinct you could call it, for knowing precisely what his audience didn't want to hear and then providing just that. In "Playing the Circuit" he made some pretence at being polite—remarking that he wasn't anti-academic and that he admired the role the university played in literary life. He also tried, without much success, to sound modest: "I wear the professorial label uneasily, not without certain justifiable embarrassment, for my own career was utterly without distinction. I haven't got a degree, not even a B.A." Along with this admission, Richler also let it be known that the majority of the candidates he interviewed for his writing workshop at Carleton didn't seem to have any interest in reading. He was surprised to learn this, he added, but then it didn't really matter since creative writing was a subject that was, after all, "unteachable."

He also expressed his disdain for academic critics—"who must categorize or die; the over-interpreters and those who deaden with explanation"—publishing their unreadable essays in journals no one reads. (Much later, in *Barney's Version*, Barney labels anyone with a Ph.D.

The New Vaudeville

"beyond the pale.") He criticized tenure—"Tenure by its very nature does allow academic deadwood to pile up"—and also Canadian kids for protesting while, unlike their American counterparts, they had nothing to protest about. No Vietnam War to oppose. No race conflict to speak of. "No-nothing paper-tigers," he calls his students—past, present and future—all style and very little substance. About his tenure at Simon Fraser University in 1969, he said, "I could only be scornful of a generation whose rebellion was not so much an attack on the roots of social injustice as it was fired by irresponsible shit-disturbing." It's an odd condemnation, coming from such a first-rate shit-disturber. But his experience in western Canada, and Simon Fraser University in particular, was bad in that memorable way Richler cherished because it provided him with lots of valuable material. "I have been congratulated for writing *The Sacrifice*, by Adele Wiseman, and rebuked for having committed *Beautiful Losers*," he said at York. "But then out in British Columbia especially, they tend to get their literary Jews mixed up."

When he wasn't attacking tenured professors and deadbeat students, he was letting his fellow creative writing teachers have it. For the most part, he considered them writers *manqué*, fortunate recipients of "a sort of cultural make-work program for the truly unemployable," doing their untalented students a disservice by not being honest with them. "A case of sheltered children sheltering children," he said.

Richler's own inclination was to be not so much the writer-in-residence as the killjoy-in-residence. As his son Daniel has said, his father always believed creative writing departments had it backwards: they shouldn't be encouraging new writers; they should be discouraging them. It was a principle he tried to uphold as a teacher, too: "If the student is untalented the most merciful thing is to tell him as much and save him time and anguish." Even so, he may have been tougher in theory than in practise. John Aylen, who runs a public relations firm in Montreal, was in Richler's creative writing workshop at Carleton in 1972, and has fond memories of the class and its reluctant instructor. "It's true, he didn't believe in teaching writing. He didn't believe it could be taught. He told us that up front. But I still think he may have believed that perhaps some talent might be there by accident.

Mordecai & Me

"It was clear to all of us that he didn't think that anything we had done was terribly good. But he wasn't unkind. He would try to find things that might be good amidst the chaff. He particularly liked anything that had an edge or was funny or sardonic or cynical. Which makes a great deal of sense, given his own work."

Several years ago I was hired to teach a writing workshop—creative nonfiction—at Concordia University, Richler's point of return to Canada in 1968. My feelings were not mixed: I jumped at the chance. Our son had just been born and my wife had left her job indefinitely and, more than ever, I felt the pressure of having to ignore my old freelancer's motto: low overhead. The job offer came only a few days before the course was set to begin, and the person who hired me had just enough time, during our brief meeting, to give me two essential pieces of advice about my new position. First, students are especially litigious these days, so no fraternizing, by which I took him to mean no flirting. Second, no one gets lower than a B- unless they really screw up, by which I took him to mean unless they try to run you over with their car.

I nodded, though I initially thought that I had misheard him. In retrospect, I don't know why. I shouldn't have had any illusions about what I was getting myself into. I had friends who had taught similar courses, and most of them had complained about how awful the experience was. I also had a friend who had been teaching at Concordia's creative writing department for years and who routinely told me stories about classes where workshop discussions invariably centred around whether it was necessary for a story to make sense. Not surprisingly, the majority of the students, all better than B-, voted no.

In the essay "Raymond Carver, Mentor," novelist Jay McInerney recounts how Carver, his former writing teacher, got stuck giving a literature course called Form and Theory of the Short Story. The title was not his choice and so he ignored it. Instead, he assigned stories he liked by Chekhov and Cheever and Flannery O'Connor, and then he discussed them in class. Everything was going fine until one student, a Ph.D. candidate, protested: "This class is called Form and Theory of the Short Story but all we do is sit around and talk about the books. Where's the form and the theory?" Carver took a moment to reply, then said, "I guess I'd say that the point here is that we read good books and discuss them.... And then you *form* your own *theory*."

Like Richler I had "moral qualms" about teaching writing; unlike Richler I wasn't in a position to say so at the same time that I was hired. I didn't have the *chutzpah* for that. Besides, if I were going to be a hypocrite, I preferred to keep it quiet. I decided I wasn't going to tell people they didn't have what it took to be a writer, either. Of course, based on the grading system, I wouldn't have to. Still, the whole thing felt like, well, a scam. So why was I so keen on selling out—and for so little?

"Because you think you have to, because you have a family to support now, because you have, yes, I know, overhead," my wife said when I came home from accepting the job and grumbled about the mistake I was sure I had just made. "Well, you're wrong, you know," she went on. "We're not that desperate. I'd rather have you happy without this job than miserable with it."

Come to think of it, she said the same thing when I started working on this book. There are, you quickly realize, definite disadvantages to being married to a woman smarter than you.

Chapter 14
Did I Wake You? #2

Be the first one to act loving or reach out.
—Don't Sweat the Small Stuff

Just when I think my unconscious has packed it in, I have another dream about Mordecai Richler. This one's a doozy. My dream analyst advised me to write down my dreams as soon as I have them, so I fumble around for a pen on my night table. For a while I made a point of leaving a pen and pad next to my bed, but it's been months since I dreamt about Richler, and I got out of the habit. Now I need a pen and paper.

"What is it?" my wife asks, her words fuzzy, her palm cupped over her eyes.

"Sorry, did I wake you?"

"Before or after you turned on the light?"

"I was looking for a pen."

"Never mind. It's all right. So what is it? Another dream?" my wife asks, propping herself up on one elbow.

"Yes."

"About *him*?"

"Sort of."

"I think I see a pattern developing," she says.

"You would. Is the light bothering you?"

"I think it's too late to ask me that question, don't you?"

"You should get some sleep."

She flashes her long-suffering smile—I like to think of it as her writer's wife's smile, more of a wince really—and then she pulls her pillow over her head. A joke, I'm guessing. Meanwhile, I scribble the dream down on one of the blank pages at the back of *Don't Sweat the Small Stuff*. There is, it turns out, a lot of helpful white space in that little self-help book. Then I switch off my lamp and let my wife go back to sleep. I decide not to bother her with my dream. I won't be calling my dream analyst, either, not at $120 a pop. Besides, I am pretty sure I can decipher this one myself.

I've heard it said that what every writer needs—his or her gender notwithstanding—is a wife. When we got married my wife was pushing forty; I was forty-three. Considering our respective ages, it was a whirlwind romance precipitated by an unexpected and not so much unwanted as unimaginable pregnancy. We'd only known each other three months when she called to tell me she was late.

"Late for what?" I said.

"Late, late."

"Oh, right."

Two positive home-pregnancy tests and a trip to the doctor later, we were engaged. Neither of us had been married before or even come close. We'd both had our hearts broken a number of times, and I'm not sure either of us, at that point, thought that marriage, let alone parenthood, was in the cards. I can speak for myself at least: I didn't. Any way you look at it, we were not off to an auspicious start. Even the easygoing rabbi from the Reform Temple, who met with us before our wedding, had doubts. If we'd been younger, he said, he might be advising us differently. As it was, he could only assume we knew what we were doing. Which is, when you

Mordecai & Me

think about it, a big assumption for a religious man to make. How could we know what we were doing? However, we are—and this never ceases to amaze me—happy.

Still, I can't help feeling my wife liked the idea of being married to a writer more in theory than she does in practise. She certainly liked it more before *Mordecai & Me*, before I started waking her up in the middle of the night on what has become a more or less regular basis. The dreams are one thing, but lately I've also been talking far too much and far too glowingly about another woman—Florence Richler. As literary wives go, she's on a par with the best, with the likes of Nora Joyce and Véra Nabokov. All three were married to difficult husbands, demanding men in one way or another. All three were more than wives; they were partners: long-suffering, silent ones. In *Broadsides*, his 1990 nonfiction collection, Richler provides a light-hearted, but not especially exaggerated glimpse into his wife's life:

> Strangers married to dentists or real estate developers say to my wife, "Oh, your husband's a writer. You must lead such an interesting life."
>
> Florence, bless her, is loyal. She doesn't break up laughing, neither does she punch anybody out. Instead, she smiles graciously and says, "Oh, yes, yes of course."

"The more you leave me out, Mr. Boyd, the closer to the truth you will be," Véra Nabokov told Brian Boyd, one of her husband's biographers. But later she added, "I am always there, but well hidden." In *Véra*, Stacy Schiff's biography of Véra Nabokov, Schiff adds that Véra's role may not have been visible, but it was vast. She doubled as her husband's navigator, chauffeur, typist, translator, proofreader, copy editor, agent, secretary, substitute teacher, and reader. She was the ideal audience: "On the one hand, she was difficult to please, on the other, her husband could do no wrong." More than once, she saved *Lolita*, in manuscript, from being incinerated or deliberately lost, insisting that it be held onto even when everyone, Vladimir Nabokov included, had decided the book would ruin him, one way or the other. She had a talent, essential for a writer's wife. She kept, Schiff says, "grim common sense from the door, shooting it dead when it approached."

Did I Wake You? #2

So did Florence Richler. She also kept the five Richler kids quiet while they were growing up—ensuring they whisper, not wear shoes in the house and even then walk on tiptoes while their father worked in an upstairs office. She was her husband's first editor and his most trusted one, the only person Richler was willing to listen to in the early stages of a book. He recognized the spot he was putting her in, but that didn't prevent him from doing it:

> Actually, being married to a writer must be hell. I count on Florence's judgment. . . . If she doesn't like something I've done, I won't submit it anywhere, but neither will I take her out to dinner. . . . And if she does approve of what I've done, I'm inclined to doubt her honesty. What if it's just compassion for an aging, often disagreeable novelist?

In an interview Florence Richler gave to *Maclean's* on the first anniversary of her husband's death, she described the mixed blessing of being Mordecai Richler's "editor-in-residence," as he called her:

> He always showed me the first draft. There was only one very serious difference of opinion as a result. I did make some various criticisms about one of the books, and it did mean that it would result in withdrawing one very significant chunk of what he had written and rewriting it. He visibly got upset. And he was going off to New York. It was the only time in all our years together that I did not get a passionate kiss and hug goodbye. . . . And I was deeply upset, I must admit.

As it turned out, Richler's New York editor Robert Gottlieb agreed with Florence's opinion and called to tell her so later the same evening. "So I was, as you can imagine, over the moon," she recalled. Even the willful and imperious Vladimir Nabokov granted his wife veto powers. In *Véra,* Stacy Schiff writes that "when Vladimir announced to colleagues that he was going to write a novel about the love life of a pair of Siamese twins, Véra put her foot down and said, 'No, you're not!'"

My wife has learned that all I want from her on those rare occasions I show her something before it is sent off is unqualified approval. Anything less and she knows I will be insufferable. A woman of many informed opinions, she is learning to keep them to herself as far as my work is concerned. It's the first part of the deal hammered out between us—a kind of postnuptial agreement. The second part is that she gets to see anything I write about her before it's published. She also gets to veto anything about her she objects to. She doesn't need a reason, either. Fortunately, she's not in my most recent dream.

In this dream, my late father and I are alone in a nondescript house, not the one I grew up in with my parents and not the one I live in now with my wife and son. The place is like a maze, and we are communicating by shouting at each other through the walls. There is a growing sense of desperation in what we are saying, but I don't know why until I realize we are under a kind of siege from a group of men outside. They are breaking windows and shouting at my father, though I can't exactly make out what they are angry about. Meanwhile, I'm trying to tell my father that we are in danger, but he can't hear me. He keeps shouting back, "What? What do you want from my life?"

The next thing I know two men are inside the house, and they are looking for Mordecai Richler. They know he's here, and they want to confront him about some insult or other. One of the men is distinctly francophone—you can tell by his accent; the other is distinctly Jewish—his accent gives him away, too, but he is also dressed like a Hassid, in a black hat and a long black coat. He has sidelocks and a beard. I'm startled for a moment when I realize it's Richler they have come for, but then I realize that's who I have been talking to all along. Mordecai Richler, not my father.

As they try to push past me into the house, I pick up the phone to call 911, but dial 411 instead. The operator says, "I think you want Emergency. This is Information. Are you sure it's Information you want?"

"Yes," I say, "that's exactly what I want."

"Are you sleeping?" I say, turning on the light again and huddling close to my wife.

"Not anymore." She wakes more easily this time, almost as if she expected I wasn't done yet. A wifely instinct.

Did I Wake You? #2

"I have a question. You're a professional. Do you think dreams could be like jokes and end with a punchline? Is that believable? Would you believe it?"

"I think dreams are our unconscious telling us to pay attention. We ignore them at our peril."

"Do you think that? Or do you know it for a fact?"

"What's the difference? Sweetheart, it makes perfect sense that *your* unconscious would tell you a joke. A joke is something you'd remember."

"Right. So you'd believe it? If you read it, I mean. You'd believe that I—"

"I have to believe in you. It's part of my job description. Writer's Wife. Now turn off the light, please, and rub my back. We need to go to sleep."

"I have to pee first."

"I'm making a doctor's appointment for you tomorrow morning."

"You are not."

"Have you noticed something? You always get the last word."

"It's my book."

Chapter 15
Prince Charmingbaum

*You know, sometimes it may be a mistake to meet the writer.
I'm quite serious.*
—Mordecai Richler

"When a woman comes into the room, or the cave or teepee, the possibilities of law, mercy, wit, and affection arise. One's stutter melts, one's blood takes on a champagne simmer and sets the brain to scintillating," John Updike writes in an essay about women, allowing in the next line that his comments could be classified, by some, as "male-chauvinist romanticism."

Like Updike, Mordecai Richler would be criticized for misunderstanding his female characters. In fact, long before there were irrelevant academic arguments over appropriation of voice, Richler was doubtful about his ability to portray women convincingly in his fiction. In a letter to Brian Moore in 1959, he said as much and hoped to remedy the problem, though he also added that he feared it was "a congenital weakness."

Prince Charmingbaum

He could never have written *The Lonely Passion of Judith Hearne*, he told Moore, "or *Jessie Hershhorn*, if you like." More than a decade later, in an interview with Graeme Gibson, Richler repeated his concern, saying that "the women in my novels tend to be rather idealized creatures, and not written about with the greatest confidence, I'm afraid."

It wasn't until after *Barney's Version* came out that he began to feel differently. "I think I'm finally pleased with the female characters in this novel," he said when I interviewed him in the fall of 1997. "I'm sure being married to the same woman for almost forty years has helped."

There was a kind of reverse taming-of-the-shrew—*Taming of the Jew?*—that happened when Mordecai met Florence. In *Barney's Version*, The Second Mrs. Panofsky—which is what she's called throughout the novel—refers sarcastically to Barney as "Prince Charmingbaum." Richler wasn't exactly a knight in shining armour himself, certainly not at first glance. In her interview with *Maclean's* after Richler's death, Florence Richler described the young man she first met as hypersensitive, awkward, and raw. He was "almost like someone unfinished," she recalled. Florence, marriage, and fatherhood became his finishing school. She also believed that one of the reasons that their marriage worked so well was because her husband never really expected a happy family life, and when he found he'd landed in one after all, he had no choice but to be grateful.

He also had no choice but to worry. This anxiety is at the heart of *St. Urbain's Horseman*, the first in the series of four big ambitious novels he wrote in the last thirty years of his life. The marriage of Jake and Nancy Hersh is at risk in *St. Urbain's Horseman*, and it's because it is such an impossibly happy marriage that the stakes are so high, especially for Jake. Early in the novel, Jake warns his interfering mother—hardly overjoyed that her son has married a *shiksa*—not to say a word against Nancy. "I love her," he says. "And so long as she loves me, I cannot be entirely bad." Still, when he is falsely accused of rape, labelled a pervert, and put on trial in the Old Bailey in London, his problems almost come as a relief. He can finally stop waiting for the other shoe to drop on his wonderful life:

> From the beginning he had expected the outer, brutalized world to intrude on their little one, inflated with love, but ultimately

self-serving and cocooned by money. The times were depraved. Tenderness in one house, he had come to fear, was no more possible, without corruption, than socialism in a single country. And so, from the earliest, halcyon days with Nancy, he had expected the coming of the vandals.

In *Barney's Version,* Barney Panofsky expresses a similar sentiment about his third marriage:

Miriam was my winning lottery ticket. My redeemer. My MVP award. Imagine, if you can, the Boston Red Sox actually winning a World Series, or Danielle Steel taking the Nobel Prize, and you'll have some idea of how I felt when Miriam agreed, against all odds, to marry me. But my epiphany was tainted by fear. Surely the gods on Olympus had taken down my number for remedial action.

In Richler's own life, though, the threat remained at bay. Still, gratitude, like optimism, did not come easily or naturally to him, although it's easy to spot traces of both in his work, starting with *St. Urbain's Horseman.* In *St. Urbain's Horseman* and *Joshua Then and Now* in particular, he would be hard-pressed to come up with his usual unhappy ending. Every novel prior to *St. Urbain's Horseman* ends either in gloom or tragedy or farce or some combination of all three. André Bennett is murdered; Atuk and Mortimer Griffin executed; Noah Adler is irrevocably alone; so is Norman Price in *A Choice of Enemies,* and Duddy Kravitz. On the contrary, *St. Urbain's Horseman* ends with Jake holding onto his wife for all he's worth. The novel's epigraph, taken from a poem by W.H. Auden, holds out the possibility of "an affirming flame" in the face of a world of "negation and despair." And so, grudgingly, does the novel. Richler also grudgingly admitted, on more than one occasion, that *St. Urbain's Horseman* was his "most autobiographical novel." He told me this, too, when I interviewed him after *Barney's Version* came out, and he did it then mostly to deflect my questions about how much he was like Barney. I was being deliberately simplistic—a first person narrator; it must be you, I all but said. He was being deliberately evasive. "I am not an autobiographical writer," he insisted.

Prince Charmingbaum

By the early 1970s, Richler was also pushing forty, and he couldn't pull off the angry young man pose anymore. He never was much of a rebel anyway, and now he didn't even have to pretend to be one. He was, despite himself, undeniably bourgeois. He had become part of the middle-class he "excoriated with such appetite," as he said in his essay "A Sense of the Ridiculous." If the first twenty years of his life provided him with all the gloom and pessimism he needed to launch his career, the next twenty years provided him with a glimpse of the security and the self-confidence he would need to sustain it.

Published in 1968, *Cocksure* would remain his most corrosive book. Which doesn't mean Richler mellowed after *Cocksure*, but he was forced to face the facts that while the world may have still been the bleak, hopeless place he had always believed it to be, his own world wasn't bad at all. Of course, being happy, especially for a writer as innately grouchy as Richler, would require adjustments. It would mean reconciling his misanthropic impulses with his downright sunny personal circumstances. It would mean getting accustomed to the fact that he was doing precisely what he had always wanted to do and that he had just about everything he could ask for. What's more, it was a situation that would last for a good long time. In 1980, after *Joshua Then and Now* was published, Richler was asked where he hoped to be in ten years time. He accurately predicted his future. "Writing another novel," he said, "and with my wife."

Even the past was starting to look better to him. *The Street*, his collection of short stories and autobiographical sketches, was published in 1969, a year after *Cocksure* and a couple of years before *St. Urbain's Horseman*. It is still full of Richler's trademark mockery, but cracks are beginning to show in the armour of sarcasm and contempt. *The Street* is, as Richler himself described it, "a mixed bag." Even its publishers (different ones for different editions) weren't quite clear what to call the book. It was variously referred to as a story collection, a collection of memoirs, even a novel, which it most certainly isn't. In an introduction Richler wrote for the 1985 Penguin edition of the book, he expressed his regret at not sticking with writing short stories. "I still consider myself something of a failed short story writer," he admitted. But he was being too hard on himself. In fact, *The Street* contains some of Richler's best short stories—"Bambinger," "Some Grist for Mervyn's Mill," and "The Summer My Grandmother Was Supposed to Die."

The Street, mainly comprised of pieces Richler wrote during the ten years he was away from Canada, is also marked by an uncharacteristic tenderness. The strong, undisguised autobiographical strain that runs through the collection reveals itself as nostalgia for a world Richler was convinced was about to disappear. "To come home in 1968," he writes in the foreword to *The Street,* "was to discover that it wasn't where I had left it—it had been bulldozed away." Mordecai Richler left Canada, a shy and angry young man, because he had the notion that being a writer and being Canadian were incompatible. There was, after all, little evidence around to contradict that belief and much to reinforce it: the success of Lionel Shapiro, for instance, or his experience with *Maclean's,* or the comment made by the Canadian distributor of his first novel who suggested he write fat books because they sell better here than thin ones. When he returned he was no longer quite so shy or angry. He was no longer an alienated outsider either. In fact, he was starting to reluctantly entertain the possibility that he might even be getting more comfortable with his life and with himself. "I don't pretend for a moment that I'm not pleased by the amount of recognition I'm getting," he told Donald Cameron, "and I guess it affects you to the extent that you're a more pleasant man, or your life is easier to bear if you've had a certain amount of recognition for your work." Richler was secure enough in his professional and personal life to come home. And even to admit to missing Canada, as he says in his essay collection *Home Sweet Home:*

> A longing, striking me at 3:00 A.M., to see big Jean Beliveau carry the puck all the way down the Montreal Forum ice one more time. Or the need, overtaking me with equal suddenness, for a smoked-meat sandwich from Schwartz's incomparable delicatessen on the Main.

If his intention initially had been to put "picayune Canada and all it stood for" behind him, he had begun to realize that "that was foolishness. . . . It was arrogant and pompous." He had also claimed that he had left

Prince Charmingbaum

Canada with no regrets, but that was impossible and he would admit as much later: "I would carry my cherished Canada with me everywhere." And he would go right on cherishing it in his own perverse way. Here's Barney in *Barney's Version* coming very close to expressing his author's feelings about his country:

> The truth is Canada is a cloud-cuckoo-land, an insufferably rich country governed by idiots, its self-made problems offering comic relief to the ills of the real world out there, where famine and racial strife and vandals in office are the unhappy rule.

It wasn't just nostalgia that drew Mordecai Richler home; it was also obligation, the realization that he had strayed too far from the source of his material for too long. His concern was that the territory he had claimed for himself would somehow begin to elude him. As early as 1960, in a letter to his Canadian publisher and friend, Jack McClelland, Richler described his dilemma. He was, he said, seriously thinking about returning to Canada to stay. There was just one big problem:

> How would I earn a living? I've got three kids. Ultimately, I fear my serious work will suffer if I stay abroad longer than ten years (eight already used up) but the truth is I can earn my nut—a good one—with three months' lazy work here. In Canada, where would my money come from? TV quiz shows? Not this boy.

But by the late 1960s the problem was starting to resolve itself. Richler was in demand at home—on university campuses and, yes, even TV panel shows. (He contemplated working as an interviewer for the CBC program *This Hour Has Seven Days.*) In addition, *Cocksure* was, despite mixed reviews in this country, selling well and it won him his first Governor General's Award in 1968. (He received the award that year for his novel and his essay collection, *Hunting Tigers under Glass,* an anomaly in the prize-giving procedure.)

Richler always expressed a special fondness for *Cocksure,* an attachment out of proportion with the novel's actual achievement. *Cocksure* is hit-and-miss funny and, if you read it now, feels trapped in its time, like a mildly off-colour joke. Whatever outrage or controversy Richler's self-described "dirty novel" attracted, its real importance in Richler's career was as a stop-gap measure, a reprieve. It was the novel he could write instead of the one he wanted to write and couldn't. That was *St. Urbain's Horseman*.

"I've been resisting writing novels all my life," Richler told a *New York Times* interviewer in 1980, after *Joshua Then and Now* was published. "I mean, hell, you go up into that room with your typewriter and when you come out again you're three years older." But Richler wasn't being exactly candid here. His resistance to the task of writing novels only started in earnest with *St. Urbain's Horseman*. After writing his first four novels in just five years, his last four would take almost thirty. He'd go for months writing a page or two and then rewriting and rewriting that page. He was stuck, good and stuck.

Writer's block was for dilettantes and tragic cases—like Henry Roth, who went sixty years between his first novel, the classic immigrant story, *Call It Sleep*, and his second, the disappointingly obtuse *Mercy of a Rude Stream*. Or Ralph Ellison, who never did live to see a follow-up published to his 1952 classic *Invisible Man*. That kind of procrastination for the sake of art was not the kind of luxury a freelancer like Richler could afford. Nor was it the kind of obstacle he had ever run up against before. Writing *St. Urbain's Horseman* was so unusually difficult, in fact, he was prepared, even eager to give it up. Any excuse would have sufficed. In his 1971 interview with Donald Cameron, Richler admitted as much, adding that if either his New York or London editors, Robert Gottlieb or Tony Goodwin respectively, had told him he was wasting his time he would have quit gratefully, happily.

A break to work on something else turned out to be what he needed, and *Cocksure*, naughty and mischievous and way over the top, provided that break. "Riding into my second year of *St. Urbain's Horseman*, disheartened by proliferating school bills, diminished savings, and only fitful progress, I finally got stuck so badly that there was nothing for it but to shove the manuscript aside," Richler would confess about his troubles at the time. "I started another novel, a year's heat, which yielded *Cocksure*."

Prince Charmingbaum

But if *Cocksure* solved Richler's writer's block, the relative ease and speed with which he finished it also underlined why he had wanted to write a novel like *St. Urbain's Horseman* in the first place. *Cocksure* was a kind of fable, as John Metcalf commented to Richler during a 1974 interview, and, as such, lacked the sureness or solidity of *Duddy Kravitz* or *The Street*, Richler's Montreal books. Richler was inclined to agree. An interesting, incongruous side of Richler comes out in interviews. There is the guardedness and the glib, recycled answers, particularly pertaining to personal matters, but there is also a surprising candour about his literary limitations—whether he's admitting he can't get women right on the page or making dismissive jokes about keeping his early work out of print.

Metcalf interviewed Richler not long after he returned to Canada, and he remembers Richler saying he felt that the thing forcing his writing in the direction of broad satire in *Atuk* and *Cocksure* and away from the realism of *Duddy Kravitz* was the fear that "he really hadn't been able to grip England from a realistic point of view. He felt that as an exile he was losing Montreal." Richler also told Metcalf that he'd come back to Montreal "in search of some kind of renewal . . . some sense of continuity." Or maybe Richler just needed to find something on which to lay the blame for the almost decade-long difficulties he was having with *St. Urbain's Horseman*. Living in London, he often quoted another curmudgeonly expatriate around town, V.S. Naipaul, who claimed the reason he wasn't writing novels set in England was that he had no idea what an Englishman did when he went home at night. That quote, Richler said, hit him hard. He had no idea either. The only thing that was clear, at least in Richler's mind, was that this time he was back for good. You couldn't call him a prodigal son anymore and maybe you never could. An Old Testament kind of guy, Richler was hardly the perfect fit for a New Testament story of forgiveness. After all, when he finally did return home, he didn't exactly make it easy for anyone to welcome him back with open arms, even on the unlikely chance they felt inclined to.

He left Canada a know-nothing kid; he came back a seasoned cynic. As such, he could hardly have been expected not to notice that his "cherished Canada" still had some catching up to do. Or that it could still be as parochial a place as it was when he had left two decades earlier. In the literary world, the difference only looked like a large one: neglect of Canadian writers had been replaced by overestimation. Richler didn't waste any time calling an overrated spade overrated. Speaking at York, he said:

> Canadian literature is still a tender if promising flower. Don't, like the proverbial Jewish mother, smother it with too much affection. The claims that are being made for it are over-large, even embarrassing. Too much attention, I fear, is being paid....

He went on to advise against "belligerent claims" that "could yet make us a literary laughingstock" as well as too much "nationalist hyperbole." He closed the speech with what sounded like a friendly warning, but was, in fact, a prediction. "It's good to be home again," he said, "and firing at closer range."

How little Canadians liked being in Richler's sights was obvious during an appearance he made on the 1971 television program *Under Attack*. Taped at the University of Western Ontario and hosted by Fred Davis, the program consisted of a panel of students and then members of the student audience all mispronouncing Richler's name (as "Rickler") and asking him his favourite kind of questions—really stupid ones. (Anyone who thinks college kids are dumber than ever today should listen to this thirty-year-old tape.) For instance: "Mr. Rickler says he sees nothing wrong with being destructive. Well, what's wrong with being constructive?" Or: "Would you rather be Canadian or American?" Richler's response in this case was, "You may as well ask would I rather be Elizabeth Taylor?" More often than not though, he just said, "I don't understand the question." Which was fair enough because most of the questions were indecipherable.

But Richler couldn't have been that upset. According to his son Jacob, Richler always dreaded the question period of a speech or a reading, but at the same time, he was also a connoisseur of stupid questions. He collected them and used them whenever and wherever he could. In his writing, he also had the chance to refine his replies. But in front of an audience, as on *Under Attack*, he wasn't half-bad either. His dismissive tone helped. When

Prince Charmingbaum

a particularly obtuse young man scoffs at Richler's choice of Jane Austen's novels as an example of literary excellence and then adds that if he had chosen someone Canadian or more contemporary he might have been impressed, Richler replies, "I didn't come here to impress you." That much is clear: he wasn't impressing anyone. What was astonishing about the broadcast was how hostile the students were to Richler. He represented, for them, just another middle-aged sell-out with a concealed inferiority complex, an inappropriate love of the ugly Americans, and, based on the reviews they'd read of *Cocksure*, a penchant for deviant sexual behaviour. (You'd think that, at least, would have made him popular on campus.)

Surprisingly, Richler was unflustered. I've only listened to an audiocassette of the program so I can't see what kind of faces he may have been making or what his body language reveals—plenty, I'm guessing—but he doesn't sound any more uncomfortable than he usually did in public. He corrected one student's misuse of *rationalize* for *reconcile*, but he was generally polite and engaged—more bewildered than angered by the tone of the questions. His patience only gave out at the end when a questioner accused him of being a fair-weather Canadian and said, in effect, that if "Rickler" thinks there is so much wrong with the country, why does he continue to call himself a Canadian? The program faded out with Richler saying, "That's a very stupid and offensive question." True enough, but it was still the question Richler couldn't seem to avoid once he had returned home for good. His situation, he realized, was lose-lose. In the York speech, Richler summed up his predicament:

> For years ... I have been treated as a turncoat, criticized for being an expatriate, luxuriating in London, England, for almost two decades. Then, finally flattered into decision, I came home—me, my wife, and five children—only to be confronted by a new accusation. "Why did you come back, Richler? Things not working out for you in London anymore?"

Returning from London also required some adjusting for Richler, as John Metcalf, an English expatriate, explained to me: "Mordecai was coming from a very bracing literary environment where people did not kiss other people's asses. Where they fought volubly in print, called each other dreadful names and fought for work. Living in London, Richler was in a very grown-up world and he came back here, for Christ's sake. He felt Canada was really just third-rate and pissy and full of self-important little people, and I think he was dead right."

In an interview with Graeme Gibson in 1972, Richler said he was still vacillating about returning and the reason was a fear of becoming "an unusual thing" in Canada. In England, he said

> there's more sense of competition.... I don't feel—I don't know whether it may sound awful or not—that five guys are going to bring out better books than me this year here. It's worrying in New York and it's worrying in London, and I think that's rather good for a writer... you can relax a bit here.

Richler's return meant there was a new kid on the block, a kid who could be, when he was so inclined—and he often was—both a scold and a bully. What he could not be, of course, was ignored, not initially anyway. Suddenly, Canadian writers were forced to measure themselves against someone with talent and an international reputation, not to mention an exceptionally good and ambitious new novel. As Metcalf explained, "What Mordecai presented in terms of a threat is that suddenly in a very small pond had arrived a monster-size frog and people said, 'If he's here and he's written *St. Urbain's Horseman*, what are we going to do?'"

What, indeed?

Chapter 16
The Big Payoff

The more books we read, the sooner we perceive that the true function of a writer is to produce a masterpiece and that no other task is of any consequence.
—Cyril Connolly

A poem is the purest form of literature and the hardest to get right. The challenge is impossible to convey; the painstaking, often preposterous amount of effort that goes into every line is enough to make even the most meticulous prose writer feel like a poseur. Which may explain why poets are so strange, and why, to put it plainly, they are not like you and me. I speak from experience. I was accosted on the street once by a local husband-and-wife team of poets whom I'd poked fun at. He'd written a letter to the editor of a Montreal weekly newspaper complaining about not being nominated for a local award, and in the letter he not only praised his wife (who was also *not* nominated), he praised himself. To make matters worse, he did so in the third person. He blurbed himself, in effect, having arrived at the reasonable conclusion, I guess, that no one else was going to. Then he signed the letter. I referred to this self-blurbing in a column, adding a quote from the critic Max Eastman, who said, "A poet in history is divine; a poet in the other room is a joke." When I greeted the two outside a bookstore a few weeks later, they both let me have it, calling me among other things, a traitor to the local literary community and "a little prick."

David Solway is another local poet whose wrong side I ended up on. A dauntingly erudite and polysyllabic man, Solway has no sense of humour when it comes to himself—an unfortunate failing for a poet in this country. A couple of years ago, he played a hoax on the poetry world by pretending to be the translator of a brilliant but unknown fisherman-slash-poet from the island of Crete. Obviously, the Greek genius, named Andreas Karavis, was a figment of Solway's lively—you might even say feverish—literary imagination. My job was to expose the hoax in my newspaper column. Solway knew this and cooperated fully. But he also called me back four times, wondering out loud whether he should deny his nondenial. He suggested I might write the story in such a way as to leave room for doubt about his imaginary friend's existence. I listened politely and then wrote the article the way I wanted, making sure to mention how many times he called me back. A few days after my column ran, I received a two-page, single-spaced letter in which Solway called me a number of polysyllabic names. No one and nothing could have hurt him more, he said. He questioned, among other things, my "moral grist." My sin was all the worse, he added, because I pretended to be one of "the good guys." Most of the names he called me I had to look up in the dictionary—and not always successfully—but I am proud to say I more or less knew what he meant when he referred to me as an "Ionescan rhinoceros." Let's just say it's not good.

I have the letter. It may be worth something some day, assuming Solway ever becomes as famous as he thinks he deserves to be. I also spent three days drafting three different responses—one conciliatory, one explanatory, and one in which I called him a big fat jerk and concluded with a comment on his rather high opinion of himself. "And how are things up on Mt. Olympus?" I asked. That version of the letter came easiest and read best. Before I sent it, though, I read it to my wife who just shook her head.

The Big Payoff

"Ask yourself," she said, "what would bother him more? You playing his silly game or a dignified silence?" As usual, she was right and while I put my angry reply in an envelope and even stamped it, I never sent it.

To come completely clean, I also used to be in love with a poet, so I know something about the toll their work takes on them. I would watch her stapling together drafts, dating them, wrestling over a word, a line break, as if her life depended on it. She would take these drafts to her weekly workshops and come back with notes for more drafts. Her colleagues would focus on a word or a punctuation mark, and she'd worry over their suggestions for days, weeks, then change it, only to change it back. A "the" or an "and" crossed out only to be reinstated a week later: more pages to date and staple together.

After we broke up, I wrote a book of essays, a novel, and the better part of a second novel largely about our relationship and still never could get it quite right, never could come close to conveying what happened between us and why. She wrote one poem about our relationship and scooped me—everything I had wanted to say, had spent so much time and so many pages trying unsuccessfully to say, and there it was, present and accounted for in ten lines.

Short stories run second, though a distant second, to poetry for precision and honesty. Every line in a short story has to sing, though, in my experience as a reviewer, they seldom do so on key. Every line has to the do the work of a whole chapter in a novel. Short story writers aren't as weird as poets, but they are fuss-budgets, too. Sticklers. Perfectionists. Compared to novelists, that is, who are a sloppy bunch, which works out well since the novel is, by definition, a sloppy form. A novel, Randall Jarrell said, is "a prose work of a certain length that has something wrong with it."

Mordecai Richler's early ambition had been to write short stories, which would then appear in *The New Yorker* like those of Mavis Gallant, a friend from his early days in Paris. But he was in too big a hurry and too anxious for success. Besides, his stories, he said, always felt like novel chapters—overstuffed. In the introduction to the 1985 edition of *The Street*, which is as close as he came to a story collection, Richler explains, "I made my first attempt at a novel, shrewdly calculating that it would not be necessary for me to shine in every paragraph: instead, I might be pardoned pages of dross for the nuggets to be found here and there." In other words, he wanted to make sure he had a margin for error. A novel provides that.

As readers, we get from novels—especially big, ambitious ones—what we want from our lives: enough order to make the whole mess tolerable. This doesn't mean the mess disappears or that it's polished out of existence, the way it might be in a poem or short story, but that it recedes for a time. It is held at bay. Or, on the contrary, it rushes over us. "It would be mad to edit a novel like *Little Dorrit*," according to Saul Bellow, who knows what he's talking about, being responsible for a few doorstoppers himself. "That sea of words is a sea, a force of nature. We want it that way, ample, capable of breeding life. . . . We wouldn't want it any other way."

Reading a good, long novel is not just quantitatively different than reading a good short story or a good poem or even a good short novel; it's qualitatively different. Its pleasures are specific. On the one hand, you are tempted to put the book aside, to stall, to make it last; on the other hand, you can't stop reading. A long novel transports you. It is not about escaping as much as it is about stepping into another world, with its own complications and heartbreaks. We also tend to forgive a long novel its flaws more readily, the way we would forgive them in a valued but erratic friend. "What made me fall in love with literature in the first place was fat novels and five-act plays," says Phillip Lopate. "I loved the repetitions of themes, the rise and fall, even the doldrums, the calms, the tedium itself, and the big payoff, which could only occur when the writer had built up a meticulous architectural structure to house it . . . my own love was for the grand arch, the passage of time, the slow transformation of characters."

St. Urbain's Horseman, circa 1972, was my introduction to the experience Lopate is talking about and to all that I would come to love best about literature in general and big fat novels in particular. Unfortunately, as introductions go, Richler's highly anticipated new novel failed me miserably. Or, more likely, I failed it.

The Big Payoff

I still have the paperback copy of *St. Urbain's Horseman* I bought thirty years ago for $1.50. I was seventeen at the time, and it was the first real grown-up novel I would own. Not a hand-me-down from my parents or sisters, not a recommendation from a high school teacher. I chose it myself—having just finished *The Apprenticeship of Duddy Kravitz* in high school—and I liked the feeling.

I cared less for the feeling of being in over my head. *St. Urbain's Horseman* is not a novel for a teenager, especially a teenager as clued out as I was. (*Duddy Kravitz*, on the other hand, may be a novel only for teenagers.) *St. Urbain's Horseman* is the existential novel—comic in its tone, tragic in its vision—that Richler had tried and failed to write early in his career. It's also as close as Richler comes to writing directly about the Holocaust. The straightforward anger of essays like "The Holocaust and After"—which begins with the line, "The Germans are still an abomination to me"—and the outlandish black humour of *Cocksure*, are, by comparison, evasive actions. *St. Urbain's Horseman* addresses the subject as directly as Richler ever would. There are documentary-style scenes featuring Dr. Mengele, and there is a current of revenge and justice—or a sense of the impossibility of both—running through the novel in the person of the mainly absent Joey Hersh, Jake's cousin, and the Horseman of the title. Jake Hersh may have been the protagonist Richler had the most in common with—he acknowledged as much—and, in Jake's obsession with the Holocaust, its horror and its aftermath, there is more than a glimpse of Richler's obsession, too.

In the essay "The Holocaust and After," Richler is appalled by the way the murder of six million Jews is trivialized in everyday life. That means a rabbi invoking the Holocaust as a sales pitch in a fund-raising drive for a new banquet hall or the novelist James Baldwin saying of the black militant Angela Davis that she looked, headed for trial, "as alone . . . as the Jewish housewife in the boxcar heading for Dachau." To Richler, the analogy is "hysterical, infuriating, and wildly inexact." He points out:

> Jewish housewives bound for Dachau, far from being alone, were crushed together in their hundreds into each airless boxcar, there to stand with their children, going for days without water,

enduring their own excreta. There were no press photographers or militants at the station to cheer them off. Or *Newsweek* cover stories . . . as in the case of Miss Angela Davis, for the understandable reason that Jewish housewives for burning were commonplace. They were not known by name, only by number.

In *St. Urbain's Horseman,* Jake Hersh daydreams about an avenger. Here, Richler fills the role himself.

Another obvious autobiographical aspect of *St. Urbain's Horseman* is that it is a book about a character enduring a midlife crisis written by a writer, at midlife, in the middle of his own career crisis. Until Richler got caught up in the frustrating stop-and-start trajectory of *St. Urbain's Horseman*—nearly a decade from conception to completion—he was inclined to write what came easiest and most naturally to him. *St. Urbain's Horseman* required a lot more effort from its author and engendered a lot more self-doubt. "I find (writing) increasingly difficult," he told Graeme Gibson not long after he finished *St. Urbain's Horseman.* "I'm more critical of my work and it displeases me more often. Now, I think most good writers, and I think of myself as a good writer, are fundamentally in competition with themselves. . . . And I'm harder and harder on my own work. It is no longer a pleasure just to be published."

With *St. Urbain's Horseman,* Richler raised the stakes for himself; he was feeling the pressure as was his protagonist, Jake Hersh. "I would never write about someone who is not at the end of his rope," Stanley Elkin said, and Richler's hero is hanging onto his world—his wife and children and his promising career as a film director—by a thread. Jake has been implicated in a sex scandal by Harry Stein, a pornographer and part-time procurer of aspiring starlets. Harry is the kind of man Jake knows he should not consort with, but, like Richler, Jake has a weakness for scoundrels. He's also a sucker for their ridiculous schemes. "What is it with me?" Jake asks his wife after getting off the phone with Harry. "Wherever I put my foot down, it's quicksand." Thanks to Harry, Jake is literally on trial, making a daily appearance at the Old Bailey, in a plot turn that is an improbable mix of Kafka and John Mortimer. His reputation already ruined, Jake's freedom is now on the line, as is his marriage,

The Big Payoff

which is, up to this point, the one saving grace in his life, "the one extraordinary circumstance." Like Barney Panofsky obsessed with Miriam Greenberg, his third wife and one true love, in *Barney's Version;* or Joshua Shapiro, trying to save his fragile wife, Pauline, in *Joshua Then and Now;* like Richler, himself, and Florence—the common element in all these relationships is the way Prince Charmingbaum wins the woman he is certain he is meant to be with after all. Through effort and perseverance, he sweeps her off her initially reluctant feet. Once swept, of course, Richler's women, with the exception of Miriam in *Barney's Version,* stay that way, transformed into Tammy Wynette "stand-by-your-man" types. Still, in *St. Urbain's Horseman,* we at least get to see Jake's Nancy reflect on the consequences of having allowed her heart to rule her head:

> Once having married, letting herself go, such was Nancy's bliss ... that she could not understand why she had hesitated. But she soon grasped that her husband was not all of a piece, as she had hoped. On the contrary, Jake was charged with contradictions. Ostensibly consumed by overweening ambition, he was, on black days, filled with self-hatred and debilitating doubts. . . . [She] feared, in agonizingly lucid moments, that if he did not rise as far as he hoped, he might yet diminish into bitterness.

But what Jake doesn't have and covets are not his problem; it's all that he has and fears losing—to disease or death, to his own foolishness or restlessness. In *St. Urbain's Horseman* and the three big, ambitious novels that would follow it, Richler grew up and so did his fiction. The later novels would be structured differently—built on flashbacks and the interplay of an idealized past and a hardhearted present. Richler's early novels, culminating with *The Apprenticeship of Duddy Kravitz,* seldom look back. They are mainly forward momentum.

The later novels, starting with *St. Urbain's Horseman,* circle whatever point their author is making, whatever meaning he is after. Richler's disgust with the world didn't lessen, but it became more measured. If he still believed, as he had as a precocious young man, that everything was for shit, he also began to acknowledge mitigating forces at work. There were other possibilities to consider: love and family and work. The existence of these things also serves to make the world a scarier place because suddenly he has so much more to lose. *St. Urbain's Horseman* is, in short, everything a big, ambitious novel should be; it is Richler's hard won masterpiece, and at seventeen, it bored me silly. Even so, I kept reading. Why? I had made an investment in the book and in literature, and I wasn't ready to forfeit it. I was young and I was prepared to make the effort to read it. I also kept a kind of record of the effort.

In an essay on bad reading habits, Nicholson Baker, who seems to spend an inordinate amount of time delightfully preoccupied with the most trivial things, says that when he comes across something he really likes in a book, he puts "a little dot in the margin. Not a check, not a double line—these would be pedantic—but a single, nearly invisible tap or nudge of the pen-tip that could almost be a dark fleck in the paper." He goes on, "I can feel secure in the knowledge that if others idly open my book, they won't be able to see at a glance what interested me—they won't say to themselves, He thought that was good?"

The things writers obsess about. Dots. I prefer check marks. I used to use a yellow Hi-Liter, too—a bad habit, I know, and not only because it has ruined countless books, but also a half-dozen shirts and a couple of couches, and those are only the ones I know about. Writing in the margins of *St. Urbain's Horseman*, I didn't even have the sense to use a pencil. There, next to the yellow highlighted passages, are all my question marks in ink. All my exclamations of exasperation and frustration: my what's-that-got-to-do-with-anythings? At his father's *shiva*—the traditional seven-day mourning period—Jake makes a scene. He doesn't believe in any of this nonsense, he tells his dismayed relatives. This, they say, is done out of respect for your father. "I never respected him," Jake says out loud and is cursed for the comment. To himself, he adds, "I loved him." Next to this passage, I wrote, "Can you really love someone you don't respect?" What was I thinking? That I would go through life unscathed?

In a few years, I'd be sitting *shiva* myself, first for my mother, then eighteen months later for my father, and I'd understand better how the ways in which we deal with loss are humiliating and surprising and infinite. We never really do it well, and that defines us. But back then I didn't know how much I still had to learn or, for that matter, how much

The Big Payoff

Richler's novel could have taught me. Rereading *St. Urbain's Horseman* recently, I put aside my old paperback copy and borrowed a library copy instead. It was too embarrassing to have to face up to, too time-consuming to have to keep forgiving my younger self for his running commentary, his annotated nonsense.

"A moment I still cherish is having met Cyril Connolly at a party," Richler told John Metcalf after he returned to Canada, "and he was good enough to walk across the room and tell me how much he'd enjoyed *St. Urbain's Horseman*." Connolly, who had said, "the true function of a writer is to produce a masterpiece," had given Richler the nod. In a letter to William Weintraub, written while he still considered London home and was struggling with finishing *St. Urbain's Horseman,* Richler had already decided he had no desire to write historical or futuristic stuff as many of his friends and colleagues were doing. *St. Urbain's Horseman* is Richler's declaration that he was only interested in writing about "the way we live now," in Anthony Trollope's phrase.

A fine, fat, funny, flawed novel, *St. Urbain's Horseman* is part slapstick, part philosophical inquiry. Full of the characteristic Richler rage, it introduces a new and refreshing nuance into Richler's repertoire of talents—compassion, even a trace of forgiveness. Where *Duddy Kravitz* came rushing out, *St. Urbain's Horseman* was hard labour, a book Richler fretted over and wrote in fits and starts. And if *Duddy Kravitz* provided Richler with his voice and made writing easier for him, as he said himself, *St. Urbain's Horseman* gave him his vision. It also made writing novels tougher. He would spend the rest of his fiction-writing life pursuing that vision.

Chapter 17
Guide to the Perplexed

One should not be too arrogant about novel writing.
—Mordecai Richler

A story about Leonard Cohen, perhaps apocryphal, goes like this: before he signed a record deal with Columbia, a music executive said to him, "Leonard, we know you're great, but are you good?" With Mordecai Richler, the reverse always seemed to be true. Everyone knew he was good, but was he great? *St. Urbain's Horseman* seemed designed to address that question. Richler received his best reviews yet. They were uniformly positive, often hyperbolic, even in Canada. Of his most important novel thus far, the usually grudging hometown paper *The Montreal Star* exulted, "St. Urbain now reaches to the ends of the earth!" the *New York Times* review called the novel "hilariously funny" and the reviewer for *Newsweek* said it was Richler's "finest . . . one of the best novels of the year . . . a minor masterpiece." Another reviewer labelled it "a sort of

Yiddish *Great Expectations*." Art Buchwald added that Richler was "a humourist to be reckoned with. . . . I think I'll figure out a way of getting rid of him." On May 31, 1971, a drawing of a rounder and more benign than usual Richler by Montreal cartoonist Terry Mosher, a.k.a. Aislin, appeared on the cover of the Canadian edition of *Time*, which raised the possibility that here, at last, "might be the elusive Great Canadian Novel." *Time* was more definite about declaring the novel "a literary and personal stock-taking . . . unquestionably his best."

Following up a success would weigh on Richler as it had in the past. It would take nine years for his next novel to come out, and when it finally did, *Joshua Then and Now* would seem to many, including Richler, I suspect, like a step backwards. In all the summing up of Richler's career since his death, *Joshua Then and Now* is, along with the early novels, most frequently left out. It is the one later work that Florence Richler skips over in her *Maclean's* interview: "I think *Solomon Gursky* is his most brilliant book. I thought *Cocksure* was the most delightful. . . . *Barney's Version* was wonderful. And *St. Urbain's Horseman*."

While most of Richler's novels began as short stories, *Joshua Then and Now* had its genesis in a nonfiction assignment. Richler was commissioned to write an introduction to a photo book called *Images of Spain* and got carried away, writing a thirty-thousand–word personal essay about being a young man on the island of Ibiza, the setting for his first novel *The Acrobats*. As always, he showed the draft to Florence, who said, "You can't bury this in a book of photographs. You'd be crazy. Develop it in your own way." The original plan was to write a memoir, but it soon became a novel.

As the title suggests, *Joshua Then and Now* is a mix of old and new obsessions. The title also provides the key to Richler's structure: the story shifts back and forth in time. Richler began using both flashbacks and flashforwards in *St. Urbain's Horseman*, but he made it standard operating procedure in *Joshua Then and Now*. He'd use a similar structure in his remaining two novels *Solomon Gursky Was Here* and *Barney's Version*. Richler had his reasons for complicating his narrative, even overcomplicating it at times. First, he was good at it. A master of the effortless transition, his characters move from time to time, place to place without ever

Mordecai & Me

confusing the reader. Instead of getting lost in the maze of "then and now," the reader is drawn into it. Shifts from the past to the present and back again are used to maintain suspense, even when nothing very suspenseful is happening. Secrets from the past are withheld until the reader has caught up with the present-day resolution. The complicated structure also effectively conceals the fact that Richler's plots are not particularly sturdy. In all his later novels, and *Joshua Then and Now* in particular, his preoccupation is not with what happens next, but with how the characters will deal with what has already happened. It is a fundamentally moral concern from a self-proclaimed moralist.

The problem with *Joshua Then and Now* is not in its structure but in how similar that structure is to *St. Urbain's Horseman*. A case could be made that Richler wasn't trying to write something different. In retrospect, this rings true. Middle-aged, married with kids, lots of them, Richler could hardly be blamed for experiencing a letdown in the decade between *St. Urbain's Horseman* and *Joshua Then and Now*. He had, with *St. Urbain's Horseman*, found the book he wanted to write, so it isn't surprising that with *Joshua Then and Now* he proceeded to recast and write it again. Jake Hersh's description of himself in *St. Urbain's Horseman* fits Joshua Shapiro to a tee: "Orthodox Jewish background, emergent working class, urban Canadian," a "Jewish intellectual journeyman's case history." Jake is a filmmaker who yearns to direct meaningful projects, but is waiting for his shot; Joshua is a journalist who writes a definitive book about the Spanish Civil War, but is best known as a minor celebrity, a talking head on a television panel show. Both rebel against their traditional upbringing; both are "ghetto-liberated." Both come from a broken home; both have "done all the right wrong things," including marrying a *shiksa*. Both are devoted to their wives while their wives have a lot to put up with. And like Jake, Joshua can't seem to put a foot down without stepping in quicksand.

"Paranoiacs are right about many things but wrong about everything," Sigmund Freud said, and both Jake Hersh and Joshua Shapiro gaze at the trees—overreacting to insignificant slights and insults—only to miss the forest. Still, they can hardly be blamed for thinking someone is out to get them. Someone generally is. Like Jake, Joshua is in trouble for alleged sexual peccadilloes. His trial is taking place in the media. His crime is his homosexual correspondence with a fellow writer. The letters are a joke—two young men kidding around, spicing up their relationship for the sake of selling their papers to whatever university library might be most easily duped. Years later, the joke backfires as the revelations about Joshua's personal life are revealed by his wife's ex-husband, a university professor.

Richler's sense of humour always had a sophomoric streak, but in *Joshua Then and Now,* it's sophomoric to the core: all nudge, nudge, wink, wink. In *St. Urbain's Horseman,* Duddy Kravitz makes a cameo appearance and complains to Jake about being unnerved by the sexual revolution. "When you come down to it, I'm a traditional Jewish boy. For me to enjoy sex, I've got to feel, well, you know ... a little bit guilty." Like Duddy Kravitz, Richler remained happily behind the times. His heroes—Jake Hersh, Joshua Shapiro, and Barney Panofsky—find marital sex dirty enough, thanks very much. As for the love that dare not speak its name, by the time *Joshua Then and Now* was published in 1980, homosexuality was well on its way to becoming the love that wouldn't shut up. Richler was old-fashioned enough to think that homosexuality, or the rumour of it, would be sufficiently scandalous to ruin Joshua's life. To summarize, Joshua is caught wearing women's undergarments, having swapped his own underwear with an adulterous male friend who had assumed incorrectly that he could keep himself from playing around by donning panties, a kind of psychological chastity belt. When this fail-safe system fails, he calls on Joshua to help him out and make the switch. Ingenious, in its way, this plot device is also antiquated. Richler's male protagonists always have a bit of the giggling schoolboy in them. Too much sexual freedom, as Duddy puts it in *St. Urbain's Horseman,* is more than some men are able to handle:

> The first time Marlene [Duddy's wife] blew me I was actually ashamed for her.... I thought, oh boy, lucky Duddy, you're really marrying a hot one. This is something really special. Now you open a novel or go to a movie and they're all going down on each other from the opening chapter or scene.... So what's so special about my marriage anymore? What makes my life such a rare item? It's ruining sex for me, I tell you.

Mordecai & Me

I also have my 1981 paperback copy of *Joshua Then and Now,* but there isn't a mark on it—no passages highlighted in yellow, no embarrassing notes to myself in the margin. That's because the book went unread. I don't remember starting it, and I'm not sure what prevented me. Even if I had already fallen into the bad habit back then of buying books I never got around to reading—a habit I would miss once I started reviewing books and had no choice but to finish them—Richler's novel should have been the exception. By then, his novels, coming out after such a long interval, were a literary occasion in this country, certainly in Montreal. The blurbs on my paperback copy should have been encouraging, too. The *Toronto Star* called *Joshua Then and Now* "the crowning achievement of his career." In *Saturday Night,* Robert Fulford wrote that it was "deeply absorbing and endlessly comic." And there's this from Joseph Heller: "It's wildly funny.... I think it's his best." But by the time I got my hands on it, I also must have been aware that the book, despite good reviews, trailed with it a sense of disappointment. It's not just that it was being perceived as not as good as its predecessor. It was being perceived as a kind of knock-off of *St. Urbain's Horseman:* similar characters, similar situations, similar concerns, weaker results.

Amusing, never boring, but questionable in its claim to moral seriousness is the way Thomas R. Edwards summed up *Joshua Then and Now* in the *New York Times Book Review* in the summer of 1980. Along with being the most influential literary publication around, the *New York Times Book Review* has another distinction. It's a powder puff. Whenever I read it, I'm struck by how rare it is to see anything worse than a quibble in its pages. The section exists largely as a showcase for Author A, who undoubtedly has a book coming out soon, to butter up Author B, who has a book out right now. The same authors generally don't review each other, but they do seem to pass the *bonhomie* along. A kind of *quid pro quo* exists: I'll scratch your talented back if you scratch mine. *Joshua Then and Now* was an exception to the rule.

Edwards, an academic—already a bad sign for a free-lancing, tenure-hating type like Richler—criticizes Richler for being a Pollyanna in reverse, for being mindlessly and relentlessly ill-willed, contemptuous of his characters and their predicament. Most of all, Edwards blasts Richler for repeating himself: *"Joshua Then and Now . . .* seems dangerously similar in theme, situation and personnel to a number of Mordecai Richler novels—*Son of a Smaller Hero, The Apprenticeship of Duddy Kravitz, Cocksure,* and *St. Urbain's Horseman.* It's as if a rich and unusual body of fictional material had become a kind of prison for a writer who is condemned to repeat himself ever more vehemently and inflexibly."

But what does Edwards mean by "dangerously similar?" Not all writers who repeat themselves are bad; and not all writers who don't are good. I reviewed three novels by the American writer John Barth in the course of six years, and by the time I finished reading the last one, I realized I could have just run my first review over again, so similar were Barth's stories and themes. This doesn't mean I didn't like all three books. The same is true for Richard Russo, author of *Nobody's Fool, Straight Man,* and *Empire Falls.* The same kind of places, the same kind of characters, even the same kind of plot runs through his novels, but I love them all and can't wait for more Russo. Richler often said that every serious writer has only one theme and many variations to play on it; if he was writing the same book over and over again, it should be noted that he was writing the same entertaining book over and over again.

And what's wrong with being, as Edwards put it, amusing and never boring? Reading *Joshua Then and Now* for the first time, I was pleasantly surprised. It exceeded my expectations and transcended its lukewarm reputation. It is, like *St. Urbain's Horseman,* fat and funny, another novel about how we live now. Richler also reveals, despite all the broad satire, a growing compassion for his characters. Joshua's father, Reuben, a Damon Runyonesque invention, is a good example. While he is mainly around for comic relief, for his earthy interpretations of Jewish law (he compares the Ten Commandments to a test you take in school: get six right and you pass), he is also a character who is fiercely protective of his besieged son and his fragile daughter-in-law. Likewise, Joshua's father-in-law, for all his Waspy, even borderline anti-Semitic attitudes, forms a touching alliance with Joshua by the end of the novel, the two united in their love and concern for Pauline.

Between the writing of *St. Urbain's Horseman* and *Joshua Then and Now,* Richler, in a turn of events even he found unlikely, became a

Mordecai & Me

beloved children's author. He wrote *Jacob Two-Two Meets the Hooded Fang*, the first of three *Jacob Two-Two* stories. The books originated as bedtime tales invented for Richler's youngest son, and one of the sweetest elements in these stories is how they maintain that feeling. All Richler's kids, with their real names intact, have roles. But Jacob Two-Two is the hero, a little boy who is "two times two," and who feels neglected at home because he is the smallest and the youngest of five children, which is how he gets his name—he is compelled to say everything twice.

In the first *Jacob Two-Two* book, Richler's pint-sized hero gets lost when he is given an errand to run by his couch potato father (like the real Richler, Jacob Two-Two's father loves eating tomatoes and sleeping on the couch) and ends up being sent to a kiddie prison for the crime of making fun, albeit unintentionally, of an adult. His jailer, the Hooded Fang, is a former professional wrestler who hates children and with good reason. Once, during a wrestling match, a kid found him funny instead of scary. After that, his career was over. But Jacob Two-Two sees through the Hooded Fang's act. He not only thinks the Hooded Fang is funny; he thinks he is nice, a closet teddy bear. In a similar way, Richler's public persona could be at odds with his private one.

In a 1971 *Time* profile, the reporter referred to Richler at home as "a man of extreme warmth and gentleness." Jack McClelland, Richler's Canadian publisher, added, "One thing that strikes me most about Mordecai is that he is a family man in every sense of the word. He is very much in love with his wife and kids and the domestic side of Richler is one of the keys to his personality. Here is this man who is so tough and hard-spoken on the outside, but who is completely devoted and dedicated to his family."

Richler credited a magazine article he wrote about professional wrestlers, and about the legendary Killer Kowalski in particular, for providing him with the character of the Hooded Fang, but there's an autobiographical aspect to this creation, too. When he was asked where the character of Madame Bovary came from, Flaubert said, "Madame Bovary, *c'est moi*." Richler could just as easily have said, "The Hooded Fang, *c'est moi*."

Guide to the Perplexed

Mordecai Richler's big, ambitious books all seem to have a bigger, more ambitious book shadowing them. Some classic work Richler can bounce his characters' ideas and predicaments off. In *St. Urbain's Horseman*, it's Kafka's *The Trial*, with its ominous promise that punishment is due us even if we have done nothing to warrant it. In *Solomon Gursky Was Here*, it's *The Book of Exodus* and the enduring Old Testament quandary: will we make it to the Promised Land? In *Barney's Version*, the questions raised mirror those raised in James Boswell's *Life of Johnson* and *King Lear*. What constitutes a good life? And how do you live it? In *Joshua Then and Now*, the bigger book is Maimonides' *Guide to the Perplexed*.

Maimonides, also known as the Rambam, was one of the rare Jewish scholars Mordecai Richler admired. It probably helped that Maimonides, unlike the rabbis whose boosterish self-help books Richler loved to ridicule, lived in the twelfth century. Called the second Moses, Maimonides was a Renaissance man before the Renaissance. In addition to being a rabbi and a scholar, he was also a philosopher and a physician. Born in Cordoba, Spain, he went into exile rather than convert to Islam and finally settled in Egypt where he became both the chief rabbi of Cairo and the personal physician to Saladin, the sultan of Egypt and Syria. Maimonides' *Guide to the Perplexed* attempts, among other things, to reconcile faith and reason and to propose a set of values men could live by. It's fair to say Richler was trying to do the same thing in novels like *St. Urbain's Horseman* and *Joshua Then and Now*: trying to find—though often without success—values a person could live by, a harmony between what we believe and how we live. "Any serious writer is a moralist," he says in "Why I Write," "and only incidentally an entertainer."

Richler also came to realize, as Maimonides had, that there was more to being a moralist than viewing the world as unremittingly bleak and corrupt. In *Joshua Then and Now*, Joshua comforts himself with this quote from Maimonides:

> Men frequently think that the evils in the world are more numerous than the good things: many sayings and songs of nations dwell on this idea. They say that a good thing is found only exceptionally, whilst evil things are numerous and lasting.

Mordecai & Me

Not only common people make this mistake, but many people who believe they are wise.

This is precisely the kind of mistake Joshua, and Richler himself, spent their youth making. Joshua tries to grow up, to put his pessimism and his spitefulness behind him, but it's an uphill battle. It would be for Richler as well.

Chapter 18
Mordecai Among the Shrinks

Don't be a grudgy type.
—Joshua's reminder to himself in *Joshua Then and Now*

One thing missing from *Joshua Then and Now* is a larger-than-life villain. There is no Boy Wonder *(The Apprenticeship of Duddy Kravitz)* or Star Maker *(Cocksure)* or even Mr. Bernard *(Solomon Gursky Was Here)* in this novel. Richler's bad guys come in two varieties—those capable of greed, hypocrisy, vulgarity, pomposity, lust and betrayal on a large scale and those capable of the same qualities on a small scale. The advantage of misanthropy is that you're not required to give anyone the benefit of the doubt. And while Richler's satiric attention was more enthusiastically drawn to the powerfully corrupt, it was more often drawn to the merely petty.

Certainly as a journalist—particularly as a book columnist for *GQ*—no target was too small. In his early days, writing for London book sections and literary magazines, Richler routinely wrote about the important books of the day and about authors worthy of his attention. He wrestled with the issues raised in the work of contemporaries like Bernard Malamud (whose novel *The Fixer* Richler found disconcertingly middlebrow) or Norman Mailer. He concluded a 1965 essay in *Encounter* about Mailer, and Mailer's latest novel, *An American Dream*, by saying,

> It's still too early to write off Norman Mailer. One still hopes he will stop clowning and settle down to the book he has talked about for so many years. But if he does have a perception that will settle for nothing less than making a revolution in the consciousness of our time then the sour truth is he is still imprisoned with it.

But starting in his *GQ* column—which lasted roughly from 1988 to 1996—he began to skip novels by his contemporaries. Instead of reviewing the new Mailer, Malamud, Updike or Roth, as he once had, he settled, more and more often, on the latest blockbuster by Patti Davis—Ronald and Nancy Reagan's daughter, of whom Richler says, "she hasn't a fresh idea or sentence in her pretty little head"—or the latest memoir by Patti's half-sister, Maureen Reagan. The Brontes they ain't. Cuckoo celebrities like Shirley Maclaine were also favourite targets as was the self-help industry and the proliferation of therapists, self-proclaimed and otherwise, with *their* latest guides to the perplexed or undersexed or oversexed or obese or self-esteem–deprived. Richler, needless to say, was not a touchy-feely guy. Like most writers, he was inclined to believe that anyone with too much self-esteem just wasn't looking at himself hard enough.

It's not difficult to draw the conclusion from Richler's reviews of self-help books that, like Barney in *Barney's Version*, he did not "hold with shamans, witch doctors or psychiatrists. Shakespeare, Tolstoy, or even Dickens, understood more about the human condition than ever occurred to any of you. You overrated bunch of charlatans deal with the grammar of human problems, and the writers I've mentioned with the essence. I don't care for the glib manner in which you stereotype people."

Neither did Richler. So why did he review—and presumably read—so many books by shrinks and pseudo-shrinks? That's easy: Richler had a

Mordecai Among the Shrinks

fondness for picking on people not nearly his own size. But if the fight wasn't fair, that didn't make him a less impressive fighter. That he liked nothing better than shooting fish in a barrel didn't mean he wasn't an expert shot or that the fish were any less dead. His description of Camille Laurin in his controversial 1991 *New Yorker* article on Quebec's language laws, and later in his equally controversial book *Oh Canada! Oh Quebec!*, shows Richler at his most devastating. Laurin, a prominent cabinet member in the Parti Québécois government in the late 1970s and early 1980s, was the man responsible for Bill 101, which imposed the law, among many others just as ludicrous, that English store signs be half the size of French signs. Rather than attack Laurin head on, as more than one anglophone activist would, Richler picked out two salient facts about him. First, he was a practicing psychiatrist before he went into politics, and second, his hair was suspiciously black. Forever after, Laurin would be dismissed as the "psychiatrist who dyes his hair black." And frankly, what more do you need to know about the man?

Jonathan Cole, the psychiatrist in *Joshua Then and Now*, is also ridiculed for his pretensions. Joshua knows Cole from his street urchin days on St. Urbain, but back then Cole's name was Yossel Kugelman. (His mother changed it, Cole tells an unconvinced Joshua.) Now he's a prominent shrink, the author of the perfectly titled self-help tome, *My Kind, Your Kind, Mankind*. Cole is also in a position to ask Joshua personal questions because he's treating Joshua's wife, hospitalized after a breakdown. Cole wants to know why Joshua is being so hostile towards him, and while there are the obvious explanations (Joshua is distraught about his wife's condition and about being questioned about his sex life by a childhood acquaintance), the real reason Joshua can't help disliking the man is remarkably petty. Joshua says to Cole:

> "I saw you once at the airport.... Waiting by the carousel. When your suitcase came, it had little wheels underneath and a handle. You pulled it like a wagon."
>
> "So what?" Yossel asked, baffled.
>
> "So you're a twit."
>
> "I've got a bad back," he protested. "I mustn't carry."

Mordecai & Me

Dialogue in Richler's work is remarkably effective at revealing character. In this brief scene, there is everything we need to know about Cole and quite a bit about Joshua, too. Cole is, for all his accomplishments, still the same wimp he was as a kid. Back then he was the only one of Joshua's crowd who collected salvage door-to-door for the war effort and didn't end up keeping the money he earned for himself. Now, a shrink on the defensive, his wimpiness reveals itself not in his having a bad back, but in his need to tell Joshua about it. For this Joshua will never forgive him. But while Joshua is granted a Richler-like talent for cutting the pretentious Cole down to size, Joshua doesn't come off well in this scene, either. He is worried about his wife and lashing out, but he is also behaving like a judgemental jerk. What kind of man holds such a trivial thing against another man? (Where is the affront in wheels on luggage? Or in having a bad back?) What kind of man remembers something like that and judges another man by it? A petty man, a small man, a writer—Richler's alter ego.

Insofar as I have a therapist—I'd rather not count my wife here—Dr. Rosemarie Krausz is mine. This is a stretch, admittedly, but a good shrink is hard to find, by which I mean a shrink who will fit my admittedly unique criteria. First, I want someone who will not charge me—I can hardly be expected to afford a therapist and a dream analyst—and someone who is a good enough sport to analyze Mordecai Richler posthumously.

I thought I had a candidate—Dr. S., let's call him. We met at a Montreal bookstore where my writer friend from Halifax was reading from her memoir about her grandfather, a man she never met and who was, by all accounts, one mean, wife-and-child-beating S.O.B. After the reading, which featured examples of some of the old man's nastier behaviour, Dr. S., more or less unsolicited, reached a diagnosis that he shared with the author and the small crowd. A classic narcissistic personality, Dr. S. said. Insecure with low self-esteem. Dr. S. also confessed that he had literary aspirations of his own. That's when it occurred to me he might be interested in working on both Mordecai and me.

Mordecai Among the Shrinks

Initially, he was. He said he'd enjoy collaborating with me on a chapter. I was a little worried about what he meant by collaborating—did he see us jointly publishing a psychiatric-slash-literary paper in some medical journal? But I let it pass. I said that I'd be in touch. The next time we spoke, he had noticeably cooled on the idea. There were ethical questions connected with analyzing a person without his permission, even a dead person in the public domain, he said. Another thing became clear: he hadn't read that much Richler and wasn't really keen on reading more. Now if I wanted to do Philip Roth, Dr. S. said, that would be a different story.

Dr. Rosemarie Krausz, a psychoanalyst and psychiatrist, had some ethical questions of her own. She also objected to my using the word shrink because, she said, it's inaccurate. After all, what a therapist does is the opposite of shrinking a person's head. *Potatoes, Patatoes,* I thought. Her goal is to open her clients up to all kinds of possibilities. On the plus side, Dr. Krausz was a fan of Richler's work. She also had literary aspirations. She was working on a novel based on her own story as the child of a Holocaust survivor. I knew this because we met when she took an eight-week course on memoir writing that I was teaching at a local library.

Her problem with my request was simple: professionals charge for their time. My problem was I didn't want to pay, though I secretly hoped she'd give me a session on the couch—I assumed she had a couch—in her office. She suggested a compromise: she would discuss Richler's work from a psychoanalytical point of view if I read her manuscript and commented on it. I suggested another option: maybe she could just read an excerpt from my manuscript and comment on it. She agreed.

I began by sending her some manuscript pages, which she promptly sent back. In red pen, she had marked the numerous places where I ended a sentence with a preposition. That kind of thing made her crazy, she had announced once in class. She also corrected my spelling mistakes. Counter-transference is what I think you call this, though I'm no shrink, so I could be wrong. She did agree, however, with my analysis of Richler and what I referred to as his "unquenchable itch to meddle and provoke." In her e-mail, she noted that Richler was an individualist, "someone who, though part of a group, is also able to distance himself from it enough to see it clearly in terms of both its strengths and limitations. The capacity for distancing is not characteristic of the majority of group members, who envy this attribute in others." She added that the Jewish community is "paranoid about its negative traits being released into the larger world community that has always hated Jews. Thus, it wants to hide these factors—sometimes even from itself! You may quote me on this."

Dr. Krausz was also puzzled by my feeling of embarrassment—confided in the pages I sent her—at my fantasizing about Richler being my mentor. "Why is this embarrassing? We all wish to be close to the people we admire," she wrote. Her comments on my work-in-progress concluded with, "What a wonderful tribute to Richler—to show all the ways you wanted to be like him." That last line, I must admit, spooked me. When we corresponded again, by e-mail, I asked if she still needed an editor. And would her couch be free any time soon?

Mordecai Richler's reputation for nastiness in public preceded him wherever he showed up—at high school reunions, university and synagogue lectures, on television panel shows and media interviews. He was a handful in social situations, too, as Jack McClelland told the reporter writing the 1971 *Time* profile. McClelland recalled Richler attending a party he was throwing for "the horsey set" in Toronto. "Under such conditions, one never knows what to expect," McClelland said, "except that he will invariably be rude and that by the end of the evening the guests are usually ready to form a lynching party to deal with Richler."

Montreal's Jewish Public Library has an audiotape of a lecture Richler gave in the fall of 1979 to kick off its annual celebration of Jewish Book Month. The topic was "Writing about Jews," but Richler began by wandering off topic, doing what he usually did at this sort of gig: reading some amusing bits cobbled together from old essays. His plan was also to read a long section from *Joshua Then and Now*, which was due out in the spring. Sandwiched between these two set pieces, though, Richler, at close range, fired away.

"I do want to tell you that I am weary of some of the more outrageous comments I have had to contend with from a number of people here. Community pillars I might turn to for advice on real estate or stocks and

Mordecai Among the Shrinks

bonds, if I were so inclined, but certainly not for guidance on anything pertaining to letters or moral distinctions. Indeed on these matters, given their self-evident intelligence and sensibility, I would, in their place, be overcome with modesty rather than proffering value judgements." Suddenly, the public-speaking drone he usually affected for such engagements vanished. This was clearly new material, written specifically for the occasion.

"You are looking at a bewildered man," he went on. "I have seemingly earned a reputation as something of a satirist over the years, but the truth is I am a very humble scribe, overworked, hard-pressed to keep up with the bad taste shown in some corners of this community. It was, after all, the Shaar Hashomayim Synagogue, not me, who presented the actor Tony Curtis with something called their Wisdom Award. Tony Curtis, a Wisdom Award. *My God,* I thought at the time, *what will the goyim think?*"

If you listen closely to the background noise on the tape, you can almost hear people squirming in their seats. And it isn't difficult to imagine the looks on the faces of the organizers of the event, the expression that says, "Everyone told us this was going to happen." Still, Richler persevered:

"This community suffers from an inability to make moral distinctions. In this community, I once met a man who made his living selling blood. He once gave an interview to the *Montreal Gazette* about how he wakes up in the morning, reads the paper and looks for a plague somewhere and rushes off to peddle his wares. Well, now, if I were to build on that and introduce such a base character into a novel about Jewish life in Montreal, it would be the yahoos who belong to the same country club as this man who would be the first to cry calumny, treason, anti-Semitism. In other words, they want to dump on the messenger not the moral menace."

There was more, but Richler concluded the impromptu attack on his audience by saying, "Some Jews prefer to be written about only in terms of unreserved praise. They find themselves absolutely adorable. These Jews confuse their writers with publicists. Put plainly, their suffocating attitude to letters is no different than the attitude in Soviet Russia. They want tributes."

Mordecai & Me

Afterwards, there were just a few questions from the audience for Richler and those had to be coaxed. One man, though, got up to ask Richler a question he had probably heard and dismissed a dozen times before. "How do you differentiate between a Jewish writer and a writer who happens to be Jewish?" The man's tone was friendly and genuinely curious, but Richler could hardly be blamed for anticipating that an insult was lurking. One usually was. He hemmed and hawed a bit and ended up with his favourite sure-fire conversation-stopper, a comment guaranteed to put any questioner on the defensive. "I'm not sure I understand your question," he said.

But the man in the audience was unfazed. "Well," he said, "I wouldn't ask you if I understood it." I'll never know if Richler smiled; I hope so. Still, it must have been a nice moment. For once, it was Richler offering up the straight line.

I first saw Mordecai Richler speak in person in the spring of 1988. He was delivering the keynote address at a convention being held in Montreal for the American Psychiatric Association. The town was lousy with shrinks, most of them from the States, all of them wearing their names on badges affixed to their chests. They may have been in town to discuss paranoia and panic disorders, but they were as bumptious as Shriners, clogging up Old Montreal's tourist shops and restaurants. When the multitude of shrinks weren't participating in an APA golf tournament or doubling their cholesterol count on French cuisine—tourism officials estimated that the convention would pump fifty-two million dollars into the local economy—they were attending a weekend's worth of workshops in a convention centre in downtown Montreal.

For the final day, the organizers planned to inject some local colour and culture into the conference and invited Richler to speak. I remember what I thought when I heard about Richler's appearance—that a week of goodwill and future U.S. tourist dollars were about to go down the drain. I was anticipating fireworks, which is why I showed up. Richler looked like he was looking for trouble, of course. Wearing a rumpled brown suit, his eyeglasses perched precariously at the end of his nose, he was dishevelled, though not as dishevelled as he routinely looked in photos or on television. In person the disarray seemed calculated, like a costume or a uniform. His voice was just short of a mumble, not gravelly so much as creaky, full of his characteristic ums and ahhs, which seemed calculated as well. With a No Smoking sign directly behind him, he happily puffed away on one of those small thin cigars he favoured—I still don't know what they're called. He didn't seem so much oblivious to the prohibition on one of his favourite bad habits as morally offended by it. He smoked, daring someone to object. In a room full of mental health professionals, adversaries of the addictive personality, no one did.

Unlike his smoking, the lecture he presented, "Canadian Conundrums," was inoffensive. It was full of recycled bits about American ignorance of Canada—like the time Lyndon Johnson forgot Lester Pearson's name—as well as a list of Canadians who were passing for Americans: from comedians to newscasters. Superman, that all-American hero, was the creation of a Canadian kid, he said, and so was Rambo, who was the invention of a professor at the University of Waterloo. The speech was pure boilerplate and, for Richler, surprisingly free of invective or mischief. For the American shrinks, he didn't have a harsh word to say. I had come because I was planning to do a magazine story on the speech. The angle I had proposed to my editor was Mordecai in the lion's den. The joke would be, I assumed, that Richler would be the one doing all the growling and clawing. But here he was, acting like a pussycat—a rumpled, chain-smoking pussycat. Even the question-and-answer period was going unusually well until a woman, one of the several hundred psychiatrists who had gathered for the lecture, asked Richler, "Could you give us some of your thoughts on our profession?"

Finally, the moment I'd been waiting for. The moment we'd all been waiting for. The audience, at least the handful of Canadians in attendance, seemed to shift to the edge of their seats at the same time and hold their collective breath. Looking around the spacious convention hall, I noticed several people smirking with anticipation. Apparently, even mental health professionals, trained to be sensitive and intuitive, can ask dumb questions. They can even repeat them. The moderator, a local psychiatrist who should have known better, wasn't helping matters. He stood

Mordecai & Me

on the podium next to Richler—too close for Richler's liking, it appeared to me—encouraging the unusually reticent author to get in touch with his true feelings about the psychiatric profession. "Oh, c'mon," he urged, all but slapping Richler on the back. "Any thoughts at all?"

And that's when Richler leaned over the lectern and mumbled, "None that I'd like to express here." This was an insult, but, for Richler, a mild one. Good sports up to a point, the audience laughed. Meanwhile, the original questioner revised her question, making it more specific. She asked Richler about his portrait of Jonathan Cole, the psychiatrist in *Joshua Then and Now*.

"Perhaps you could describe the character for the people in the audience who haven't read the novel?" she persisted.

Even from the back row where I was sitting I believed I could see Richler's mind working, spotting a sly grin working its way into his otherwise annoyed expression. *Here it comes.* But he just adjusted his microphone and cleared his throat. "No, I couldn't do that," he said, almost timidly.

According to the shrink from Philadelphia who was sitting next to me, Richler was holding back, not expressing his true feelings. "See that, he's repressing."

I nodded and thought, *You don't know the half of it.*

I wrote my story up the only way I could: Mordecai Richler was mellowing. And while I didn't come right out and say so, I could hardly imagine a more disheartening conclusion to have to reach. My first look at Richler in action and he was, relatively speaking, toothless. It was as disappointing as Don Quixote wised up, or Babe Ruth emaciated. What I didn't know then was that there was only a little more than a year or so to go until the publication of *Solomon Gursky Was Here*, a book that would prove that that day among the shrinks was an aberration. Richler would be back to his old surly self soon and with a vengeance.

Chapter 19
Dream House

In 1971 ... on July 10, Sam Bronfman, one of the most successful tycoons this country has ever produced, died at home, proof positive that, contrary to report, an unexamined life can be worth living.
–Mordecai Richler from a review of *Mr. Sam,* Michael Marrus's biography of Samuel Bronfman

In the fall of 1989, I was in the audience at the Jewish Public Library to hear Mordecai Richler speak again. He was on hand to read from his new novel, *Solomon Gursky Was Here,* and that's what he did for about forty-five minutes, bent over the microphone, eyes on the page, seldom glancing up. Like the two hundred or so people in the room, I was waiting for the question-and-answer period to begin and for *the question,* the inevitable one, to be asked. It came immediately; Richler didn't even have a chance to take a sip of water. An elderly woman was already at the microphone set up in the aisle, demonstrating the kind of courage I can only assume comes with age. In any case, she was not going to be put off. Her question was simple and direct, and it was the one on the mind of everyone in the auditorium.

"So," she said, "your book, is it about the Bronfman family?"

It was, among other things, a great straight line. I imagined Richler, after a long pause and an exaggerated slow-burn, saying, "Next question." Then smiling. A variation, except for the smile, on what he'd done at the psychiatric convention—guaranteed to get the crowd on his side. But then I wasn't really imagining Richler; I was imagining myself. In his place, that's what I would have said and done. I would have jumped at the opportunity to make an evasive, ice-breaking joke, to make the audience comfortable. I would have gone for the easy laugh.

In his own place, Richler, who was, for a reluctant public speaker, always very good off-the-cuff, seemed this time to have an answer, an indignant one, rehearsed. He raised his shoulders for the first time in the evening, looked the impertinent questioner square in the eyes and said, "I will not have seven years of my work reduced to gossip." Then he said, "Next question." Too late for a laugh.

In any case, that was telling us. But what was it telling us? Seriously, who else is *Solomon Gursky* about if not the Bronfmans? Jewish immigrants who go from being bootleggers to liquor barons, who turn some brains, good timing and guts into an empire. A complicated, ambitious novel (Richler's most ambitious in many ways), it is, at its core, a simple story about reinvention—about an immigrant family's search for a way to make a new life in "a cold country that was as indifferent to them as they were to it." Who would understand what that sort of reinvention required better than Richler? As a kid, in his cold-water flat, his nose was always pressed up against the glass of success. In the essay "St. Urbain Street Then and Now," he describes the mix of envy and resentment he experienced living within spitting distance of "our heart's desire," the adjoining upper-class suburb of Outremont with its "tree-lined streets and parks and skating rink and (oh my God) furnished basements . . . where the girls didn't wear shiny discount dresses and gaudy shell necklaces, but frocks that had been bought retail." The purchasers of those dresses, their fathers, "were in property or sweaters or insurance" and were "learning how to golf."

For all his prepared protestations at the Jewish Public Library, Richler was unabashed in his novel. There's even a quote lifted straight out of

Dream House

Peter C. Newman's book about the Bronfmans. Asked if he gets ulcers, Bronfman patriarch Mr. Sam says, "I don't get ulcers, I give them." In *Solomon Gursky Was Here*, Mr. Bernard uses the same line.

"Literature is closer to gossip than art," the novelist Mary McCarthy said and every writer who is remotely honest with himself knows this is true. But Richler still had his disclaimer crafted for *Solomon Gursky*. In an author's note at the end of the novel, one reminiscent in its defensive tone of the author's note that began *Son of a Smaller Hero* some thirty-five years earlier, he protests too much. "I made the Gurskys up out of my own head," he says. (Lawyer Michael Levine, on retainer to the Bronfmans at the time, was asked by Charles Bronfman, Sam's eldest son, to check out *Solomon Gursky* to see if anything in it was actionable. Levine cleared the novel and, indeed, liked it so much he ended up taking on Richler as a client.)

In fairness, Richler had taken a long time between novels again—nine years between *Joshua Then and Now* and *Solomon Gursky*—and had poured more of his imagination, more history, too, into his new novel than he had into any other. *St. Urbain's Horseman* was an ambitious undertaking, but *Solomon Gursky* trumped it, at least in sheer *chutzpah*. *Solomon Gursky* is Richler's epic or at least his declaration that he could write an epic. If it's not his best novel, it's certainly his most show-offy, an amalgam of hard research—about the North, about London in the late nineteenth century, western Canada at the turn of the twentieth century—and look-Ma-no-hands flourishes.

In its flights of fancy, *Solomon Gursky* does feel like a reaction to the criticism Richler kept hearing after *Joshua Then and Now*—namely that he was repeating himself. And so *Solomon Gursky* remains his most deliberate and self-conscious attempt at trying something different. It combines mythology with slapstick, history with broad farce. I read and reviewed it when it came out in 1989, but didn't grasp until I reread it recently how hard Richler was swinging for the fences and how close—much closer than anything else he wrote—this ambitious, uneven, flawed and high-flying tale indeed comes to being the Great Canadian Novel. Just look at the ground covered: more than a century of history—from the Franklin Expedition's doomed voyage in the 1840s to corporate buy-

Mordecai & Me

outs in Montreal, circa 1983—and five generations in the family tree of the Gurskys, a clan of Russian-Jewish immigrants, pirates, dreamers, mystics, basket cases, and self-made billionaires. Extravagantly adventurous and malevolently comic, Richler's saga of pride, prejudice and nation building has enough loopy characters in it to make Dickens wince. Everyone manages to be both a caricature and credible human being. There is, for example, the surprisingly noble and utterly distasteful Bert Smith, who tries but fails to bring down the corrupt Gursky empire. A withering portrait of Canadian uptightness, he is Inspector Javert to Solomon's Jean Valjean. Then there's the surprisingly softhearted Henry Gursky, an ultraorthodox Jew, the white sheep of the family, who lives among the Inuit, converting them to Judaism and waiting for the Messiah to come so the world will finally, happily, end. For his trouble, Henry gets lost in the Arctic wilderness and eaten by his half-native son. The son's excuse for this combo of cannibalism and patricide is that his father, unlike the other members of the expedition, was kosher. The question of whether his father was dead when he began his snack remains unanswered.

The task of holding the shifting, back-and-forth narrative together falls to Moses Berger. Affectionately described by his best friend as "an enormous failure, a tragic waste," Moses is the narrator of the story in all but first person point of view. Everything we find out about the Gurskys he finds out first. A self-proclaimed "Gurskyologist," he is determined to tell the real story of the family's remarkable climb up the corporate and social ladder: from irredeemable scoundrels to respected community leaders. Vindictiveness may not be the best motive for a biography, but it's the one Moses is stuck with. His plan is to discredit Montreal's wealthiest family. Once he's dug up the dirt on the Gurskys, Moses also intends to present it to his father, L.B., a failed poet turned speechwriter, gratefully embedded in the deep pockets of Gursky patriarch Mr. Bernard.

Richler created some vulgar characters in his time—Duddy Kravitz, comes to mind, as does Atuk, Harry Stein in *St. Urbain's Horseman,* the Star Maker in *Cocksure,* Joshua's father, Reuben Shapiro, and The Second Mrs. Panofsky in *Barney's Version*—but Mr. Bernard is in a class by himself, self-serving and manipulative on a grand scale. In one memorable scene, he shows up for a crucial business meeting with his stomach in

Dream House

knots and, unable to control himself, lets loose a resounding fart. With a quick glance at his main flunky, the poor put-upon Harvey Schwartz, Mr. Bernard's embarrassing problem is solved. Ruthlessly abused in the office and mercilessly henpecked at home, Harvey is a loyal soldier. Without missing a beat, he falls on the grenade, as it were, excusing himself to the washroom and taking the blame for his boss's bowels.

Still, for all his cruelty and vulgarity, it's hard to see Mr. Bernard as anything other than a force of nature, a monument to the straight facts of upward mobility. In the end even Richler can't help admiring him for being such an unrepentant S.O.B. Give your villains the best lines, a writing teacher told me once, and Richler does. On his deathbed Mr. Bernard's pestering, sentimental wife asks if he believes in God. "Don't you understand anything?" he tells her. "If God exists, I'm fucked."

Even while he is setting himself the task of compiling an inventory of Gursky sins, Moses can't avoid being seduced by the family's spectacular rise any more than Richler or his readers can. Moses' obsession with exposing the Gurskys eventually transforms into an obsession with understanding them. What he discovers is that more than avarice and acquisitiveness exist in their past. Like any good comic novel, *Solomon Gursky* has its serious side, which comes down to a question as old as the Diaspora, as enduring as the immigrant tale: "How shall we sing the Lord's song in a strange land?" The strange land, this time, is Canada. With the Gurskys, Richler doesn't just have a song to sing; he has a whole opera. The question isn't whether he made it all up out of his own head, as he insisted, but whether he had to. *Solomon Gursky* is a triumph of literary invention, notwithstanding the fact that Richler didn't have to invent very much of it.

A few years ago, I interviewed Charles Bronfman at his elegant office in the centre of downtown Montreal. He was living in New York and wasn't often in town, so the meeting had to be set up some six months in advance. It had already been cancelled twice, then unexpectedly rescheduled. I dealt with two different secretaries. I also had to fax ahead a list of the questions I was going to ask and have them approved. The questions were innocuous enough and were part of my research for a biography I had been hired to do of Manny Batshaw, an elder statesman in Montreal's Jewish community and one of its most successful fund-raisers. The eighty-four-year-old Batshaw, a sweet, unassuming man, had just retired after seventeen years in Charles Bronfman's employ as a consultant on the Bronfman empire's philanthropic activities. This was the reason Bronfman deigned to talk to me at all; he was doing a favour for a loyal and valued employee. He told me what I already knew—that Manny was a prince—but that didn't matter. I just needed to quote Charles Bronfman. It was a necessary bone thrown to the people who had raised the money required to publish the book and pay its work-for-hire author.

I was surprised that meeting Charles Bronfman had become a big deal for me, too, though I was doing my best not to admit to being either impressed or intimidated by the prospect. I had met important people before—John Updike, Saul Bellow, Margaret Atwood, and Richler, too— and had managed not to gush. If anything, I had always been too reserved. But this was different. This wasn't a writer; this was someone with real power, real influence. As Charles Bronfman answered my pre-approved questions, I couldn't help thinking about how much money he was making or perhaps losing in the forty-five minutes allotted to me. I also couldn't help noticing that Charles Bronfman was a surprisingly unaffected man: bald and thin, almost nondescript. Another surprise: he was absolutely unguarded. He swore expertly and unselfconsciously, without any sense that he should worry about using four-letter words in the company of a stranger, a stranger who was also, on occasion, though not this one, a journalist. If he didn't care in the least what you thought of him, it was because he knew you couldn't afford to think badly of him. You certainly couldn't afford to say you did. He could pontificate, too, straying, on occasion, from my list of harmless questions to pass on some wisdom his father, Mr. Sam, had in turn passed on to him. According to his father, the secret of altruism was to understand one simple truth: help someone and they'll never forgive you. There was a glint in his eye when he said this, and I thought, *Yes, you could write a novel about this guy.* In fact, you could write one about what he just said. You could also write a novel about your own ambivalence—your feelings of awe and uneasiness

Dream House

at just being in the same room with him. If you could convey that to a reader and only that, you would, indeed, have something.

Richler knew this and while he could go on saying, for the record, that he had made the Gurskys up out of his own head, that wasn't the point. The point was he didn't have to. He knew it, too. Richler had already gone on record—long before he started working on *Solomon Gursky*—by saying that the Bronfmans rags-to-riches saga was a story worthy of Isaac Babel, no less. Clearly, Richler had been contemplating the challenge of writing about the Bronfmans for a long time. More evidence of Richler's personal attachment to the story comes in a review he wrote of *Mr. Sam: The Life and Times of Samuel Bronfman*, Michael Marrus's innocuous biography of Sam Bronfman. Richler's review was written in 1992, after he was done with *Solomon Gursky*, but probably still feeling a proprietary interest in the subject. He takes both the biographer—he refers to Marrus as "a housebroken academic"—and the Bronfman family to task for "forking out for a politically correct eulogy." Richler's main complaint is that "instead of being defiant, or at least amused, about the gaudy origins of the family's billions, Sam, in his time, and now his progeny, [have] remained unaccountably ashamed." To this he adds a heartfelt, "Too bad."

In *Solomon Gursky Was Here*, Richler conveys the feeling of exhilaration that the toadying L.B. Berger experiences coming down from a visit to the Gursky's mansion high on Montreal's defining landmark, Mount Royal:

> Then came the summons from Sinai. L.B. was invited to an audience at Mr. Bernard's opulent redoubt cut high into the Montreal mountainside, and he descended from those heights, his head spinning, pledged to unheard-of abundance, an annual retainer of ten thousand dollars to serve as speech writer and cultural adviser to the legendary liquor baron.

Richler was excessively hard on L.B. Berger and hard, too, on A.M. Klein, upon whom he based the character. In his review of the Marrus biography, Richler recounts the many ways in which A.M. Klein, "the poet, the Joycean critic, and novelist," grovelled, writing hosannas honouring his patron as well as speeches, annual company reports and, in Marrus's words, "birthday and anniversary greetings Sam then sent to friends and family members, and even, in all likelihood, some highly personal correspondence, such as a long letter to his son Charles on the occasion of his bar mitzvah." Klein was also called in to help design a personal coat of arms for the Bronfman family, "an outlandish conceit," as far as Richler was concerned. But Klein took the whole business very seriously, to the point of giving instructions to a heraldry expert: "The ideal that is cherished is that of mankind throughout the world, held together by pacts of friendship and loyalty."

Richler talked repeatedly about his goal of making unsympathetic characters sympathetic, but even for him, some characters were simply beyond the pale. Richler knew the temptation of selling out, and he had stubbornly resisted it. He had little or no sympathy for anyone who hadn't.

I can't say the same for myself. As I was leaving Charles Bronfman's office, which was roughly the same size as the apartment my wife and son and I were living in then, the billionaire shook my hand—he had, I thought at the time, an unnecessarily firm handshake—and complimented me on the quality of the questions I'd asked. The softballs I'd thrown him, he meant. Make that the softball questions he already knew were coming. As a journalist, I should have been ashamed of myself. Instead, I felt myself melting inside. Swooning like a schoolgirl with a crush.

I wish I could say that if he had offered me a cushy job right then and there, an annual retainer, I would have told him thanks, but no thanks, but I can't. I wish, at least, I could pretend I didn't know what my response would have been if such a circumstance had come up. But I knew. If Charles Bronfman had said, "Jump," I couldn't imagine myself saying anything other than, "How high?"

Indeed, for the rest of the week, I fantasized about his people calling my people, which is me, of course, and saying he had enjoyed the interview, and would I like to come in and discuss an opening he had for a speech writer, an authorized biographer, a lackey? In my humiliating, but persistent daydream, I called him C.B.

"He said he liked my questions," I told my wife when I got home from the interview. "What do you think he meant by that?"

Dream House

Irony is wasted on the noble and well-intentioned. In the spring of 2002, the Montreal women's division of the Combined Jewish Appeal came up with a nifty plan to raise money for the needy by gussying up Samuel and Saidye Bronfman's old Westmount mansion, also known as Oaklands. It was a win-win situation. They could be as ostentatious as they wanted and still be doing it all in the service of a good cause.

The project was called A Decorator's Dream House, and the idea was to get twenty-six local interior decorators and designers to refurbish the mansion's empty rooms. Montrealers, mostly wealthy, predominantly Jewish, would then be invited to tour the place at sixty dollars a pop, the proceeds going to Jews who, for all the organizers knew, lived in tragically unfashionable bungalows. The mansion, which is currently owned by Samuel Bronfman's grandson Stephen, is about as high up Mount Royal as you can get without falling off the other side. Despite its ideal location, it has been vacant for more than a decade, which provided the added incentive of restoring—at least for the couple of weeks the charity drive was on—a bit of history, not to mention a bit of gossip. But history can't be restored, not intact anyway. Gossip, on the other hand, is like rust; it never rests. It proliferates.

On a sunny day in June, I paid my sixty bucks and drove my rusting, mufflerless 1991 Ford Escort up the mountain, forgoing the valet parking and squeezing myself into a spot on the street between a brand new Lexus and a Mercedes SUV. The refurbished Bronfman house, so tasteful and ostentatious at the same time, may as well have been Disneyland, with its parade of giddy gawkers. Undreamed of luxury was the ride we had all lined up for. There were minks in the closets and breakfast trays on all the beds, excluding those in the servants' quarters. There was a champagne bucket, complete with champagne bottle, by the bathtub in the bathroom that adjoined the master bedroom. The grounds, about the length of a couple of football fields, but much wider, were maintained impeccably. The whole place had an eerie quality of still being lived in. It was as if the Bronfmans—Sam and Saidye and the kids—were going about the business of being affluent and pampered, and were oblivious to the steady stream of envious intruders snooping around. It was as if we were invisible, not them.

Mordecai & Me

I was there for the purposes of research, so once inside I headed straight for the bookshelves, looking, I suppose, for a book by Richler, maybe a signed copy of *Solomon Gursky* or, even better, a defaced copy. I found generic titles instead, a three-volume set on *Great Jews in Sports* and *in Music* and *Stage and Screen*. What, no *Canadian Jewish Review: Hugs, Pain and Chocolate Chips Cookies*, the fictionalized title Richler attributes to one Westmount matron and aspiring author in *Solomon Gursky*? But before I could decipher what these titles added up to—I also noted, more incongruously, copies of Leonard Cohen's *Energy of Slaves* and Primo Levi's *Tragedy of an Optimist*—I was informed by one of the many guides roaming through the house that the books, like everything else I was seeing, had been chosen by the various interior decorators. People with more taste than power.

Wandering into what I assumed was the kitchen, I asked another guide where the refrigerator was—don't the rich have a use for such an appliance? Or do they just dispense with leftovers?—I was informed that I was not in the kitchen, but the butler's pantry. There were twenty rooms in all, restored and refurbished in impeccable taste. Only the basement had been untouched by professionals, and it was in the basement that washrooms were allocated for the paying visitors. The walls of the basement were covered in diamond-shaped, padded sections of orange Naugahyde, bordered by silver studs. Very 1950s. Very tacky. It was the one and only glimpse of a genuine human mistake anywhere in the place, and it was refreshing. In *Solomon Gursky*, Libby Gursky, Mr. Bernard's devoted wife, ushers a young Moses Berger to the bathroom in the basement—there are arrows directing needy visitors to the "Guest Facilities"—so he won't be peeing or worse where the rest of the family does. I imagined these basement bathrooms were what Richler had in mind.

"I don't blame you for taking notes," an attractive well-coiffed woman in her late fifties said to me as I left the grand dining room, the table meticulously set. "It's really something, isn't it?"

Yes, but what? Moses Berger never reconciles his love-hate relationship with the Gurskys. Moses was, Richler writes, "insecure in opulent surroundings but absolutely adoring it, coped with the contradiction by indulging in snide remarks." I understood the temptation. About Richler

Dream House

and the Bronfmans, the story that persists is the one about his 1976 meeting with Saidye, Mrs. Sam Bronfman, at the movie premiere of *The Apprenticeship of Duddy Kravitz*. When the matriarch of the Seagram empire told Richler that he'd come a long way for a boy from St. Urbain Street, Richler replied, "You've come a long way for a bootlegger's wife." ("From the Rambam to the rumrunner. We've come a long way, don't you think," is how Moses Berger puts it in *Solomon Gursky*.)

I suppose I had come up the mountain to sneer as well, but who could deny it? The place really was something. When I left I walked past the valet parking booth to my car, dreading what I predicted would be its sputtering, mufflerless start, and I felt a mix of unwarranted contempt and embarrassing awe. *Who lives like this?* I thought. *Who wouldn't want to?*

Chapter 20
Grumpy's

Yanofsky? Don't I know that name from somewhere?
—Mordecai Richler

Late in the fall of 1991 I had a drink with Mordecai Richler, though it was not my idea or his. I had been hired to write a profile of him for a city magazine. Unsolicited and perhaps sensing my anxiety, my editor told me before I accepted the job that Richler was being unusually agreeable these days. He had, to my editor's surprise, already gone into a studio without any fuss to pose for a photograph. This was going to be a cover story, set to appear in April 1992, to coincide with the publication of *Oh Canada! Oh Quebec! Requiem for a Divided Country,* Richler's mocking polemic on Quebec nationalism. I would have ninety minutes with him: from four to five-thirty, my editor added. Did I think that would be enough?

We were to meet on a Thursday at a bar called Grumpy's, one of his downtown haunts. He and Florence were living in their home in the

Grumpy's

Eastern Townships by then, but they came in once a week to their Montreal apartment. For decades, his writing routine, no matter where he happened to be, was unaltered: he would stop working late in the afternoon and have a drink or two at a nearby bar before dinner, so he would be squeezing me into his daily ritual. Be careful what you wish for, someone once said. But then I hadn't wished for this meeting so much as daydreamed about it. I was prepared—in this case, overprepared. I arrived early, leaving myself more than enough time to do some obsessing about, among other things, what drink I should order.

Leaning against the bar in Grumpy's, I was suddenly aware that here I was, a writer well into my thirties, and I didn't have a drink I could call my own. I couldn't even remember the last time I leaned against a bar. I was a stereotypical Jewish male, a Jackie Mason joke: I had a better idea of what kind of cake to order than what kind of booze. My one choice was out of the question. I'd spent most of the 1980s on unsuccessful dates, nursing a white wine spritzer, but I wasn't about to order that, not in the company of a man who had proudly admitted to having more than his share of "luminous brain cells" extinguished by Rémy Martin. While I waited I toyed with the idea of ordering a scotch, but knew that would be a mistake. Not only did I not know which kind to order, I didn't know in what manner to order it: neat? On the rocks? Over easy? I considered asking the bartender for advice, but then thought again. After all, Richler was a regular here. I could imagine what the bartender would tell him once I was gone. In the end I ordered a beer—imported. Richler, when he arrived, rendered my debate with myself moot and asked for a coffee.

He also seemed on edge, guarded more than grumpy. His head was down when we met, though he did make a half-hearted attempt at placing me. The name was familiar, he said. Did he know it from somewhere? Did I teach? At Concordia, wasn't it? Had we met there?

"No," I said, "I didn't think so." Which was a curious answer, I realized immediately after it was out of my mouth. *I didn't think so.* Wasn't I sure that I didn't teach at Concordia? (I would teach there a decade later.) Besides, I knew where we first met: it was that evening at the Ritz when he won the two grand for *Solomon Gursky*. I also knew where he might know my name from—from a glowing review of the novel I'd written for the *Village Voice* a couple of years earlier. It had been blurbed in an ad that ran in the *New York Times Book Review,* which I'd kept, figuring, correctly so far, it would be the only time I'd see my name in that section.

There was another possibility. He might know my name from the nasty review I'd written a year earlier in the *Gazette* of his eldest son Daniel's first novel, *Kicking Tomorrow.* I don't think I was predisposed to dislike the book, but once I decided I didn't, I may have been keener than usual to say so as colourfully as I could, knowing perhaps that Richler Sr. would be reading it.

Why, I wonder now, did I go after *Kicking Tomorrow* with such glee? Some secret resentment that the author's father's name was paving the way for him while those of us without famous fathers had to make it on our own. Or maybe some secret jealousy that he had the kind of access to his father I could never have. In any case, the review was bad enough to make me hope that that wasn't where Richler remembered me from, though I'd been reviewing books long enough to know that writers never forget a bad review or the name of the person who wrote it. I was guessing that writer-fathers of writers—especially a father as devoted as Richler was reputed to be—weren't likely to forget either.

What I didn't realize at the time, and should have, was that if Richler, not a forthcoming man anyway, was more guarded than usual, it was probably because he had other things than me on his mind. Like the fact that he had—after a long career of pissing people off and taking considerable pleasure in doing it—finally outdone himself. Nothing he wrote, before or since, would result in the kind of violent reaction sparked by his thirty-one page article about Quebec's silly language laws in the September 1991 issue of *The New Yorker,* which was then sparked all over again, seven months later, by the book the article inspired.

In a postscript at the end of *Oh Canada! Oh Quebec!* Mordecai Richler recounts the fallout from *The New Yorker* article and confesses to being unprepared for how much of it there was. "I had not expected *The New Yorker* piece to endear me to Québécois nationalists, but I was astonished by some of the reactions all the same, in English as well as French

Canada." Perhaps what surprised Richler most about the criticism was that the majority of it centred on a brief part of the article—his account of anti-Semitism in Quebec in the years leading up to and including World War II. Even commentators who disagreed on most things—like the hard line separatist Lise Bissonnette, editor of *Le Devoir,* and the more federalist *La Presse* columnist Lysianne Gagnon—agreed that Richler was out of touch when it came to such a sensitive, complex subject. He was accused by academics, francophone and anglophone alike, of dealing in "ancient history."

Hardly ancient, he counters in his postscript, though perhaps more personal than he was letting on. I've lived my whole life in Montreal, and I haven't been subjected to anything I could classify as anti-Semitism, notwithstanding the occasional remark from politicians like Jacques Parizeau or prominent community leaders like the publisher Pierre Peladeau, who said that Jews in this province take up too much space. On the other hand, my grandparents and parents, my uncles and aunts, all had stories to tell about being taunted or tormented by French-Canadian kids, of street fights and name-calling, a practise that went both ways. If my relatives were *maudits juifs,* their adversaries were *frogs* and *pea-soups* and *Pepsis.* There was no shortage of epithets on either side.

"We would return to the Main once more when we wanted a fight with the pea-soups," Richler writes in *The Street. The Apprenticeship of Duddy Kravitz* offers this summary of the tribal battles on the streets of Montreal in the 1930s and 1940s:

> The biggest sign in Felder's tiny tenement store, DON'T BUY FROM THE GOYISHE CHIP MAN—FELDER IS YOUR FRIEND FOR LIFE, was no longer needed. The last time the chip man, an intrepid French-Canadian, had passed with his horse and wagon, the boys, led by Duddy Kravitz, had run him off the street.

If others considered Richler's rehashing of old wounds old news, Richler didn't. He was "the grudgy type," remember, and this was one grudge he had no intention of letting go. In fact, when Lise Bissonnette steered clear of the issue of anti-Semitism in her initial criticism of his *New Yorker* article, Richler brought the subject up on her behalf. In a rebuttal in the *Gazette,* aimed at Bissonette, he makes it clear that there was more he could have said, but that he was limited by space and not incidents. In his postscript to his book, Richler cites "chapter and verse"—like the comment of *Le Devoir* founder Henri Bourrassa in 1906 that "Jews are the most undesirable class of people any country can have . . . they are vampires on a community instead of being contributors to the general welfare of the people." Reciting a litany of *Le Devoir's* anti-Semitic comments, Richler is in fine form. In his postscript, he's also not about to forgive the present-day St. Jean Baptiste Society for the petition it delivered to the Canadian Parliament in 1938, opposing "all immigration and especially Jewish immigration." Or, for that matter, to forgive critics like prominent Quebec banker Michel Bélanger, who entered the fray over Richler's *New Yorker* article before he had bothered to read it. "Foreigner is not the expression for Richler," Bélanger said. "I think the right expression is he doesn't belong."

Still, in fairness to his critics, Richler often did seem to be in over his head writing about contemporary Quebec. There was always some question about how well or how poorly he spoke French, but, in any case, he did not speak it publicly and admitted to being "deeply embarrassed" at not being bilingual. He maintains in his postscript to *Oh Canada! Oh Quebec!* that he reads French well enough to understand the nasty things being said about him in *Le Devoir.* He also admits that Quebec politics wasn't always an obsession with him. He was gone for most of the 1960s and for Quebec's Quiet Revolution. Back in Canada in the 1970s, he spent more time ridiculing Canadian nationalists than their Quebec counterparts. His experience of French Quebec, as he acknowledges in an essay in *Home Sweet Home,* is, for someone born and raised in the province, "a pathetically limited and distorted one." And if French Canadians were the enemies when he was growing up, they were not "entirely unloved," as he points out in *The Street:* "Like us, they were poor and coarse with large families and spoke English badly. Looking back, it's easy to see that the real trouble was there was no dialogue between us and the French Canadians."

It's also true that if *Oh Canada! Oh Quebec!* made Richler a marked man in his own home, there was a time when Richler seemed almost sympathetic to the cause he would come to despise. Visiting Quebec in

1970, on assignment for *Life* magazine to do a story on the October Crisis, Richler points out that the separatist movement hasn't appeared out of nowhere and for no reason:

> Trudeau was obviously right when he pointed out that it had been the acquiescence of French Canadians, as well as the avarice of the English Canadians, that had allowed the Québécois to drift as second-class citizens for too long. . . . And yet—and yet—[René] Lévesque was also right when he insisted that Quebec . . . was simply not a province like the others. They had *bona fide* grievances.

In "Language (and Other) Problems," an essay in *Home Sweet Home*, Richler also expresses a grudging admiration for the accomplishments of the newly elected Parti Québécois: "The separatists had endured to form a government out of what Trudeau, only a few years earlier, had disdainfully dismissed as not so much a party as a particle. Some particle."

In the same essay, Richler displays some sympathy for the PQ's language lesiglation, Bill 101, the same legislation he would devote a book to ridiculing a few years later. Once again he draws a parallel between French Quebeckers and Jews:

> Bill 101 . . . was something the English-speaking people of this province had, to some extent, brought on themselves by the infuriating refusal of so many in high and influential places to learn French. The truth is that for years in this society . . . it was the WASPs who were at the pinnacle and the adorable, saucy French Canadians who were expected to tote the bales. Through all the years of my boyhood here, hardly a French Canadian (or a Jew, for that matter) could be seen in the exclusive WASP dining and country clubs.

Richler also admits to taking a certain vindictive and vicarious glee in seeing the upstart PQ stick it to the WASP establishment. More startling, he commends the new PQ government for its social democratic policies and its honesty, "something of a departure in this traditionally patronage-ridden province." Less surprisingly, he makes fun of Charles

Mordecai & Me

Bronfman for his hysterical warning to an audience of Jewish community leaders that a PQ victory in 1976 would be a catastrophe. "Make no mistake," Bronfman said, "those bastards are out to kill us." Finally, there was this startling statement from Richler: "Though I didn't vote for them, I welcomed the victory of the PQ in November 1976." This doesn't prove that Richler was once a closet separatist, but it is evidence that his mind, circa 1976, was probably more open than the critics of *Oh Canada! Oh Quebec!* would have ever guessed. In the intervening years, Richler's mind closed considerably. There was a purely political reason for that; there was also a deeply personal one. Politics first.

Mordecai Richler left Canada as a young man because it was a dull place; by the time he was turning sixty, one referendum behind him and one still to come, he couldn't be blamed for thinking dullness wasn't so bad. Whatever sympathy Richler might have expressed for the nationalist movement in Quebec in its brief heady days was unlikely to last long. He couldn't resist a straight line after all, and Quebec nationalists provided him with plenty. *Le Devoir* editor Lise Bissonnette accused Richler of writing satire in *The New Yorker,* an accusation Richler took as a compliment, though one he didn't entirely deserve: "Honesty compels me to protest that no living satirist could improve on what actually has been happening here.... Whenever I have described Quebec's sign laws at dinner parties, whether in New York or London, the other guests have ... warned me never to put [the details] in a novel—nobody would believe anything so patently absurd."

Absurdity prevailed, and Richler was like a fat kid in a candy store: everywhere he looked there was something juicy to feast on. Shrinks dyed their hair black, and hard-line separatists like Jacques Parizeau, a graduate of the London School of Economics, couldn't resist using expressions like "by jove" and "jolly good." Meanwhile, one of the men who had kidnapped and killed Quebec government minister Pierre Laporte was out on parole and holding court at his book launch, referring to the murder as an act of "sincerity and conviction." Another one of Laporte's murderers, Paul Rose, also paroled, told an audience of sympathetic college students that the Canadian Supreme Court ruling against French-only language legislation was "very extremist." Tongue troopers were also set loose on the province, measuring the size of English signs, which were required to be at most half the size of French ones. Apostrophes were disappearing from the names of venerable institutions like Eaton's, which became Eaton, and Steinberg's, which became Steinberg. Meanwhile, the PQ house leader, Claude Charron, was arrested for shoplifting a sports jacket from the downtown Eaton's department store. "Parti Québécois supporters, far from being appalled," Richler writes in "Language (and Other) Problems," sided with Charron, "many of them ceremoniously tearing up their Eaton's credit cards. Eaton's or Eaton, they charged, was a notorious anglophone institution."

For Richler, it was all too much to resist. Who needed satire? Who even needed an imagination? Still, it didn't hurt that Richler could use his gifts as a novelist and not just a journalist when he was summing up a man like Jacques Parizeau. "Parizeau," he wrote, "was not a convincing people's tribune. A rich man's son, a sybarite, given to maladroit off-the-cuff pronouncements, he seemed more like the silent movie banker come to foreclose the mortgage on Charlie Chaplin. Quebecers never warmed to him."

In the case of René Lévesque, the grudging admiration Richler expressed for him at the start of his remarkable rise to power had changed considerably by the time he wrote *Oh Canada! Oh Quebec!* Five years after Lévesque's death, Richler offers this parting shot:

> My enduring feeling about [Lévesque] is that if he had chosen to hang me, he would, even as he tightened the rope round my neck, have complained about how humiliating it was for him to spring the trapdoor. And then once I was swinging in the wind, he would blame my ghost [for] . . . imposing a guilt trip on a sweet, self-effacing, downtrodden francophone.

Unlike Parizeau, Lévesque was beloved in Quebec, and this kind of comment was not likely to win Richler friends. Then again, what else was new? In an essay in *Maclean's* a year after Richler's death, Daniel Poliquin, the Franco-Ontarian translator of *Oh Canada! Oh Quebec!* pointed out that Richler "saved his best rants for Quebec," and that he turned on his

Quebec contemporaries with an "almost feral glee." Here, Poliquin added, "the indignation of the Old Testament prophet teamed with the acid wit of a seasoned Catskills performer to produce *Oh Canada! Oh Quebec!* Nationalists were not amused, to say the least."

Poliquin's description of Richler's book is telling. As a work of political punditry or investigative journalism, *Oh Canada! Oh Quebec!* is not especially impressive. Richler was never big on legwork, less so the older he got, and it shows in *Oh Canada! Oh Quebec!* Most of his research is done from a barstool or over the breakfast table, perusing the daily newspaper. The book is full of quotes borrowed from journalists—mostly the anglophone journalists of the *Gazette*—covering the political scene. Richler was aware of the debt he owed, and this was his only book with footnotes, other than *Barney's Version,* where the footnotes, an addition of Barney's punctilious son, are invented. But what *Oh Canada! Oh Quebec!* lacks in newsworthy reportage, it more than makes up for in sheer nerve.

Rabbi Allan Langner singled out *Oh Canada! Oh Quebec!* as the book of Mordecai Richler's he liked most. When I talked to him about Richler, he recalled a conversation he once had with a francophone acquaintance. This was around the time Richler's *New Yorker* article appeared, and the rabbi's friend was looking for an explanation. Why, he wanted to know, did Richler have to be so hard on French Canadians?

"I remember I said, 'Oh, but you've never read what Richler has to say about the Jews.' Really, I thought he was pretty tame in *Oh Canada! Oh Quebec!* I think he was much more careful talking about French Canadians than he ever was talking about Jews."

As it happens, the publication of *Oh Canada! Oh Quebec!* put Montreal's Jewish community in a forgiving mood towards their old nemesis. Montreal Jews were about to experience gratitude—a new and entirely unexpected feeling when it came to their ongoing relationship with Richler. The thorn in their side was about to become a feather in their cap. Like the hypersensitive B'nai Brith types he was so fond of making fun of, Richler had become a one-man anti-defamation league.

He wasn't letting the nationalists get away with anything—particularly the notion that Quebec nationalism was territorial not ethnic. Not with designations like *pure laine* or chants like *"Le Québec aux Québécois,"* which did not include, as Richler was fond of pointing out, "anybody named Ginsberg or MacGregor." He was also appalled by the excuses still being made for characters like Lionel Groulx, a Catholic cleric who wrote virulently anti-Semitic tracts in the 1930s and 1940s, but who was nevertheless considered "the spiritual father of modern Quebec" by federalists as well as separatists.

"What astonished me was that the things I wrote about Groulx all seemed so evident," he told me during our interview. "I thought people might say that it was old news, but not that it was controversial or open to debate. They have seminars now where speakers say Groulx was a complicated man, a spiritual anti-Semite, whatever that means. Well, he was a fascist lover, a nasty little prick, and to pretend otherwise is odious."

When Richler wasn't being accused of living in the past, he was accused of longing for it—nostalgic for a time when francophones in Quebec were exploited by the English-speaking minority, when they weren't served in their own language in department stores like Eaton's, when they were told "to speak white." But that was nonsense, Richler pointed out that afternoon at Grumpy's. "When people say I'm nostalgic, they're accusing me of being nostalgic for power. What power did I have growing up? Look, it's quite clear that I have much more power today than I've ever had in my life. I'm also perfectly happy to see French Canadians in a prominent economic position."

For all that, it was still hard, then and now, not to view *Oh Canada! Oh Quebec!,* as well as the article in *The New Yorker* that preceded it, as a quixotic, even sentimental gesture. Richler was a moralist, after all. It was natural for him to believe that the things he was likely to long for were not coming back—for instance, a time, as he told me, when "Montreal was a much more cosmopolitan city, when the two cultures enriched rather than excoriated one another."

It's no coincidence either that *Oh Canada! Oh Quebec!* is dedicated to Richler's five children. When I interviewed him in 1991, all of them, with the exception of Jacob, his youngest, had long since left Montreal for places with more opportunities. (Jacob would eventually leave, too.) Richler also knew they weren't coming back. In the book, he expresses his anger about "families being broken up" and about everything being "done to make anglophone youth . . . feel unwelcome in Quebec." In this complaint, he's speaking for himself and also for Montreal's aging Jewish population. He's expressing a community's anger and sadness, and in doing so, he became, for a brief time, our champion—a most unlikely defender of the faith.

The role did not sit well with him, he explained to me, laughing easily for the first and only time during our meeting. "It was very funny for me to be suddenly seen as pro-Semite. It can get tiresome let me tell you. The phone rings three times a week, now: 'Will I go to a father-son breakfast?' 'Can I talk to the Hadassah?' What do they want from my life? This kind of thing was just never a problem before."

Writing about Quebec, Mordecai Richler also uncovered an irony about Canada: there is something in this fractious, regionalized country that unites us—our fear of being made to look foolish, especially in front of the Americans. After all, this wasn't the first time Richler's loyalties had been called into question. For his old Baron Byng classmates, who heckled him at reunions, he undermined the school's reputation; for Ruth Wisse, he was not a real Jewish writer; for CanLit nationalists, he was a turncoat—not a real Canadian, Farley Mowat said of him once; for western Canadians, he was the guy who called Edmonton, in the *New York Times*, no less, "a used-building lot"; for Quebec nationalists, he was not a real Quebecker.

Not surprisingly, he resented being told where he belonged. He also resented some of the more mercenary motives that were being attributed to him. Maybe he was the one being sensitive now, but he could hardly be blamed for detecting a trace of anti-Semitism in the criticism. The implication was that he was a Jew after all and that he was just doing this kind of thing for money. Ray Conlogue, a *Globe and Mail* arts reporter working in Quebec at the time, began a column about Richler's 1991 *New Yorker* article this way: "Every two or three years Mordecai Richler mounts the lucrative podium of a well-known American magazine to deliver himself of a thunderbolt directed against the province of Quebec."

English Canadians, especially Toronto journalists slumming in Quebec, go through three phases, *Gazette* columnist and documentary filmmaker Josh Freed once told me. First, they fall in love with the place and can't imagine leaving. They can't get enough of French culture. They insist on speaking their newly acquired language, even when they are not required to. They are more Catholic than the Pope. They would vote for separation if they could. Then they get bored or they can't find a school for their kids. Then they're gone. Conlogue was in phase one back then. According to Richler's postscript to *Oh Canada! Oh Quebec!*, Conlogue called *The New Yorker* and gave an editorial assistant there an earful. The editorial assistant, Richler points out, wrote down the exchange. "You do understand," Conlogue said, "that Richler is a disaffected, English-speaking, Jewish writer, outside the mainstream, and having him represent us is like having an Hispanic speak for all of America."

If *Oh Canada! Oh Quebec!* seems in retrospect like a book Richler was fated to write, it was also, as he made clear to me at the time, an enormous pain in the ass. He viewed it then as a sacrifice of his time and energy. The book had been a distraction; he felt that he had better, more important things to do with his writing time.

"What angered me is the thing in *Le Devoir* and other papers about how much money I made writing the article when I could make a lot more money writing a novel or a film," he told me. "Look, I spent about eight months writing a book about a very parochial subject. It's been published in London and New York as a favour to me, really, because I'll be lucky to sell a couple of thousand copies there. A book on Canada and Quebec—I mean who gives a damn?"

The irony, which could hardly have been wasted on Richler, was that he had come full circle. The young man who had left this country because it was too parochial had, some forty years later, written a book he knew was sure to be parochial. So why did he write it? Because, he told me, "this is the place I'm from." He ended his 1984 essay collection *Home Sweet Home* and, seven years later, his postscript to *Oh Canada! Oh Quebec!* with the same declaration:

> I could not live anywhere else in Canada but Montreal. So far as one can generalize, the most gracious, cultivated, and innovative people in this country are French Canadians.... Without them, Canada would be an exceedingly boring and greatly diminished place.... This is still a good neighbourhood, worth preserving. So long as it remains intact.

It would be a considerable stretch to say that Richler, in his role as commentator and gadfly, had any quantifiable impact on the political decisions made in Quebec in the last ten years. To the province's nationalists, he was a dinosaur; to the federalist forces, he was a dinosaur and a liability. He couldn't be trusted to be a team player or to keep quiet about compromises that might be reached on the issues of language or collective rights. What he was, in the end, was what he had always been—a freelancer, a gadfly flying solo, a rumpled Zorro, scratching out his own political opinion on the province's complicated landscape. What he stood for was what he had always stood for—the right of the individual to make his own stupid mistakes. Whatever else he was up to when he wrote about Quebec politics, he was taking a stand and he was not going to budge.

At the televised tribute held for Richler a year after he died, his old friend Jack Rabinovitch told the story of running into Richler at the Ritz Bar not that long after *Oh Canada! Oh Quebec!* had come out. Rabinovitch was on his way to dinner, but Richler forced him to have a drink with him and then another. Richler indicated the presence of Bernard Landry in the bar. Richler was convinced that Landry, who was not yet premier of the province, but was a prominent member of the PQ, was giving him a dirty look. So Richler was digging in his heels, much as he had when he was heckled at his Baron Byng reunion, an event Rabinovitch was also present for. Richler was determined not to leave the bar first. More drinks were ordered and then some more. He's not going to chase me out of this place, Richler told his friend. Rabinovitch never did get to have dinner that night.

Grumpy's

As the first anniversary of Mordecai Richler's death approached in the summer of 2002, plans were underway to honour him. Michael Levine, the lawyer overseeing the Richler estate, was organizing a gala tribute to be held in Montreal's Monument National, a refurbished theatre on Boulevard St. Laurent. On the one hand, it was to be by invitation only, a gathering of Richler's family, friends, and cronies, with an intimate guest list of about seven hundred; on the other hand, the event was going to be televised nationally a week later on the CBC. Levine had lined up actors to read from Richler's work, and a handful of celebrities. Montreal *Canadiens* hockey great Jean Beliveau, a Richler favourite, was going to put in an appearance. Robert MacNeil, the Canadian-born former host of the PBS *MacNeil-Lehrer Newshour,* was set to host. Rumour had it that Richard Dreyfus, the actor who played Duddy Kravitz in the 1976 movie, would be in Montreal to reprise the character. To coincide with the tribute, *Maclean's* was bringing out a special issue dedicated to Richler and his enduring influence on Canadian literature and life. The *National Post* was going to run a special Richler section. But here in Montreal, the local newspaper, the *Gazette,* had managed to overlook the story and was about to be scooped in Richler's own hometown. Which was how I ended up writing a freelance piece for the paper at the last minute, a few days before the tribute. It would be part appreciation, part news story. For the second part, I had a call in to Michael Levine's office to discuss the event at the Monument National.

"Are you going to ask for an invitation?" my wife wanted to know.

"I don't think so."

"Don't you think you should be invited? You are working on a book about him."

"First of all, no one's authorized me to write a book about Richler. I don't know that I'd be welcome. I also don't know if I want to go."

Really, I didn't. I'd only been working on *Mordecai & Me* for a few months at that time, and I was already beginning to wonder what I'd gotten myself into. Other, more conventional biographies of him would be coming; I knew that. Other writers were talking to Richler's family and friends. I was alone, with my obsession. And I suppose I thought it best to keep it that way.

Mordecai & Me

"Besides," I added, "I'm not sure the whole thing's in very good taste. It's kind of like a public unveiling. There is an exploitive, even voyeuristic quality about it. The man is dead after all."

My wife, bless her heart, refrained from saying what she was thinking. Something, I assumed, about the pot and the kettle both being very black. Instead, she said, "I'd still like to go and I think you should. Why don't you ask Michael Levine when you talk to him? We could get a baby-sitter, dress up for a change."

As it happened, I didn't have to ask Levine for an invitation, he volunteered it. He even offered two invitations, so I didn't have to ask for one for my wife. It was for her sake, I told myself, that I said yes. Chapter 65 of *Don't Sweat the Small Stuff:* "Be Flexible with Changes in Your Plans."

My newspaper piece, titled "Our Curmudgeon," ran in the *Gazette* a few days before the tribute along with a sidebar on the event at the Monument National. My wife bought a new dress. I took my one suit to the dry cleaner. Then on the day of the tribute, a legal-sized Manila envelope came for me, forwarded from the *Gazette*. Inside, there was a tearsheet of my article. Handwritten, in blue marker and neat block letters, there was a message, in point form, scrawled diagonally across the page. It said:

> MORDECAI RICHLER WAS A CRIMINAL GUILTY OF SPREADING HATE—PROPAGANDA
> - HE IS DEAD, WE ARE ALL GLAD HE'S DEAD. ANYBODY WHO PRAISES HIM IS MAKING HIMSELF AN ACCOMPLICE OF HIS CRIMES
> - WE HOPE HE WILL BURN IN HELL FOR ALL ETERNITY, WE WILL GO SPIT ON HIS GRAVE
> - HE WAS A SUB-HUMAN PIECE OF GARBAGE
> - ANY PICTURE OF HIM TURNS OUR STOMACHS
> SIGNED
> ALL FRENCH CANADIANS

My first reaction was, I confess, delight, the kind of delight I suspect Richler would have taken in such a message landing on his doorstep. *Material,* I thought. But it also occurred to me that this was my first real piece of hate mail, and it had come courtesy of Mordecai Richler. I'd received plenty of snotty remarks about my work, the occasional angry and incomprehensible letter from screwy poets, but never anything threatening. I'd ridden his coat-tails to this moment of backhanded glory. I was an accomplice. His what? Apologist? He was dead a year, and he was still hated. I suspect it would have been reassuring for him to know that even after he was gone the jerks were still behaving like jerks.

Pleased with the note, I could hardly wait to show it to my wife. "Look," I told her, "it's from *all* French Canadians. But I'm guessing they didn't all sign it."

A sensible woman, my wife said, "This is not a joke." Less sensibly, she insisted I tell someone about it.

"Who?"

"Your editor at the paper. Michael Levine's office. The tribute is tonight; they should know about this."

"It's just some nut. Besides, it's not exactly a threat."

"It's close to being one," she said. "I think you have to let people know about this."

"I can't. It would be embarrassing. Wimpy. Do you think Richler would have let this kind of thing upset him? He would have loved it. It would have ended up in the Mordecai Richler Papers. And his next novel."

Richler listened to his wife, my wife pointed out, so for her sake, for the sake of the new dress she'd bought and the babysitter we'd hired and our rare night out, I left a message with Michael Levine's secretary, explaining the situation, but I never heard back. I also called my editor and asked if the newspaper had some protocol for this kind of thing. They did not, he said, doing his best not to laugh.

"That's okay," I added, mumbling. "I'm only asking because if I don't and if something does happen and the place blows up tonight, I don't want to be lying in the rubble and the last thing I hear is my wife saying, 'I told you so.'"

As it turned out, ninety minutes to interview Mordecai Richler, back in 1991, was more than enough, more than I needed or wanted. You learn as

Mordecai & Me

an interviewer to try to keep things conversational. You can stretch an interview out that way. You can also get your subject to feel comfortable and say things he might not otherwise say. This was not an option with Richler. Of the many talents Richler possessed, small talk was not one of them. He also wasn't especially good at or interested in making an insecure interviewer feel at ease. The more clipped and less forthcoming his replies became, the more I worried about asking a stupid question. After forty minutes, I wrapped the interview up. As I was leaving, Richler slid off the barstool he had been sitting on and went to look for a friendly face, someone he could have a scotch with, I was betting.

His last comment to me was an indication of some of the anxiety he was feeling in that period between *The New Yorker* controversy and the imminent publication of *Oh Canada! Oh Quebec!* "I know this is going to start things up again," he said, adding a promise. "But after this I'll be resigning from my role as a political commentator." He was right about the first part. *Oh Canada! Oh Quebec!* did keep the heat on. His promise was another matter. He didn't come close to keeping it. But then Richler was, in his own perverse way, a true Quebecker. When it came to the subject of independence, he was incapable of leaving well or bad enough alone. In 1998, in another postscript to his *New Yorker* article and *Oh Canada! Oh Quebec!*, Richler comments on the closely fought and divisive 1995 referendum. This time around, Richler even leaves the house, lunching with Lucien Bouchard, Jean Charest, and Jean Chrétien. From the comfort of his writing desk, though, he gets in shots at everyone from Bernard Landry to Preston Manning, whom he refers to as "the Christian fundamentalist in the prairie woodpile." Richler is also amused by Manning's reform colleagues who occasionally quote Adolph Hitler—"What luck for rulers that men do not think"—in their newsletters. Landry, who was the PQ deputy premier in 1995, had written a threatening letter to the U.S. Secretary of State, warning that if the American government continued to support Canadian unity, Quebec nationalists would not forget who their enemies were. On the night the 1995 referendum was lost, Landry also showed up at a downtown hotel and berated an employee of Mexican origin for robbing his yes side of victory. "A few days later," Richler writes, "Landry allowed that he had been 'animated' but not abusive, and refused to apologize. Then he discovered that there was a videotape."

Richler went on to write a weekly column in the *Gazette*, which was syndicated across the country and dealt regularly with the subject of Quebec. The Chekhovian theme of the declining anglophone presence in Montreal is also picked up in his last novel *Barney's Version*. "At breakfast," Barney says, "I dutifully went through the *Gazette* and the *Globe and Mail*, doing my best to keep up with the comedy we're living through in Canada's one and only 'distinct society.'" Barney also refers to his fancy apartment building in downtown Montreal as "an old fart's castle . . . a fortress for besieged anglophone septuagenarians":

> Most of my neighbours have unloaded their Westmount family mansions and shifted their stock portfolios to Toronto for safekeeping, as they wait for the Québécois *pure laine* (that is to say the racially pure francophones) to vote in a second referendum on independence of a sort, yes or no, for this provincial backwater called Quebec.

"If you're attacked enough you can't miss," Tom Wolfe once said, and Richler kept giving his enemies, old and new, reasons to despise him. A character in *Barney's Version*, a B'nai Brith-type fund-raiser, prays for anti-Semitic incidents—swastikas on synagogue walls, racial slurs in the media—so he will get a bump in pledges from the easily worried pillars of the Jewish community. Likewise, Richler thrived on human folly. He collected, catalogued, and chronicled it. He was never happier than when evidence of the dumb things people did and stood for showed up on his doorstep, unsolicited but welcome and just about ready-made. Getting under people's skin and on their nerves wasn't just a hobby for Richler, it was his life's work, and it would have pleased him to know that, even posthumously, he remains as much of a pain in the ass as ever.

Part Four
Mordecai Richler Was Here
1992–2002

Chapter 21
How to Make Enemies and Influence People

Nothing delights me more than a biography of one of the truly great that proves he or she was an absolute shit.
–Barney's Version

The detente between Mordecai Richler and Montreal's Jewish community couldn't have been expected to last long. Whatever concerns Richler might have had after *Oh Canada! Oh Quebec!* about becoming B'nai Brith's Man of the Year—"Plaques, plaques, and more plaques," Richler writes in *Solomon Gursky* of the Jewish community's fondness for testimonial dinners—were put to rest when his travel memoir *This Year in Jerusalem* was published in 1994. Richler was zeroing in on his own tribe again. French Quebec was off the hook for the moment; Jews were back on.

Late in the summer of 1994, the *Suburban*, a weekly Montreal newspaper with a large proportion of Jewish readers and a position on Israel slightly to the right of Ariel Sharon, attacked Richler in a column written by a veteran journalist with the apparently real, but still suspiciously

How to Make Enemies and Influence People

Richlerian last name of Nimrod, first name Dan. Richler's book hadn't come out yet—an excerpt had appeared in *Saturday Night* magazine—but that didn't stop Nimrod from speculating on what the whole book might be like. What's more, one Nimrod column was not enough to do the job. More would be required to purge all the animosity the Jewish community, not to mention Nimrod, had built up against Richler over the past three decades. So Nimrod wrote another column and then another. Bashing Richler became a regular feature like the restaurant page.

Assisted by provocative headlines—JEWS DON'T NEED FRIENDS LIKE RICHLER—Nimrod's main point was that Richler had built a lucrative career and a considerable reputation for himself by betraying his community and, consequently, pleasing his gentile readers with his demeaning portraits of "Jewish" characters. Nimrod, not the most nimble of stylists, insisted on putting the word Jewish, as it pertains to Richler, in quotes—as in Richler's "inexhaustive [sic] supply of utterly corrupt and decadent 'Jewish' characters." Whatever else there is to say about him, Nimrod proved a refreshingly unsubtle literary critic. In assessing Richler's writing, he mixed textual analysis with a desire to vent. The result was some pretty snappy hyperbole: "Of all the damnable, stereotyped Jewish characters in English fiction—from Ahasuerus to Shylock, from Svengali to Fagin and Barabas, the Jew of Malta, none of the truly great craftsmen of English literature succeeded in creating such a monstrosity as is embodied in Richler's Duddy Kravitz."

Nimrod also felt an obligation to warn unsuspecting young readers about Richler. "The older generation is all too familiar with Mordecai Richler's literary adventures," he wrote, "and the harm they have caused to the reputation of Jewish individuality and collectively [sic]. This is not the case with the younger generation, which can be taken in too easily by the Richler fame and notoriety due to their superficial knowledge of his life and credo." But what was somehow cheering about Nimrod's tirade in three installments was how long he had been nursing his grudge: thirty-five years, more or less, ever since Richler, in *The Apprenticeship of Duddy Kravitz*, demonstrated what Nimrod called his "allergy to himself and his race." Richler's gift for making enemies, it seems, was only matched by his ability to retain them.

Mordecai & Me

To not know Mordecai Richler very well—only in passing or second-hand or by reputation or as the result of an occasional offensive comment—was to not like him very much. Dr. Shulom Friedman, a Montreal ophthalmologist, was in the same class as Richler at Baron Byng High School. In his waiting room, there's a framed photograph of the Baron Byng graduating class of 1948, with its unlikely president, Mordecai Richler, front and centre. "He was President," Dr. Friedman tells me. "So I guess someone must have liked him."

In the photograph, Richler is seventeen, lean and handsome in his own way. He is having, what would be for him, a rare good hair day, which is to say his hair is combed. But there is also the typical unruliness in his expression. It could be arrogance or shyness or discomfort; as usual, it's hard to tell. It's as if he were still making up his mind about how he wanted to come across—as a dashing rogue or an S.O.B. who didn't give a damn what anyone thought of him. Those two sides would always be in conflict, of course, never entirely reconciled and never entirely distinguishable from one another.

Dr. Friedman also has a scrapbook in his waiting room. It's fat with clippings about Baron Byng and Richler. He shows me a newspaper photo taken of him with his arm around Richler's hunched shoulder. Richler is holding a drink and posing, but he appears to be doing so reluctantly. A fact Dr. Friedman confirms. "This is from the Baron Byng reunion, the forty-fifth in 1993. I asked for the photo; I don't think he remembered me."

This, despite the fact that it was Richler who brought Dr. Friedman and his wife together. The Friedmans' love story appeared in Concordia's alumni magazine in 1996: Mordecai Richler, the not-yet famous author, working as a stringer for the *Montreal Herald*, was getting two cents a line to report on college events. (He'd found his true vocation, he would later say, and gave up his job as a pin boy at the bowling alley, even though it paid three cents a line.) On this occasion, Richler was wandering the halls of Sir George Williams (later renamed Concordia), working on a story about the hazing of freshmen. He recognized Friedman from their high school class and interviewed him. Then he talked a young woman—"a freshette"—into posing with Friedman for a photo to accompany the

How to Make Enemies and Influence People

piece. In the photo, the two are sporting atomic hats, beanies with propellers, which were inexplicably popular at the time. Unlike most couples, they got to see each other at their worst on their first date. They've been married for forty-eight years.

"Did you ever tell Richler that story?" I ask.

"Oh no," Dr. Friedman says, reminding me again that he was not really friendly with Richler. Besides, Friedman figures, the story was a little too heart-warming for Richler. "My only recollection of him was that he was a little arrogant, a little stand-offish."

"Then or later?"

"Both. But one thing I will say. He called a spade a spade. I have to give him that," Dr. Friedman adds reluctantly.

Kermit Kitman is in a rare category—he's one of the few people Richler admired. Kitman came to Montreal in 1945 from Brooklyn to play baseball for the Brooklyn Dodgers Triple A team, the Montreal Royals. He was a good centre fielder and fast, by his own estimation more than fifty-five years later. But being in the Dodger farm system with a centre fielder named Duke Snider coming up behind you, your chances of making the major leagues were, Kitman knew, nonexistent. Still, Kitman had his moments. He hit a home run in his first Montreal at bat. He also went to spring training in Florida in 1946 with Jackie Robinson. Robinson, who was a year away from breaking baseball's colour barrier, was on his way to the Montreal Royals to play professionally in a white league for the first time, and he and Kitman talked about what awaited Robinson.

"All the other players were staying at the hotel, except me and Jackie," the eighty-year-old Kitman tells me when we meet at his home. Spry and with a Brooklyn accent unaltered by all the decades away from home, he's just come from his office, where he still goes most days. "I was married, with my wife along, and Jackie was staying with a preacher's family in the coloured part of town. It was Florida and segregated. But Jackie and me were always early, and because we were, we couldn't get inside the clubhouse. We would lie down in the grass till the bus arrived and take a suntan. That's a true story, though I kidded Jackie about not needing one.

This went on for about a month, and he used to ask me what it was like in Montreal because I was here the year before him. I guess he was a little nervous and wanted to know how he would be treated. I told him he wouldn't have a problem."

For a ballplayer in those days, Kitman was a practical fellow. Unlike his teammates, he attended university and he knew the lifestyle of a ballplayer—minor or major league—was not for him: the travelling, the uncertainty, the coarseness. "I didn't like the life," he says. He had, he tells me, "a Jewish head." So he married a Montreal girl, learned the *shmatte* business and settled down in a mansion high—Gursky high, Bronfman high—in upper Westmount.

But to Richler, who had been a kid when he first saw Kitman play at Montreal's De Lorimier Downs, a stadium in the east end of the city, Kitman was a hero—a Jewish athlete you could brag about, at least in the beginning. "One of ours," Richler called him. More than thirty years later, in 1969, Richler was on his way into Jarry Park to see the Montreal Expos play the first major league baseball game outside the United States, and it was Kitman he was keen to meet.

"Yeah, it was opening day," Kitman recalls. "I was going into the park, and a lawyer I knew walked over to me and said that there was someone he wanted to introduce. Richler told me his name, but I didn't know who the hell he was. I remember that I didn't like that he had a drink in his hand, a glass with ice. This was on the street. He told me he used to watch me play. He was nine years younger than me. I was twenty-three when I was with the Royals, so he must have been about fourteen. I said nice to meet you, shook his hand and that was that. Next thing I know he's calling to tell me he's sending me a copy of his book. I think I got it upstairs. What was it? *The Street*, yeah, that's it. I think he called me a *shmuck* in it."

Actually, Richler called Kitman "a shmo-head." In *The Street*, fan worship gradually gives way to heckling when Kitman doesn't turn out to have the stuff to make it in the majors. But then this shouldn't be surprising—no pedestal was strong enough to hold Richler's heroes for long. "Kitman was our hero," Richler writes. "It used to give us a charge to watch that crafty little Jew, one of ours, running around out there with all those tall dumb southern crackers. . . . Kitman, alas, was all field and no hit. He never made the majors. 'There goes Kermit Kitman,' we would holler . . . 'the first Jewish strike-out king of the International league.' This we promptly followed up by bellowing choice imprecations in Yiddish." Still, Richler never forgot his childhood idol. "He would let me know every time I was in a book he wrote," Kitman says. "I must have been in five."

That Mordecai Richler inspired strong feelings in those people who knew him, whether slightly or well, does not come as a surprise. What is surprising is how disinclined many of those people are to either forgive or forget. When I first came up with the idea for this book, I started looking around for an agent. Most didn't get back to me, or when they did, it was with a well-rehearsed thanks-but-no-thanks, sent by e-mail, several weeks later. But one agent did phone me back the same afternoon I submitted my proposal. Initially, I took this to be a positive sign. I was wrong. She didn't want to be identified by name, but she did make a special and immediate effort to call and tell me, politely, that she had known Richler personally and would not feel comfortable involved in any project that contributed to the Richler myth.

"Everyone goes on about what a loyal friend he was, as an example," she said. "Well, he simply wasn't. I knew someone who was a close friend of his and just gave up the friendship." It was too exhausting to be his friend, she added, too much of a one-way street. "He created such a feeling of tension around him," she said, "that when he was genial, the people around him were not so much appreciative of his company as relieved."

I told her that mythologizing Richler wasn't my objective. But by then she was on to the second reason she thought my idea for a book about Richler—or any book about Richler, for that matter—was a bad one. There was, she said, no market for it, not even in this country. What's more, she said, if Richler was starting out today, no one would publish him—the Jewish comic novel was dead.

On the day Richler died, Guy Bouthillier, president of the St. Jean Baptiste Society, managed to take what was, for him, the high road and limit himself to a creepy bit of condescension. If only Richler could have understood "the aspirations of modern Quebec," Bouthillier remarked, "he could have helped others to understand them."

Robin Mathews, a professor at Simon Fraser University, began his reply to my e-mail about his relationship with Mordecai Richler by saying, "I don't much care whether I talk about Mordy or not." He then went on to cite at some length and in some detail just a few of the things that had always bugged him about Richler and that, frankly, still did. Professor Mathews wasn't going to let the simple fact that Richler was dead let him off the hook.

"We first began to dislike each other when I answered an article he wrote in 1966," Professor Mathews e-mailed back. Mathews had responded to a Richler article in *Saturday Night*, which suggested that his generation had looked to New York as its spiritual home. Born just a couple of years after Richler, Mathews, a staunch Canadian nationalist, felt no such attachment and wrote the magazine to say so. His disagreement with Richler deteriorated from there. Mathews's name comes up periodically in Richler's writing and public appearances. Richler even went to the trouble to insult him on national television when he was on *Under Attack*, saying he was "appalled by such people as Robin Mathews."

"He wrote about me often as that crazy professor at Carleton University who wanted to keep all foreigners out of Canadian universities," Mathews continued in his e-mail. "Typical Richlerism." It was at Carleton in 1972 that Mathews, who was on faculty, and Richler, who was writer-in-residence, met and forged an enduring enmity. The two participated in a public debate in which Mathews found fault with what he called one of Richler's "Pay Me to Crap on Canada Articles."

"It was this kind of self-loathing we were subjected to by M.," Mathews's e-mail continued, recounting the debate. "I thought M. would rise up with rapier wit and give me a very, very bad time, and the fight would be on, and I'd have to fight for my life. No. Mordy ran away.... Mumbled that he could have gone to California and made a lot more money than he had coming back to Canada, and then his mumbles disappeared into incoherence. The great Mordecai Richler. I judged him for a bully. He was willing to tear me up and crap on me (and a whole lot of other people) when I wasn't (or they weren't) nearby; but when I was nearby, Big Bad Bold Mordy turned tail and ran away. I found him unlovely."

My correspondence with Professor Mathews continued via e-mail. He had, as it turned out, more to say. Especially after I suggested that whatever he thought of Richler personally, he'd be hard-pressed to argue against Richler's contributions as a novelist. Mathews was not hard-pressed. He wasn't so much nursing a grudge against Richler as cherishing it; he was also cherishing his conviction that anyone praising Richler had been misguided and still was. Apparently, that included me.

"But you belong with the great audience of the knowing," he concluded. "You know Mordy's grandness as a writer (if not a human being). You march with the well-informed and the sensitive to literature.... Very good wishes to you, and the very best of luck with your work, Robin Mathews."

I considered writing back, at least once more. Was that a crack, I wanted to know, that bit about me marching with "the well-informed and the sensitive to literature"? Of course it was. Once again, as in the hate mail I had received the day of the Richler tribute, I was being accused of being an apologist, an accomplice. But I let the correspondence drop. The truth is I felt responsible for opening an old wound because I had wounds of my own. I also had my reasons for holding a grudge against Richler. But unlike the outspoken Professor Mathews, I was more reluctant to share them.

"Why do you think he dislikes Richler so much?" my wife asked me after I showed her Robin Mathews's e-mails.

"I can't speak for him. I wouldn't, but—"

"But? But you have a theory?"

"I can speculate. He dislikes Richler for the same reason I dislike him sometimes. Because he could be a son of a bitch and because he had talent, and whatever else you want to say about the man, that rankles. Because he accomplished exactly what he wanted to, instead of being an academic, writing books no one will ever read. Or, in my case, a hack, reviewing other people's books. Because when Richler died and all the tributes started pouring in, Mathews probably couldn't help thinking that he was the only one thinking, 'What a joke!' Sort of how I felt when Yann Martel won the Booker. This is an ugly business. What have I been trying to tell you? I have issues."

"Sweetheart?"

"I know, I know, it's all small stuff."

Chapter 22
Did I Wake You? #3

All writers are vain, selfish and lazy, and at the very bottom of their motives there lies a mystery. Writing a book is a horrible, exhausting struggle. . . . One would never undertake such a thing if one were not driven on by some demon whom one can neither resist nor understand. For all one knows that demon is simply the same instinct that makes a baby squall for attention.
—George Orwell

"Did I wake you?" I ask my sleeping wife. It's two o'clock in the morning, but this time I don't even bother to check if she's sleeping. I realize I'm going to have to wake her up in any case, so I lie next to her and nudge her shoulder and cough loudly. Then I crack my knuckles. I switch on my reading lamp. What I have to tell her I can't possibly keep to myself, not till morning. She is, in our bed, a person in the wrong place at the wrong time.

"What's wrong? What time is it?"

"Around two. You won't believe who I just saw being interviewed on *Charlie Rose*. Guess. Go ahead." I can feel her sigh more than hear it.

"Is this another dream? Did you see Richler?"

"No, it's not a dream. It was real, it was *him*. He was on, talking to Charlie Rose."

Mordecai & Me

"Who?"

"Yann Martel."

"Oh, that him," she says. She doesn't sound particularly surprised, just drowsy. And, of course, there's no reason for her to be surprised or me either for that matter. It's a few weeks after Martel won the Booker Prize and he's ubiquitous and unavoidable: all over the newspaper, television and radio both here and in the States. It's perfectly normal for him to be talking to Charlie Rose, a PBS interviewer who, despite his inability to pronounce simple words like poetry—he calls it poitry—has a soft spot for artists and writers. Maybe that's what's surprising—how perfectly normal it all is.

"And he was good. I mean really good—funny and personable and relaxed. What am I going to do?"

My wife raises her head from the pillow. "Sweetheart," she says and then pauses. "Be happy for him."

"Sometimes," I mutter, as I leave the bedroom, "I wonder if you know me at all."

Dr. Rosemarie Krausz's home, a loft across from the Molson Centre, is something to see: thirty-five hundred square feet of impeccable taste. When I arrive, a crowd seems to be gathered: Dr. Krausz's teenage son, a cleaning lady, a dog, Dr. Krausz's boyfriend and his teenage son. But Dr. Krausz assures me they will all be leaving soon or out of the way, with the exception of the cleaning lady and the dog. She wants me to know that I will be able to speak freely.

"Now where would you like to sit," she says once we are more or less alone. "We could stay here at the kitchen table or go over there." She gestures to the living room and to a rather comfortable-looking couch.

"The couch?"

"Yes, if you want. Why are you smiling?"

"Well, you're a shrink—sorry, I mean, a psychoanalyst and that's your couch."

"I wasn't going to sit behind you. This is my home."

This is my first visit to a psychoanalyst, and I can't help remembering

Did I Wake You? #3

an old TV show, a kind of *Laugh In* rip-off, hosted by the Winnipeg-born comedian David Steinberg. In one skit, Steinberg plays a Groucho Marx-style shrink. The bit starts with Steinberg asking the patient to sit down. When the patient hesitates Steinberg's voice becomes very soothing and he says, "Please, go ahead, sit anywhere, anywhere you want, it doesn't mean anything." Then when the patient chooses a chair, Steinberg jumps up, wags his finger and shouts, "Mommy complex!"

Rosemarie Krausz, a petite, handsome woman, is intimidating in her own subtle way. It's her curiosity, I guess, and her capacity to judge, even if judging is probably not what she would call it. She is also hard of hearing, which you would think would be a disadvantage for a person in her line of work. Then again, maybe there's an advantage to making people repeat their most intimate thoughts and feelings again and louder.

Before I know it I'm telling her my dreams, the same ones I shared with my dream analyst. But unlike my analyst she doesn't care that I can't remember them accurately. In this respect, she's a lot like a writer of autobiographical fiction. She realizes that any embellishment I may add, or anything I may misremember, is as relevant as if I told her everything just the way it first presented itself to me. Like my dream analyst, she also comes to the conclusion that what I see in Richler is a father figure. But she doesn't see anything odd about this.

"What comes through from what you gave me to read is the feeling of a son looking up to a revered father, thinking, 'Boy, I'd like to be like him. But can I be?' You wrote me that that was embarrassing, but why should it be?"

"I don't know," I say, but I'm thinking, *What a question! I'm forty-seven years old, for heaven's sake. What do I need with a father figure?* To change the subject, I offer to tell her my dream about Yann Martel. I warn her I no longer remember it very well. She says it doesn't matter. If this is going to work, she says, all that matters is that I'm honest. Then, a bit out of the blue, she adds, "There's something I've been meaning to ask you. How come you've never gone into analysis?"

I shrug and change the subject again. "This is for you," I say and hand her a signed copy of my novel.

She thanks me and says, "I'm going to read this."

"In that case, you'll have a field day."

Mordecai & Me

"Writers seldom wish each other well," Saul Bellow said. Which is fair enough, but then what? What happens when *not wishing* other writers well isn't enough? When it backfires, as it tends to? Well, for starters, you should probably shut up about it. "Envy is the central fact of writing life," Gore Vidal said and the fact least talked about. There was more about Mordecai Richler and Yann Martel I was keeping from Dr. Krausz, and while I knew this would jeopardize our little experiment, I didn't care. I figured I'd already embarrassed myself enough in front of a former student.

A few days after the Booker Prize nominees were announced—a list that included two other Canadians, Carol Shields and Rohinton Mistry along with Martel—I received a call from an arts reporter for a local CBC television program. She was preparing a profile of Martel as a run-up to the prize ceremony and she wanted someone to talk about *Life of Pi*. Explain its success. Would I do that? I was tempted. I don't have rules I live by, but if I did, one would be to never say no to being on TV. "Being on TV is like being alive, only more so," John Updike said about his experience with the medium. That has been my experience as well. Still, in this case, I reluctantly declined. I confessed that while I had read most of *Life of Pi* I couldn't bring myself to finish it. I found all that description of life on the lifeboat and the hero's survival strategies interminable. Asked once how much research he did for fact-based novels like *Ragtime* and *Billy Bathgate*, E.L. Doctorow replied, "Just enough." The opposite seemed true in *Life of Pi*. Martel had done his homework and then some; he learned everything there was to know about being shipwrecked with a Bengal tiger, insofar as that was possible. I just didn't care. How often was something like that going to come up? "As for the tiger, well," I said, "don't get me started."

A few weeks later, on the day the Booker Prize was handed out, TV came calling again. This time a producer for the local CBC supper hour news show asked if I could come in and talk to the anchor, Dennis Trudeau, about the Booker Prize ceremony. The show was going to be covering the Canadian angle, in particular the local angle. After all, Martel was a Montrealer, "one of ours." The plan was this: bring in Martel's parents, some relatives and family friends, and tape them as they

Did I Wake You? #3

watched the live BBC feed announcing the winner, which was scheduled for five-thirty, local time, an hour before the CBC coverage began. If Yann Martel won, the local station would have an exclusive. Family stunned, tearful, celebrating, jumping up and down like game show contestants. Real reality TV. Meanwhile, Dennis Trudeau would immediately interview Martel's father and ask him how he felt. That sort of thing—the sort of thing television was invented for.

But what if he doesn't win? I was told that it would still make good television, though maybe not as good. (Disappointment and failure play better in literature than on TV.) So what about me? What do you need me for? I asked. Context, the producer said. The plan was for me to go on the air live with Dennis Trudeau after the winner was announced and the family interviewed, and talk about the significance of literary prizes, this prize in particular; and if a Canadian did win, what significance it would have for Canadian literature. Once again, I knew I should say no, but this time I didn't. The producer told me to be at the studio for five. They wanted me to come in early and watch the BBC televised ceremony with Martel's family. So that's what I did. In fact, I arrived at the CBC at the same time as the Martel family. Yann's father, Emile Martel, a diplomat and a respected poet, couldn't hide his excitement. His cell phone rang while we were talking. It was his son calling from London, he told me. Yann was staying calm, his father said. His father, on the other hand, wasn't. And why would he be calm? He had every reason to be proud, to be overwhelmed by this extraordinary event. I couldn't help imagining my parents in a similar situation and how they would feel. How they would be endearingly insufferable, overdosing on *naches*. Then I dismissed the thought. There was already enough to be jealous about without me thinking about how his parents were alive and mine weren't. As Martel's family and I were led to the studio, the only thing I could think of was that he wasn't going to win. I would have put money on it, given odds. I was convinced and felt like a shit for being so pleased with my prediction.

I trailed after the Martel family into the studio. They were being seated for their on-camera segment when a stagehand saw me and called for another chair.

Mordecai & Me

"Not for me. I'm just observing," I said. "I'm not part of the family."

"But part of the family of literature," Emile Martel said, which only made me feel worse. Then the producer whispered in my ear, so the Martels wouldn't hear, that they had received a tip from the BBC earlier in the afternoon. They had been assured that a Canadian would win. Martel's odds were suddenly twice as good—decreasing from six to one to three to one.

The odds on my own predicament, on the other hand, were suddenly half as good. What if Martel did win? Well, for starters, I would be asked what I thought of the book. If I expressed my honest and admittedly snippy opinion, it would sound like sour grapes, like a monumental case of it. Which was, to be honest, more or less what it was. Then again, if I went on the air and said the book deserved to win, what kind of wimp would I be? What kind of bandwagon jumper? I could either be embittered and envious or a suck-up. Those were my choices. A writer's life, encapsulated. I could also keep on rooting, for my own petty, personal reasons, for Carol Shields.

Of course, Martel won. Of course, his parents were thrilled. They even jumped up and down. They were jubilant and moved and Emile Martel spoke eloquently about what the victory meant to his son and to him. It was great television; even I could see that. Suddenly, I wished I had a copy of *Life of Pi* with me so I could finish it on the spot—in the hour or so I had until I went on the air—and proclaim my change of heart. In any case, I had decided what I was going to do. I was going to shut up. Discretion was the better part of valour, and of simple, ordinary decency. Who was I to drizzle on this parade? That was my plan anyway and remained my plan until an hour later when another producer fetched me from the green room and told me, as I went up to the studio for my live interview, that they were really glad to have me on, that I would give some balance to the Martel segment. Balance? What did she mean by balance? Well, she said, everyone is celebrating and everything, and then we have you and you didn't like the book. How do you know that? I asked. But I knew. I remembered my conversation with the CBC arts reporter a few weeks earlier.

So, live on the air, immediately after the audience at home had watched the Martel family celebrate their son's triumph, after what was arguably

Did I Wake You? #3

the biggest splash made by a writer in Canadian literary history, Dennis Trudeau turned to me and, with a news anchor's talent for insinuation, said, "This wasn't your choice, was it? You didn't even like this book."

It was a leading question, but no more than I deserved. I talked about the tiger and tried to make sense, but all I could think of was the Martel family, and how after they returned home from a celebratory dinner, they were probably going to sit down to watch a tape of the program, and how even if I got really lucky and they had programmed their VCR incorrectly or, being cultured people, had no VCR, there would be a whole slew of messages on their answering machine—what were the chances they didn't have an answering machine?—congratulating them and then adding an, "Oh-by-the-way, who was that little prick bad-mouthing Yann? What's *his* problem?"

So much for the family of literature.

Chapter 23
Ask a Stupid Question

You have to begin with the self. That's where the hot spots are.
—John Updike on *Charlie Rose*

Dan Nimrod, *c'est moi*, I suppose. I, too, have a problem with Mordecai Richler's 1994 memoir *This Year in Jerusalem,* though mine is not related to what Richler reveals about himself. Nimrod called him "a man allergic to his race," but the opposite was true. Richler was addicted to his race; he couldn't have stopped writing about being Jewish if he wanted to. No, my problem with Richler's so-called memoir is how much he's still *not* revealing about himself. From the start, from that defensive disclaimer in his second novel, *Son of a Smaller Hero,* Richler had managed to have his autobiographical cake and eat it, too. He would write about his own life, making little or no effort to disguise it, and then announce with a straight and defiant face, that it was all fiction. At the same time, his personal essays, always glib, always self-deprecating, always entertaining, were,

Ask a Stupid Question

with a few notable exceptions like "My Father's Life," never especially intimate or revealing. Maybe that's why I expected *This Year in Jerusalem*, Richler's first full-length memoir, to be different.

I was expecting too much. *This Year in Jerusalem* is more reportage than memoir, and what memoir there is reads like a scrapbook filled with diverting but predictable encounters with the old St. Urbain Street and Baron Byng gangs. There are recollections of Richler's days, circa 1948, as a surprisingly idealistic teenager in Habonim, a Zionist youth organization. His plan back then was to leave Canada and, along with several streetwise buddies, enlist in the war for Israel's independence. This fantasy owed more to Hollywood movies like *Beau Geste* than to any real attachment to the new Jewish state. Idealism also had its limits as far as Richler was concerned. He joined Habonim because he'd heard girls in a left wing organization were more likely to put out. Which was, according to Dan Nimrod, just one more example of Richler's sins, casting unfair aspersions on nice Zionist girls. (To be fair to Richler, he never claimed he got anywhere with these alleged pushovers.)

Reading *This Year in Jerusalem*, it's difficult to shake the feeling that it is a book Richler could have written with one of his two hunt-and-peck typing fingers tied behind his back. His observations on the perils of religious fundamentalism and his support for an independent Palestinian state, while admirable and fair-minded, fall into the what-else-is-new? category. On the personal side, there are fewer revelations. Everything from Richler's poisonous relationship with his paternal grandfather to his long and happy marriage to his "protestant bride" is glossed over as if, well, as if it's none of our business.

So, yes, I expected more. Maybe I'd been spoiled by a recent spate of memoirs by accomplished male novelists who were, like Richler, on the other side of sixty, but who seemed eager to comment on everything from their medical conditions to their dying fathers. The authors who had embraced the sexual revolution of the late 1960s had discovered in the early 1990s that the ability to do your own thing depended, more and more, on being able to do it with a healthy prostate. The authors who had fled their conventional families thirty years ago had returned to accompany their ailing fathers and mothers to their medical appointments.

Mordecai & Me

Still, they were all coming clean, talking revealingly about the personal source of their material and inspiration. Philip Roth's *The Facts* and *Patrimony,* John Updike's *Self-Consciousness,* and V.S. Naipaul's *The Enigma of Arrival* all came out around the same time as *This Year in Jerusalem.* And what these authors would discover, unlike Richler, was that the decision to write a memoir, like it or not, compelled them to reveal more of themselves than they ever had before—even in Roth's case—and probably more than they ever intended to. Updike and Roth, at least, were writing their memoirs as a kind of pre-emptive strike against the dreaded and sure-to-be looming literary biographer. In the end, though, both men were probably harder on themselves than any biographer would be.

That's not the case with Richler. Instead, in *This Year in Jerusalem,* he deliberately steps back, creating a distance between himself and his subject, as if he will go only so far and no further. To be known, yes, but only on my own conditions, is how he put it in his 1970 essay "Why I Write." In *This Year in Jerusalem,* almost twenty-five years later, those conditions feel more like barriers. Barriers that had—looking back on Richler's career—always been present. Which just feels like a lost opportunity to me, a shame really. Richler goes on avoiding what Updike refers to as "the hot spots" and chooses, as usual, the sore spots. For a writer who never shied away from taking anyone on, from Sam Bronfman to René Lévesque, Mordecai Richler missed the chance to take on his most complicated creation—himself.

When I teach autobiographical writing, I begin with the same lecture: don't think of the *I,* once it's down on the page, as *You.* Remember that no matter how closely you believe you are adhering to the facts, or the facts as you know or remember them, that *I* on the page is a character and, as with any character, you must use it strategically. I understand this distinction as a teacher and a writer; as a reader, I am suggestible and literal-minded. I want gossip, a story to believe. I don't believe in hidden layers or unreliable narrators. If the first person is talking, I'm listening. I'm inevitably sucked in by that little pronoun, so formal and upright, so trustworthy on the page. Barney Panofsky, the narrator of *Barney's Version*, the only novel Richler wrote in the first person, is not Mordecai Richler. But that's not the issue. Is he close enough? That's the issue.

After *Barney's Version* was nominated for the Giller Prize in the fall of 1997, I interviewed Richler for the last time, though it would not be the last time we met. I asked him, then, why he had never used the *I* before in his novels. "It didn't occur to me before," he said gruffly, as if I were required to believe him. But how could it not have occurred to him? Novels like *Son of a Smaller Hero*, *St. Urbain's Horseman* and *Joshua Then and Now* are plainly first person stories, even if they are written in the third person. He chose not to use the first person, I suspect, for that very reason—because he wanted, as always, to pretend there was a distance from stories he was not the least bit distant from.

The predicament he faced with *Barney's Version* was that this time the nature of the novel—about a man trying to tell his story before it was too late, before it all becomes a blur—could not be accomplished in any other way than through the confessional voice of its main character. Still, make no mistake about it, Barney Panofsky is Mordecai Richler in most of the big and little ways that matter: from his craving for Jewish soul food to the types of characters he disdains, like puffed up politicians and CanLit types. There's his ex-wife, too, Miriam Greenberg, another Florence Richler homage. Though in *Barney's Version* Miriam finally gets to do what Richler's other fictionalized wives aren't permitted to—make an overdue exit and divorce Barney.

Translated into Italian a couple of years before Richler's death, *Barney's Version* became an unexpected bestseller. More than that, though, it became a cultural phenomenon. According to William Weintraub, Richler was astonished by the reaction and made one visit to Italy to promote the book after it came out. He was planning to return before he became ill in the spring of 2001. In Italy, he was transformed into an adjective. The word *Richleriano* became code for someone who does not tolerate political correctness. But the Italians didn't know the half of it. Barney's musings about "dykes on mikes," his disdain for health food stores, his prank faxes about the search for a female heavyweight contender and even his slugging his first wife are quaint compared to the kind of commentary Richler was including in his novels long before the term politically incorrect existed. In *St. Urbain's Horseman,* Jake Hersh's Uncle Abe delivers an uninhibited and not entirely unsympathetic speech about the changing times:

> And what do they want, our Jewish children? They want to be black.... Their hearts are breaking for the downtrodden French Canadians. Well, only two generations earlier, these same French Canadians wanted only to break their heads. And if it's not the blacks or the French Canadians, it's the Eskimos.... It's the burden of being white, it bugs them. How long have we even been white? We were kikes, that's all.

Wherever a line existed between satire and the limits of good taste, Richler was keen to cross it. Read *Joshua Then and Now* and try not to cringe at the scene where Joshua, in pursuit of Pauline, catches her in the toilet stall in the men's room having sex with a West Indian writer. As he urinates, Joshua sings *Old Man River*. A few pages later, his explanation for why he is behaving so badly only makes matters worse. "I'm in love with a nigger-loving whore," he says.

By comparison, *Barney's Version* is a gentler novel, with a gentler protagonist. There's something a little less sanctimonious about Barney Panofsky than his predecessors Jake Hersh or Joshua Shapiro. He's more of a regular guy, more of a *nebbish* than those two. In *St. Urbain's Horseman,* Jake is referred to as "bloody Jake Hersh" for his mocking tone and his superiority complex. In *Joshua Then and Now,* the novel ends with Joshua being told by his wife, "You turned out to be more moral than we were." We are, it's clear, expected to believe her. Jake also has the notion that he would have made a pretty good rabbi, except for the fact that he doesn't believe in God. In her interview with *Maclean's* on the first anniversary of her husband's death, Florence Richler recalls the self-righteous and intimidating young man she met in London:

> And most of the time, one would wish that he would leave very soon, so that we could all be our foolish and ordinary selves. There was something about this foreign man that kept one alert to what

Ask a Stupid Question

we said and did.... I remember when he left town ... a very dear friend of mine said, when we were all commiserating with one another, "Oh dear, what will we all do without Mordecai?" And [another] man said, "Yes, we've lost our conscience."

In this respect, Barney Panofsky is not quite like any Richler protagonist or like Richler; he's easier to take. As for his problems, they're not self-imposed or self-indulgent or imaginary for a change. They're not particularly complicated either. He is getting old and frail and losing his faculties; it's as simple as that. What is most endearing and most irresistible about him is how badly he wants this not to be the case, how unwilling and unprepared he is to bow out gracefully. "Dying, a blight common to earlier generations," Barney says, recalling the good old days, "did not enter into our scheme of things. It wasn't on our dance cards."

Barney hates being a grandfather. "It's indecent," he says. "In my mind's eye, I'm still twenty-five. Thirty-three max. Certainly not sixty-seven, reeking of decay and dashed hopes." For his part, Richler started complaining about getting old when he was still relatively young and, from then on, it became a habit. At thirty-eight, according to his friend and *Saturday Night* editor Robert Fulford, he already saw "youth slipping away from him ... his teeth loosening, his 'hangovers more onerous.'" With *Barney's Version,* Richler, at sixty-seven, shows he wasn't prepared to bow out gracefully, either. It was his argument—a compelling one—that he wasn't washed up just yet.

I finally asked Mordecai Richler *that* stupid question, and what I got in return was not a stupid answer, but the look. The one that was part bewilderment, part exasperation, part anger (like the Hooded Fang confronting Jacob Two-Two, it occurs to me now) and invariably accompanied by a long, disconcerting silence. It seemed to say, "I have no idea what you're talking about, and, what's more, I'm pretty sure you don't either." The question in question was, "Do you want to be liked?" Sitting across from Richler at his new favourite downtown bar—Ziggy's had replaced Grumpy's—I had what I thought was a good reason for asking it. I wanted to know if Richler was sensing a shift in critical and public reaction to him now that *Barney's Version* was out and was the odds-on favourite to win the Giller. A novel by Richler—especially his first in almost a decade—was bound to attract its share of attention, but there seemed to be something else going on this time, particularly with this book. Something like Richler Revisionism.

Sometimes celebrity culture extends to writers, a fact Richler never liked, but was well aware of. "I fervently believe that all a writer should send into the marketplace to be judged is his own work; the rest should remain private. I deplore the writer as a personality, however large and undoubted the talent," he said in his 1965 review of Norman Mailer's novel *American Dream*. But, if anything, the necessity for a writer to become a personality—or to have one—grew as the interest in what was in their books decreased. In an essay entitled "Pedlar's Diary," about his publicity tour for *Barney's Version*—the same tour on which I interviewed him—Richler reminisced about the old days:

> Publication wasn't always such an ordeal. . . . When my novel came out . . . I would sit at home waiting for cherished friends to phone and read aloud my worst review, just in case I missed it. Those, those were the days when novelists could be condescending about traveling salesmen, men who lugged their sample cases from town to town, but we have long since joined the club.

There wasn't anything especially new in Richler's sample case. He was difficult to interview, not a forthcoming man in the best of circumstances. John Aylen, his former creative writing student at Carleton, became a friend and a drinking buddy towards the end of Richler's life, and he pointed out to me that the one thing you needed to be friends with Richler was an ability to keep quiet. "Mordecai was not a big talker," Aylen said. "I try not to talk when I have nothing to say, and I can remember long, long silences between us when we were alone. I suspect he appreciated that." Michael Coren, who had obtained Richler's permission to write his biography before eventually abandoning the project, conducted about seven hours of interviews with Richler. "He was a good guy, but not very talkative," Coren said. "He didn't carry a conversation very well."

Ask a Stupid Question

By the time *Barney's Version* was published the media's tolerance for Richler's particular combination of rudeness and shyness seemed to be growing. Richler was a curmudgeon, true enough, but he was our curmudgeon. Like a surly waiter at a popular restaurant or a prickly character actor, his flaws, over time, became indistinguishable from his virtues. What's more, compared to the kind of revelations contained in most recent literary biographies exposing celebrated writers as womanizers or plagiarists or Nazi sympathizers or bad tippers, Richler's grouchiness seemed harmless.

Besides, in Richler's case, the most damning things to say about him had already been said, repeatedly, long before *Barney's Version* was published. Canada's aging smart-ass was being outed as kind of a nice guy— or at least nicer than anyone previously suspected. Richler's private persona was described by one old friend as "gentle and warm and generous." In a review of *Barney's Version*, written by another old friend, John Fraser, the former editor of *Saturday Night*, Richler was exposed as a lovable prankster and a hoot to be around. Another reviewer of *Barney's Version*, who made it clear how little he cared for Richler and his politics in the beginning of his review, went on to concede that the new novel reveals a much softer side to its author. During a CBC radio panel discussion, Richler was practically canonized, praised as a national treasure, a kind of dishevelled, cigar-smoking, bad-tempered Anne Murray.

Which may be why I wanted to know if the man who had made a career of skewering everyone in sight over the last forty years was concerned about acquiring a good reputation at last. Then, just in case, I repeated my stupid question. He'd heard me the first time.

"What do you mean do I want to be liked?" Richler replied. "I want my work to be well thought of. But myself? I never think of that one way or another. Look, I don't take the temperature every day. I've also been very critical of a lot of things in the past, and I continue to be critical, so I'm fair game. I don't solicit affection."

Nevertheless, affection, of a kind, a perverse kind perhaps, was coming. Like it or not.

Chapter 24
The Influence of Anxiety

One is involved with ten or twelve people in this world and not more.
–Mordecai Richler from an interview with Graeme Gibson

Mordecai Richler didn't like seeing children grow up to write revealing books about a famous parent, especially a famous writing parent. "It is a form I have trouble with," he admits in his 1990 review of *Home Before Dark,* Susan Cheever's memoir of her father's complicated secret life. "I think authors, anyway, should be proof against their children interpreting them in print. I would rather they erred on the side of reticence."

But why should authors be immune? Why should their children be more reticent than, let's say, Joan Crawford's kid or, some day in the not-too-distant future, Michael Jackson's offspring? Richler, always dead set against special pleading, does some of his own here. What may have worried him is the distance Susan Cheever travels between her intention and her destination. She begins with the notion of writing "a slim volume of anecdote and remembrance," but that's not how it turns out. "I don't think I would have started this book," Cheever says, "if I had known where it was going to end, but having written it I know my father better than I ever did while he was alive."

Richler had kids of his own—five—and, as it turned out, four of them would end up doing some writing of their own. As it also turned out, being the children of a writer, and writers themselves, they could hardly be expected not to recognize a foolproof character when they saw one. If Richler were reluctant to admit that his own life was at the core of most of the characters he created and the stories he told, his children would have no such reservations. When Richler made the case in his review of *Home Before Dark* that a writer's kid should refrain from exploiting his or her parent's life, he must have known what was coming—specifically, his son Daniel's debut novel, *Kicking Tomorrow*, which was published in 1991. Richler could hardly have failed to recognize himself in the portrait of the protagonist's father.

When we first meet Robbie Bookbinder, the rebellious and rather obnoxious hero of Daniel's story, he's at odds with his father. Robbie wants to know what the old man does for a living. Meanwhile, his father—"flopped on the couch, a bottle of Canadian Club on the carpet between him and the TV, the husk of an orange peel high up on his swollen beerbody abdomen"—is too busy watching a *Canadiens* hockey game to answer. When he does, his speech is full of "aums" and "ahhs." Even down to the inarticulate grunting, he is a dead ringer for Daniel's famous father. This portrait of the middle-aged artist as a couch potato would be repeated. Noah Richler's prologue to his father's posthumous 2002 collection, *Dispatches from the Sporting Life*, begins:

> In 1972, my father brought his family back to Canada after nearly twenty years in England. I learned in no time that his preferred place on Saturday nights from September to May was on the living room couch, watching *Hockey Night in Canada.*

Then there's *Sister Crazy*, Richler's eldest daughter Emma's literary debut. Clearly not a novel, not exactly a collection of linked stories either, *Sister Crazy* feels most of all like a memoir, and the only good reason it can't be called one is because of its author's insistence that it is not. (Like father, like daughter.) I reviewed *Sister Crazy* when it came out in the spring of 2001, and I was not unkind to the book. (I had been much harder on *Kicking Tomorrow* a decade earlier.) I came to the conclusion that Emma Richler was a writer with potential, a welcome and ultimately deserving addition to the family business. But I also said that you'd have to be wearing a blindfold to read *Sister Crazy* and not see it for what it was—thinly veiled autobiography. So while it may be unfair to drag the real Richlers into a discussion of a work of fiction, I went on, how could I or anyone else be expected not to? Here, after all, is the story of the fictional Weiss clan, a family with a well-known grouchy dad, a long-suffering and saintly mother, and five precocious kids. Sound familiar? And there's more, particularly in the second chapter, "Angel's Share," which, coincidentally, provides one of the best portraits around, fictional or not, of Richler as a scotch-drinking, cigar-smoking, tomato-eating, mechanically inept couch potato. Honestly, I said in my review, who else could this guy be? If anything, I should have praised her more for capturing her old man so convincingly:

> My dad is a sportswriter. He also writes children's fiction under a pseudonym. In these books, he writes about . . . a world full of human failures, cranks, and despots, some with endearing and poignant flaws, others with thunderous bad taste and hilariously inflated egos. He finds these types, these faltering embarrassing types, really funny. These are his people.

Emma's fictionalized portrait of her father (the father in Daniel's novel is a sportswriter, too) is also the darkest on record. There are no Susan Cheever-style revelations in *Sister Crazy*, but this father is a man his hypersensitive daughter has a hard time understanding and, more important, pleasing. Emma's narrator, Jem Weiss, lives for those moments when her father pays special attention to her, but they're moments fraught, too, with the likelihood of misunderstanding, even disaster:

> My dad walks with me. He is gripping my neck, loosely he thinks, in a manner suggesting fellowship and affection. It feels

The Influence of Anxiety

good although his grip is a little like those sinks in the hair salon, designed to hold your head in place but actually inviting disaster, such as permanent spinal injury and wholesale numbing of the nervous system. But I like walking with my dad this way. The world is ours.

Emma's descriptions of her narrator's father are full of ambivalence. He is a "grumpy" and "tight-lipped man," intimidating but devoted to his wife and kids. For her part, Jem longs to be a boy; she thinks that would make it easier to win her father's favour. He is also a practical joker, a prankster, an enormous amount of fun to be around, which is why Jem is so desperate to please him when she is in his company.

One of the most interesting aspects of *Sister Crazy* is that it is not the story of a dysfunctional family, but of a family that functions almost too well. What Emma's narrator can't adjust to is a real world that seems so dull compared to the lively, witty world in which she grew up. "When does childhood end?" she wonders. The hardest time Jem has in the book is trying to make the real world "measure up." This is a point of view I'm now willing to admit I understand well, perhaps too well. It's not that I think of Mordecai Richler as a father figure (shrinks and dream analysts notwithstanding); it's that I wanted, when he was alive, when our paths crossed every so often, to be part of his inner circle. Why? Because it looked like so much fun.

In a tribute Jacob Richler wrote to his father in the *National Post*, Jacob recalled a man who gave as much wicked thought to the notes he left behind for his kids as he did to the plots he created for his novels. "Seventeen now, girlfriends happily began ringing up the apartment looking for me," Jake wrote. "And for once—just this once Dad took pleasure in relaying phone messages of a sort, which he left for me, typewritten, on the dining room table." Caroline phoned, Mordecai Richler wrote his teenage son, "She doesn't want to speak to you again. She hates you. She thinks you're a turd. Well, it's a point of view."

Mordecai Richler, like his hero in *Barney's Version*, was also unable to resist the temptation to send prank faxes. When Jacob started working at *Saturday Night*, his father had the pleasure of knowing his correspondence would be seen by everyone in the office, especially if he labelled it "private and confidential." On one such fax, he wrote this p.s. to Jacob: "I wouldn't worry about what could just be a harmless rash, but, yes, I do think it would be considerate to wear gloves at the office until you've checked it out." Richler never switched to a computer—he continued to bang out his fiction on a sturdy old electric typewriter for which he had a harder and harder time finding ribbons—but the fax machine was invented for him. It was an instrument of pure fun, as friends like John Fraser could attest. When Fraser was Master of Massey College, Richler sent a fax accusing Fraser of demanding a kickback for appointing Richler Massey's writer-in-residence.

"Everyone knows the story of his encounter with Saidye Bronfman," William Weintraub says over lunch, reminiscing about his fifty-one year friendship with Mordecai Richler. "But there's another, lesser known Mordecai story I like. He was at some fancy party somewhere, and a woman, well-put-together, you know, the hair, the make-up, all of that, came up to him and said, 'Oh, Mr. Richler we'd just love for you to talk to our group.' Mordecai's response was, 'You should know that I charge two thousand dollars for a speaking appearance.' So the woman said, 'But Mr. Richler, we're the *Hadassah*.' And Mordecai raised his index finger to his eyes, then pointed it at the woman and said, 'Three thousand.'"

Weintraub met Richler in Paris in December 1950, introduced by another expatriate Montrealer, Mavis Gallant. Though Weintraub was five years older than Richler, he was struck, from the start, by Richler's determination and seriousness when it came to his literary career. That Richler's ambition didn't put Weintraub off probably says more for Weintraub's easygoing nature than Richler's charm. But then Weintraub, who'd just lost his job at the *Gazette* for more or less calling his managing editor a pig, wasn't ambitious in the same way his new young friend was. Weintraub admits as much in *Getting Started*, his memoir of the 1950s and of his friendship with Richler, Gallant, and Brian Moore. "Unlike Mordecai and others I'd met in Paris, I didn't aspire, at all costs, to literary heights," Weintraub explains in *Getting Started*. His goals seemed more attainable: "I simply wanted to earn my living as a journalist and live an interesting—perhaps very interesting—life." This doesn't mean that Weintraub didn't feel jealous of his friends' early success. Last to write a novel of his own, Weintraub watched as Mavis Gallant began her long association with *The New Yorker,* Brian Moore wrote *The Lonely Passion of Judith Hearne* and Richler wrote one novel after another. "One of the principal roots of my gloom was envy of the triumphs of Mordecai and Brian as compared with my own puny accomplishments," Weintraub confesses in his memoir.

In retrospect, it's difficult to imagine how a friendship between Weintraub and Richler got started, let alone endured. There was Richler, prickly as always with his youthful arrogance and self-righteousness thrown into the mix; and Weintraub, a bit lazy by his own admission, and also one of the most accommodating men you're likely to meet. Still, they had more in common than it appeared—Jewish Montrealers, lovers of literature. As Weintraub's memoir demonstrates, they were remarkably generous with each other. Richler worried about Weintraub's depressions, and Weintraub worried about Richler's brashness. They comforted each other through their first divorces and rejoiced in their early successes. Their friendship even survived frequent loans of money. "I sent Mordecai the manuscript of *Getting Started* when it was done," Weintraub recalls, "and he was a little miffed that I was only writing about the times he borrowed money from me and never how I borrowed money from him."

Weintraub admits Richler could be a very demanding friend, but he could also be loyal. "When he wanted you to do something for him, he wasn't at all shy about asking. But it did seem to work both ways. He would reciprocate. He was a lot closer to publishers than I was, for instance, and with my second novel *The Underdogs,* he certainly helped me out. He put in a good word with Jack McClelland. McClelland said he had reservations about the second half of the book, and Mordecai said to me that he promised Jack that I was going to deal with that. I did.

"And yes, of course, Mordecai could be hypercritical of people, merciless in his excoriation of those he didn't admire. But on the other hand, he could be very considerate. When I gave him the manuscript of *Getting*

Mordecai & Me

Started to read, he came across one or two things that might be mildly offensive to somebody we both knew, and he asked me to take them out. He felt that it might be wounding to the person in question. That wasn't really as out of character as people think."

In recent years, Weintraub's friendship with Richler changed. For one thing, Richler had stopped asking long ago for Weintraub's feedback on his manuscripts the way he once had with *Son of a Smaller Hero* (which Weintraub disliked) or *The Apprenticeship of Duddy Kravitz* (which Weintraub immediately recognized as a breakthrough). "In later years, he was more confident in himself. He also had Florence to show his work to," Weintraub says.

"I was also seeing less of him in later years. He and I had been drinking together, and I gave it up because I felt it was doing me some harm. So we ceased to be drinking companions. That was his method of relaxation after work—to go to a bar downtown. I used to do that with him, and then I was not doing it."

Still, as literary friendships go, Weintraub's and Richler's was unique and enviable. Tested by the different paths the two men took, and by their different levels of success, they still continued to cheer for each other and confide in each other. Their taste in literature and companionship and all things, really, did not change much since they were young men in Paris.

"One of the last times I saw him, I drove him to the Snowdon Deli so he could pick up some 'soul food' to take home—*blintzes* and *verenikes*, which he couldn't eat much then. Then we went for coffee. And he asked me how he could find out about computers. He was going to put some stuff about computers into his new novel and he knew nothing about them.

"I also visited him in his apartment not long before he died. I was going to New York, and he asked me to get him some of those cigars, those Davidoff ones, I think they were called. But he didn't want Florence to know."

After Richler's death, William Weintraub was approached by Michael Levine, the lawyer for the Richler estate, about writing Richler's official biography, but he declined. "I didn't think about it for very long," he says. "Too much work." Weintraub made a career for himself as a filmmaker at

The Influence of Anxiety

the National Film Board. But in 1996 he revived his writing career with *City Unique*, a book about Montreal in the 1940s and 1950s, its sin city heyday. On the cover, above the title, there is a blurb from Mordecai Richler calling it "an engaging, evocative book about Montreal's primetime." Now, as Weintraub and I part company, he grimaces and confesses he's working on another novel, his third, and his first in more than twenty years. He also confesses he's not having much fun. "Who needs another novel?" he says.

At Ziggy's, in the fall of 1997, I didn't expect that the stupid question I asked Mordecai Richler about *Barney's Version* was going to be the last stupid one I got to ask him. Sure, once I left Ziggy's I'd vowed never to interview him again, as I had in the past, but in a few years, when his next book came out, I expected to be sitting across from him at another bar, Sneezy's or Dopey's, a fidgety freelancer, in my fifties by then, asking him more questions he preferred not to answer. That was one scenario I envisioned that afternoon. The other was that the next time we met would be soon, so he could congratulate me on my book. The truth is I wasn't really thinking much about his novel that afternoon; I was thinking of my own, my first, *Jacob's Ladder*, which had been published just a month earlier. To be more specific, I was thinking about whether or not Richler had read it and, if he had, whether he had liked it.

Under other circumstances, this thought would never have occurred to me. I would have just assumed he hadn't read it, that he didn't even know it existed. But on this occasion, I had reason to believe otherwise. I knew for a fact that he had been sent the book. I also knew that he was obliged to read it or at least glance at it. It was one of the four books nominated for the Prix Parizeau, a literary award Richler had dreamed up a year earlier as a joke at the expense of then Quebec premier Jacques Parizeau. Parizeau, an ardent, long-time separatist, had revealed his true colours after losing the 1995 referendum for Quebec independence by the narrowest of margins. Crushed and likely more than a little tipsy, he had delivered an angry us-vs-them speech, blaming the loss of the Quebec nation on "money and the ethnic vote."

Mordecai & Me

It was the kind of comment that went a long way toward confirming everything Richler had been harping on about Quebec nationalism for almost two decades—that it was insular, xenophobic, and anti-Semitic. (Both of Parizeau's slurs seemed aimed at Jews, though not exclusively Jews.) Richler responded to the ugly aftermath of the 1995 referendum in his favourite way—with a prank. With the backing of his old friend Jack Rabinovitch, the man behind the Giller Prize, Richler announced the Prix Parizeau, an award for the year's best work of fiction written in English in Quebec. The sole criteria was that the prize, worth three thousand dollars, could only go to a writer who was not *pure laine*. (The Prix Parizeau was reminiscent of the William Lyon Mackenzie King Memorial Trophy Richler invented for *Joshua Then and Now*. It was in honour of Canada's "ostensibly bland and boring" but secretly "somewhat demented prime minister.")

Translated literally, the term *pure laine* means virgin wool, but it's more like purebred. It's a reference to French Quebecers who could, if they were so inclined, trace their ancestry back to the province's first French settlers, sort of like the Pilgrims who came over on the Mayflower. *Pure laine* was not a term you heard a lot anymore. In a multicultural society, it was deemed politically incorrect. Still, Richler was operating under the assumption that ethnic nationalism was at the root of Quebec's desire to separate from the rest of Canada. That he was attacked in the Montreal media, English as well as French, for making such an assumption and for establishing the Prix Parizeau, only proved, to his mind, that he was absolutely correct. He had more than a little experience with what happened when he hit a nerve, and he couldn't be blamed for thinking he'd zeroed in on another one.

For an English-language literary award in Quebec, the Prix Parizeau generated its share of controversy. Still, most observers assumed that the prize was just a one-time deal. I was worried they were right. My own novel, which had been delayed a season, had not appeared in time to be eligible for the first Prix Parizeau, so I was keeping my fingers crossed. While my novel had been overlooked for most of the other literary awards it had been submitted for, I couldn't keep myself from thinking that if Richler did like a running gag as much as I suspected he did, and if he kept the Prix Parizeau alive, I was a lock.

The Influence of Anxiety

So in the fall of 1997, when the Prix Parizeau surprisingly resurfaced, my confidence bloomed into overconfidence. With good reason, I think. First of all, the competition was not what you would call fierce. Although four books were nominated for the award, what hadn't been reported anywhere—and what I certainly wasn't going to tell anyone—was that only four books were submitted. Due to the controversy surrounding the award and Richler, most local publishers or publishers of local authors or the authors themselves decided not to participate. This was, in other words, the Special Olympics of literary competitions—everyone was a winner. And there were other encouraging signs. Set quite coincidentally during the 1995 referendum, *Jacob's Ladder* is the story of *fin-de-siècle* anglophones, Jews mostly, the children and grandchildren of St. Urbain Street, living their sad diminished lives (like characters in a Chekhov play, I liked to think) in a North Shore suburb of Montreal. There was even an allusion to Parizeau's concession speech—his "money and ethnic" remark—in the book. Finally, I couldn't have been less *pure laine* if I tried. I am pessimistic by nature, but even I couldn't imagine not being the front-runner, if not a flat-out sure thing. Finally, I had a hunch one of the three jurors, William Weintraub, would be in my corner. John Aylen, whom I didn't know at the time, was one of the other jurors.

But it was the third juror, I realized, who was going to make the difference. That was Mordecai Richler. So when he didn't mention my novel during our interview a few weeks before the Prix Parizeau was to be announced, I put the best spin on it I could. I assumed he wanted to remain neutral, not tip his hand. Still, what occurred to me at the time was how if the situation were reversed, I would never have been able to shut up about such a thing. I would have wanted him to know I'd read his novel, read it and liked it, and maybe even given him some indication, some subtle hint, that, yes, he could start thinking now about how he was going to spend that three grand. In retrospect, I realize there were at least two reasons why my novel didn't come up the day I interviewed him. The first was he hadn't gotten around to reading *Jacob's Ladder* yet or to making a decision on it. The second was that he had read it and already decided to vote against it. Which is what he did. At least I can safely make that assumption since at the Prix Parizeau ceremony, held at yet another downtown bar—Winnie's this time, with my acceptance speech memorized and burning a hole in my pocket—Richler announced that I had not won the prize after all. Obviously, I'm putting that the wrong way. He didn't announce anything of the kind. He announced the winner. Which wasn't me.

After David Manicom, a poet who'd written a collection of short stories called *Ice in Dark Water,* made his acceptance speech, William Weintraub came over to congratulate me on *Jacob's Ladder* and to tell me how much he enjoyed it. What was implicit in his comments was that his vote had gone to my novel. (He would tell me so directly later.) What was also implicit in Weintraub's comments was that Mordecai Richler had not voted for my book. In my undelivered acceptance speech, I thanked my family and friends and my publisher and the jurors. But I saved my last and most fulsome thanks for Richler. I told the story I've already told about how I had announced in a creative writing class in college that Richler was my favourite writer. Now, I planned to say, I felt like he was more than that—more like a kindred spirit. I would shake his hand firmly, and knowing him as well as I thought I did, he would mumble and lower his gaze, embarrassed. But a connection would finally be made, a bond formed. My invitation to the inner circle was assured. Thinking back now on what I didn't get to say and do, it's well worth three thousand dollars not to have to carry around the memory of getting up in public and making such a fool of myself.

I recently got my hands on Harold Bloom's *The Anxiety of Influence,* though I have yet to read it. Even so, the description on the back cover of the paperback edition tells me enough. Bloom's theory is that the relationship between a precursor and an individual artist is inevitably fraught with anxiety. "All literary texts," the blurb on Bloom's book reads, "are strong misreadings of those that precede them." When it came to Mordecai and me, what more did I need to know? I hadn't just been misreading his work, I had been doing it deliberately and for a long time. Aside from a few superficial similarities, we could hardly have been more different. There was no real reason for me to assume he would like my novel. I had wanted him to, that's all. It was, it turned out, just a dream.

In *Saul Bellow Drumlin Woodchuck,* Mark Harris says, "Writers walk around in other people's fantasies, nightmares, psychiatric sessions. Sometimes they are really there, and sometimes they are not." Sometimes, in other words, you see what you want to see. Big surprise. Mordecai Richler and I were not kindred spirits. One fact proved it: I always had been and still was desperate for someone else's approval; Richler never was.

"Mordecai believed in himself," William Weintraub told me almost a year after Richler died. "His whole attitude was take it or leave it. It was, 'I said that and I'm not ashamed of it, what the hell. I'm not going to sit down and explain it to you. If you don't like it, too damn bad.'"

Chapter 25
Swan Song

Every poet begins by rebelling (however "unconsciously") more strongly against the consciousness of death's necessity than all other men and women do.
—*The Anxiety of Influence*, Harold Bloom

Even before *Barney's Version* was nominated for the Giller Prize in the fall of 1997, it was inevitable that a new novel by Mordecai Richler was going to be viewed as an event and that Richler himself was going to be viewed as a kind of CanLit elder statesman, whether he welcomed the prospect or not. Mostly, he didn't. If he was suddenly being treated in a way he never had before—deferentially, that is—it meant one of two things: he wasn't doing his job as a satirist properly or he was getting soft.

A new Richler novel would also inevitably fuel speculation that this latest one might be his last. The long silences between his last four novels—nine years between *St. Urbain's Horseman*, *Joshua Then and Now* and *Solomon Gursky* and eight more until *Barney's Version*—made that seem like a distinct possibility.

Swan Song

When I interviewed him I asked him about the rumours that this was going to be his swan song, and, once again, I was greeted by a long silence and by the look. His answer was also dismissive—he must have had me down for a hopeless case by then. It was a variation on what he'd said over and over again in interviews and essays, including the first time I interviewed him in 1991. "I'm stuck with my original notion, which is to be an honest witness to my time, my place, and to write at least one novel that will make me remembered after my death. So I am compelled to keep trying," he told me. He sounded like he was reading a prepared statement. He was sincere, but bored with the inquiry, too. He was a novelist; what else would he be expected to do?

Barney's Version provided him with something to build on. He was, according to his longtime New York editor, Robert Gottlieb, just hitting his stride. It was William Weintraub's favourite Richler novel. And, along with *Solomon Gursky*, a favourite of Florence's as well. With its pitch-perfect combination of subject and style, and the dissolute and declining Barney Panofsky raging against, or at the very least ducking, the dying of the light, *Barney's Version* reads more like another breakthrough—*Duddy Kravitz* or *St. Urbain's Horseman* revisited—than a farewell. It is a novel about decline and deterioration, written in the shadow and, no doubt, under the influence of Richler's first brush with cancer a few years earlier. A fact that just serves to make it a better, more compassionate and courageous book.

A young writer tackles the subject of death because he knows he'd better—with a sense of obligation, as if it were a requirement for his literary resumé. You get that sense reading Richler's early novels. The martyrdom of André Bennett in *The Acrobats* (he's done in by a former Nazi), or Noah Adler's mother bowing out on the last page of *Son of a Smaller Hero* (a final guilt trip laid on her son), or the botched fake suicide by the main female character in *A Choice of Enemies*, are all either overly romantic or overly cynical. But Richler, even as he got older, was never very good at being philosophical about the subject of death. It was enough for him to be terrified of it, and the fear of death pervades his later novels. Jake in *St. Urbain's Horseman* and Joshua in *Joshua Then and Now* are perpetually awaiting catastrophe; meanwhile, the Star Maker in *Cocksure* and Mr.

Mordecai & Me

Bernard in *Solomon Gursky* are both determined to live forever. But it's not until *Barney's Version* that you get the sense that death is more than a plot device, that it is, instead, the author's primary preoccupation. Reminders of it are everywhere. From the thin, elegant cigar burning down on the novel's cover, to the Samuel Johnson quotes Barney favours: "But death, you know, hears not supplications, nor pays any regard to the convenience of mortals." Whenever he travels, Barney carries a copy of Boswell's *Life of Johnson* with him. "I want them to find it at my bedside," he says, "should I expire during the night."

There's also Barney's dinner with Hymie Mintzbaum, an old mentor and the man who got Barney started as a producer of bad TV shows. Having argued the last time they met, Barney is still pleased to meet Hymie at an upscale Hollywood restaurant. Until he sees him, that is. Hymie, once built like a linebacker, is now thin and frail. The victim of a stroke, he's dozing in a motorized wheelchair, a bib around his neck. His speech is slurred, incomprehensible, and he's at the mercy of a condescending waiter who is, in turn, under strict orders from Hymie's imperious daughter. Barney immediately cancels Hymie's prescribed meal of steamed vegetables with a poached egg and no salt, and orders him brisket and *latkes* with booze. Barney cuts Hymie's food and the two get drunk together. They are enjoying themselves until Hymie's daughter shows up and puts an abrupt end to the party. Emboldened by alcohol, Hymie aims his motorized wheelchair at his daughter and then at the waiter who squealed on him. At least, that's how Barney would like to remember the incident. He may, he admits, be indulging in some wishful, but faulty thinking. He has kept a note, however, that Hymie scrawled him that read, "I don't want to die yet."

All these gestures are minor variations on Barney's own major attempt to forestall his decline. The truth about death, its inevitability, is not only banal, it's impossible to argue with. Yet Barney and the people he cherishes most do argue, do bargain, do deny, do try to duck death. It was an instinct that came naturally to Barney and his creator. Richler kept on smoking and drinking and eating all the wrong foods long after he'd been warned not to, perhaps because heeding the warning would have meant acknowledging his mortality. In *Life of Johnson,* Samuel

Swan Song

Johnson's biographer, James Boswell provides his revered subject with a softball question: "Is not the fear of death natural to man?" Dr. Johnson replies, "So much so, Sir, that the whole of life is but keeping away thoughts of it."

Duddy Kravitz, Mr. Bernard, Moses Berger, Jake Hersh, Joshua Shapiro—Mordecai Richler's best and most memorable characters—all share a fear of dying. In *St. Urbain's Horseman,* even literature can't lessen the fear. Jake writes, "To read of meanness in others, promiscuity well observed or greed understood, to discover his own inadequacies shared no longer licenced them, any more than all the deaths that had come before could begin to make his own endurable."

Richler didn't confront death in his work so much as confront his fear of confronting it. "Fundamentally, all writing is about the same thing," he told a reporter for *Time* in 1971, "it's about dying, about the brief flicker of time we have here and the frustration it creates." That frustration is at the heart of *Barney's Version.* Barney is not so much a survivor as a hanger-on—hanging on for dear life. This is Barney's most endearing quality, and it may be Richler's, too. Richler was not an old man when he started *Barney's Version*—he was in his early sixties—but it still reads like an old man's novel, in the best sense. It is Richler's *Lear* and like Lear, Barney is, in the final tally, a man more sinned against than sinning.

"I think I snubbed him," I tell my wife, as she turns to me in bed. I didn't mean to wake her this time, but if you sleep in the same bed with someone every night for four years, after a while you get a sense of when they are troubled. Biorhythms, my dream analyst would probably call it. I call it tossing and turning.

"Who? Who did you snub?"

"You know, *him.* Mordecai Richler. And no, it's not another dream. This really happened, but I'd forgotten about it till now."

I was at a launch for a couple of friends who'd written a book about Montreal's fabled literary history. There was a chapter on Richler in the book, and a friend of one of my friends—a Richler drinking buddy—had talked Richler into making an appearance at the launch. It was, for

Mordecai & Me

Richler, a generous thing to do. For me, it was an opportunity to tell him off, which is what I was intent on doing as I watched him from across the room, waiting for my chance. I had to catch his eye, that's all. So I began to walk towards him, rehearsing my opening comments. Something like: *I expected better from a colleague and a fellow freelancer. I expected better from you. I mean we write for the same paper.* The closer I got to him, the more convinced I was that I wasn't going to back down. I really did have something to get off my chest. Something like: *Just because you are who you are and I am who I am doesn't give you the right to, well, I think you know what I'm talking about.* Clearly, my speech needed more rehearsing, but before I could retreat to a corner to gather my thoughts, Richler saw me coming. He looked straight at me, also unusual for Richler, and did the thing I least expected him to. He smiled, kind of warmly. He recognized me, perhaps from the picture that accompanied my book column in the newspaper, perhaps from the photo on the dust jacket of the novel he had rejected for the Prix Parizeau, or maybe from our last interview. It also looked as if he were about to say something, hello, probably, or nice to see you, but maybe something more. When I realized that, I just kept walking past him to the boxed wine and cheese cubes at the back of the bookstore.

"That does qualify as a snub," my wife says.

"It was all to do with the Galganov affair. Before your time, I think."

"No, I remember the Galganov business."

"Are you sure?"

"I was at that book launch, too, sweetheart. I remember you going on about—"

"Were you? I don't remember."

"Gee, thanks. You know what, I think I'll go back to sleep now."

"Good night."

I'm guessing that when my wife married a writer, there were some things for which she was prepared, but pettiness on such a grand scale was not among them. The Galganov business, or affair, as I prefer to call it, began with a review I wrote of a book called *Bastards* by a man named Howard Galganov. Head of his own advertising agency and a self-proclaimed Quebec anglo-rights activist, Galganov earned a tiny but boisterous place in Quebec's wacky political history. He organized some protests outside department stores—they were singled out for not advertising in English—and started a lobby group; he also ran unsuccessfully for a federal seat and for mayor of the suburb where he lived, also unsuccessfully. But he parlayed his notoriety into a stint on the radio as a noon hour talk show host. He was, among other things, an incredible blowhard, viewed as an extremist by Quebec nationalists and federalist moderates alike, and as an embarrassment by most of the English-speaking community. In fact, what he was saying wasn't such a big deal. It was the manner in which he was saying it—loudly and vulgarly—that got him attention.

Galganov was also extraordinarily inept on the radio, which made him, for me anyway, endlessly interesting to listen to. So when he started promoting his self-published book, *Bastards*, a collection of rants from his radio show, I thought it would be fun to review. In my experience as a reviewer, most bad books are competent but dreary. *Bastards* is the exception; it is magnificently awful. The reasons to read it are many, but chief among them is the way Galganov curses the people he disagrees with—calling them "sniveling, pathetic crybabies" and "separatist pieces of dirt." Then there's Galganov's *laissez-faire* approach to proofreading, which is a polite way of saying he doesn't proofread at all. Or his idiosyncratic use of the semicolon. He puts; them; any old; place. The review was a joy to write, and what was most appealing about it was that I managed to make fun of Galganov and Quebec nationalism at the same time. Two birds, one stone, that's called.

The review ran in the *Gazette* book section on Saturday, and I could hardly wait until Monday, when I knew that Galganov was sure to attack me on the radio. I was, I confess, a regular listener, and on Mondays he was angrier than ever, having had an entire weekend to gather grudges and fume over perceived insults to either him or Quebec's beleaguered anglo community. But when Galganov finally did get around to mentioning my review, he seemed more perplexed than angry. He said that even though he didn't know what I was talking about, he liked the review, and he was considering using it as a preface for the sequel to *Bastards*—*Sons of Bitches*, I'm guessing.

Mordecai & Me

The following weekend I was attending a "Books and Breakfast" series at the Ritz-Carlton for a column I planned to write about one of the authors scheduled to speak. I was seated at a table full of strangers, mostly well-off Jewish couples in their fifties and sixties, who were talking about Mordecai Richler's column in that morning's *Gazette*. The subject was Howard Galganov's new book and Richler was hilarious. Never better. Had I seen it? Seen it? I said, I wrote it.

When I got home I read Richler's column, and what I expected to be just a coincidence—another column about *Bastards* a week after mine—didn't seem so coincidental. Some of the references were similar: I had joked about Galganov calling the pundits at a local commercial radio station elitists; so had Richler. This wasn't particularly troubling since there was every reason to believe that two people reading a book as silly as Galganov's would latch onto the same examples. Harder to explain was the example Richler gave of one of Galganov's more colourful epithets. He quoted Galganov referring to some group or other as "scumsucking, elitist limey bastards." But the thing was, Galganov hadn't said that, I had. In my column, I had conjured up a Galganovian spin on the *Declaration of Independence.* Imagine, I wrote, Thomas Jefferson's famous lines this way: "We hold these truths to be self-evident, that all men are created equal. . . . And if you don't like it, you can rot in hell you powder-wigged, scumsucking, elitist limey bastards." Galganov may have hated everyone, but even he had no reason to find fault with the pre-revolutionary British. He never used the word *limey.* Which indicated a couple of things: first, Richler probably hadn't read *Bastards* as closely as I had. Second, he had read my column, though not that closely either, and copied my quote. It wasn't exactly plagiarism, but it was in the ballpark.

I mentioned it to my editor who mentioned it to Richler's editor, but, seeing as how he was a star columnist and I was relegated to the book pages, nothing more was said about it. But that wasn't what rankled—what rankled was the day after Richler's column ran, Galganov spent the first fifteen minutes of his program cursing Richler and challenging him to come on his show for a debate. Of course, Richler maintained a dignified silence.

"And you didn't," my wife says.

"What?"

"Maintain a dignified silence. Remember, I told you to write to the publisher and you said what good would that do. And I said if you weren't going to do anything about it, what was the point of complaining? And you said—"

"No point complaining? And you call yourself my wife."

"Right, that's exactly what you said. Then you drew horns and glasses on Richler's newspaper photo and showed it to me. That was kind of sweet, I thought. You were sharing your feelings. See, it wasn't before my time."

"I'm glad we cleared that up. Now you can go back to sleep."

"I will, as soon as you promise me one thing. None of this Galganov business gets into the book."

"You have my word."

"Good." My wife leans across me then to kiss me, I think. Instead, she reaches over to my night table and turns on the light.

"Remember Chapter 60," she says, opening *Don't Sweat the Small Stuff* to the table of contents. "Turn Your Melodrama into a Mellow-Drama."

"Your point?"

"That you can be bigger than all this."

"How long have you known me?" The question is meant to be rhetorical, but she answers it anyway.

"You can try," my wife says.

She's right. I can. What's more, I should. There's an embarrassing postscript to the Galganov affair. Rereading *Solomon Gursky Was Here*, I realized that on at least two occasions, I plagiarized Richler without being conscious of it. In his novel, there is a character with one blue eye and one brown eye; in my novel—which I started writing not long after I read *Solomon Gursky* in 1989—there is a character with one green eye and one brown eye. In his novel, the similarities between Chinese dumplings and Jewish *kreplech* are noted; in my novel, a character makes a speech about brotherhood in which he notes that Chinese dumplings and matzo balls, like people, aren't that different.

"It's like you always tell me," my wife says, "bad writers borrow, good writers steal."

"I think I stole that somewhere."

Mordecai & Me

Barney's Version is a fitting swan song, after all. It is a novel full of petty concerns played out in the shadow of the one big unavoidable concern—obliteration. Barney is determined to set the record straight and insists that's why he's telling his story in the first place. "To come clean," he says, "there are only insults to avenge and injuries to nurse." But there's another reason Mordecai Richler is telling Barney's story: Barney, like his memory and identity, is gradually disappearing. From the start of his career, Richler talked a good game about how a writer should be "the loser's advocate." In his first novel, *The Acrobats,* his anti-hero André Bennett says, "Look, every human being is to be approached with a sense of wonder." But the more outrageous and scathing his fiction became the more selective his sense of wonder became. The characters he loved were invariably full of appetite, scoundrels and schemers, boozers and pranksters, con men and crazies. The characters he mocked were hypocrites and poseurs—suburbanites. It so happens they were also men and women who believed in God and their community, who did charity work, who were proud of their kids, who called their mothers every day. They were people who took no chances, who led ordinary, uneventful lives. Occasionally, Richler put himself in their shoes, but the fit was never comfortable. In *Duddy Kravitz,* Uncle Benjy earns some sympathy, mostly for dying. In *St. Urbain's Horseman,* Jake's Uncle Abe also gets a chance to tell his smug, superior nephew off: "You think I was born fat and bald, with a heart condition. Wasn't I young once, and aren't you going to grow old? Aren't we all made of flesh?" Uncle Abe goes on to defend his choice to live a respectable life and carry on a time-honoured tradition:

> I brought them up, Irwin and Doris [his children], and when the day comes they will bury me. I wear my father's *talith* in *shul*, next Irwin will wear it, and then his son and his son's son. It's a good life. I enjoy it. I am not one of your bitten Hershes, a wanderer, coming home only to poke snide fun and stir up trouble. A shit-disturber.

Richler has the last word, though: Irwin, we already know, is a twit, and Jake's sympathies would always remain with the shit-disturbers. So would Richler's, but in *Barney's Version* he makes a more sustained and deliberate effort than usual to understand characters he seldom understood or cared about before. The Second Mrs. Panofsky, an insufferable *yenta*, grossly obese, a sucker for New Age crystals, is nevertheless sympathetic. Barney acknowledges she was not a bad person: "Had she not fallen into my hands but instead married a real, rather than a pretend, straight arrow, she would be a model wife and mother today." Chaim Charnofsky, the horribly narrow-minded father of Barney's first wife, also has a side to his story. Here, his nephew reluctantly presents it:

> [Chaim] is an embittered man, yes, but with cause, and many have reason to be grateful to him. Myself foremost. Chaim was the first of the Charnofskys to come to America from Poland, and from the very beginning he denied himself, pinching pennies, and sending for relatives. If not for his devotion my parents would have remained in Lodz, where I would have been born, and Auschwitz would have been the end of our story. . . . But the children of many of those whom Chaim brought over here, men and women who have prospered in America, now regard him as an embarrassment.

Even the novel's main villain, Terry McIver, a CanLit mediocrity, in Barney's view, and the writer whose slanderous memoir provokes Barney to write his own memoir, is cut some slack in the end. When McIver dies unexpectedly, Barney relents, "McIver, to give him his due, perservered against long odds. He rode a small, unnecessary talent to recognition in his own country, which is more than I ever did or dared. I should not have been so cruel to him." It's a curious, unexpected confession. It makes you wonder, if Richler had lived, what would have been next? Heartfelt apologies for Robin Mathews? Jacques Parizeau?

Richler may not have cared about being liked, as he made it clear to me in our last interview, but he cared about whether Barney was liked. He cared about the readers' sympathies and whether Barney would be able to attract them. On this count, he didn't have to worry. Barney may be, in his own words, "an impenitent rotter" and "a malevolent man," but he's also a teddy bear. He is more playful than politically incorrect; he is inevitably redeemed by a kind remark or gesture. He's also loved by

Mordecai & Me

family and friends; we know he will be mourned and remembered by them. *Barney's Version* may be about one man's solitary disintegration—about how "nobody truly ever understands anybody else"—but Barney is not alone in the end. "Who in the hell could love Duddy Kravitz?" Duddy asks during a cameo appearance in *St. Urbain's Horseman.* From the moment we meet Duddy, this is a legitimate question. With *Barney's Version,* the question comes full circle: "Who in the hell could not love Barney Panofsky?" There is never any risk in *The Apprenticeship of Duddy Kravitz* of its hero becoming lovable. It's not in Duddy's plan. For that matter, it's not in Jake's or Joshua's, either, just as it wasn't in Mordecai Richler's. But in *Barney's Version,* Richler finally succeeds in giving his readers what they may have been longing for from the start—a *mensh,* a flawed man who is ultimately good-hearted. The road from Duddy Kravitz to Barney Panofsky may have been straight, even narrow at times, but it was still a long way for Mordecai Richler to travel.

Chapter 26
An Appreciation of a Kind

> *Biography is a spectre viewed by a spectre.*
> —Saul Bellow to Mark Harris

In his disapproving review of Susan Cheever's *Home Before Dark*, Mordecai Richler made note of the daughter's "picky footnotes" to her father's journals—for example, her correction of a trivial error about who won the 1938 World Series. Later, Richler included this filial fastidiousness in *Barney's Version* through the character of Barney's eldest son and literary executor, Michael Panofsky. The conceit of the novel is that it's a memoir being published all but posthumously, while Barney, lost to Alzheimer's, resides in a nursing home, in "a near-vegetable state." The structure of Richler's narrative, a kind of pinball action from one bout of forgetfulness and remembering to another—"table talk," Barney calls it—is deliberately full of digressions and provides an evocative glimpse into its hero's mental deterioration. After the fact, Michael, a successful lawyer, sees to the manuscript's publication, adding an afterword and a series of irritatingly irrelevant footnotes. Michael plainly loves his father, but that doesn't keep Richler from portraying him as an anal-retentive prig.

So Barney ends up with a Boswell of his own after all. And even if Michael may not be ideal, Barney can be grateful for one thing: at least his son is not a writer. *Barney's Version* is full of Richler's inside jokes, his sniping, through Barney, at the writing life. Starry-eyed when he arrives in Paris, Barney leaves with one thought in mind, to steer clear of all artists and writers in the future. "I've never known a writer or a painter anywhere," Barney says, "who wasn't a self-promoter, a braggart, and a paid liar or a coward, driven by avarice and desperate for fame."

Margaret Laurence once referred to writers as a tribe. A multitude of cliques is more like it—often a clique of one's own. As for the fame writers are so desperate for, there's only so much of it to go around, and don't think we don't know it. Which explains why we always do our best to cut each other down to size. The better the writer, the better he is likely to be at wielding the knife. In *A Moveable Feast*, Ernest Hemingway's posthumous memoir of his days in Paris in the 1920s, Hemingway chronicles a road trip through the French countryside with F. Scott Fitzgerald. The outcome is a masterpiece of comradely character assassination. With friends like Hemingway, Fitzgerald didn't need his wife, Zelda, to emasculate him. Hemingway casts doubt on both Fitzgerald's talent—he deemed Fitzgerald a kind of idiot savant and *The Great Gatsby* a brilliant fluke—and his virility. Of course, it's Fitzgerald who makes the mistake of asking if his penis might be too small. "Too small for what?" Hemingway all but asks.

Literary animosity is older than paper. Aristophanes considered Euripides a "maker of ragamuffin manikins." Ben Jonson called Shakespeare lazy; Tolstoy couldn't bear Shakespeare either. Mark Twain couldn't abide Henry James and neither could H.L. Mencken, who called James "an idiot, and a Boston idiot to boot." Evelyn Waugh said, "James Joyce went mad to please the Americans." Truman Capote famously said of Jack Kerouac's improvised style in *On the Road*, "That's not writing, that's typing." Gore Vidal, commenting on Capote's death, called it a

An Appreciation of a Kind

good career move. Of Norman Mailer, Vidal said, "No one reads him. They hear of him." Mailer replied, "Nobody Gore knows reads me," and then punched or threatened to punch Vidal out to be on the safe side. James Baldwin called Mailer a middle-class Jew, and Mailer, who was a middle-class Jew, didn't take it as a compliment. Mary McCarthy said that every word Lillian Hellman wrote was a lie, including "and" and "the." Of John Updike, John Cheever wrote in his journals, "I would go to considerable expense and inconvenience to avoid his company," adding, "his work seems motivated by covetousness, exhibitionism and a stony heart." Tom Wolfe referred to Updike, Mailer, and John Irving as "the three stooges." Richard Ford, after receiving a lukewarm review in the *New York Times* from fellow novelist Alice Hoffman, took one of Hoffman's novels out in the backyard and shot it; then his wife shot it. And Vladimir Nabokov didn't care for anyone. When asked what he thought of his contemporaries' books, Nabokov said, "They seem to be all by one and the same writer—who is not even the shadow of my shadow."

Some tribe.

"The children don't play nicely together," is how Mordecai Richler describes the intramural bickering displayed in Norman Podhoretz's literary memoir, *Making It*. In his review of the book, Richler is discussing one particularly "brilliant, influential, but astonishingly smug body of New York writers"—Podhoretz, Dwight Macdonald, Leslie Fiedler, Baldwin, Mailer *et al.*—but he could have been speaking of writers in general. He could have also added that given this propensity for writers not to play nicely, the literary biography has a built-in and fatal flaw: writers themselves usually end up telling the stories of other writers. They can do it well or they can do it poorly, but however they do it, they have a hard time not looking petty or judgemental or foolish. Which is what makes writing about other writers so much fun to read.

Well, fun for some. From a young age, Richler demonstrated a predisposition for righteous indignation—as a kid on St. Urbain Street, he was always up on his high horse about one thing or another, and when someone didn't live up to his moral expectations, he wrote them off. He did that with his grandfather and later with his mother. (Although that was mutual; she didn't appreciate her son's comic portrait of her as an interfering Jewish mother in *St. Urbain's Horseman* or as a stripper in *Joshua Then and Now.*) But when it came to writers and artists, Richler could be forgiving—at least towards those he felt were worthy of forgiveness. So while John Buchan, a former Governor General of Canada and the author of the novel *The 39 Steps,* and Ian Fleming, the creator of James Bond, are criticized for the anti-Semitic characters in their work, H.L. Mencken, an unapologetic Jew-hater, gets off with only a slap on the wrist from Richler. The reason: Richler admired his writing from the time he was a kid. The same goes for Hemingway and Faulkner and Céline. Richler's double standard—one set of rules for writers and artists he admired and a harsher set for those he didn't—is evident in a piece he wrote about Woody Allen. Included in his 1998 nonfiction collection *Belling the Cat,* the piece is prefaced by Richler's note that it was first published in 1991, in *Playboy,* "long before Woody Allen's troubled private life attracted so much media attention." Then Richler adds, "I have not brought it up to date, as it were, as a matter of principle. Woody Allen's private life is his business, not mine."

At first glance, Richler's reticence seems admirable, but look again—it's also convenient. Remember, Richler considered himself a moralist and, given that self-designation, it should have been difficult for him—if not impossible—to pass up the chance to pronounce on a man who was, after all, sleeping with Mia Farrow and her adopted daughter at the same time. If that wasn't bad enough, Richler also managed to ignore the fact that Allen's nebbishy, but honourable movie alter egos never stop fussing, albeit amusingly, about society's decaying values.

While Richler could say from atop his high horse that Woody Allen's private life was none of his business, he hardly felt the same way when it came to writing about businessmen like Sam Bronfman, the Reichmans, politicians like Brian Mulroney and athletes like Gordie Howe and Pete Rose. Their personal peccadilloes provided juicy material and were, as far as Richler was concerned, fair game for gossip and speculation. For example, in his review of *Mr. Sam,* the Michael Marrus biography of Sam Bronfman, Richler gleefully recounts Sam Bronfman's efforts to become respectable by placing suits of armour in his Westmount mansion and dressing up his servants. Richler also can't resist making note of Bronfman's wife Saidye crooning "Baby Face" to her husband at his eightieth birthday. In "Hail Brian and Farewell," a *Saturday Night* article included in *Belling the Cat* under the title "Bye Bye Brian," Richler comments on Brian Mulroney's dissembling personality: "All politicians lie, but few as often, or as mellifluously, as did Sincerely Yours, Brian Mulroney, who lied even when it wasn't necessary, just to keep in shape, his voice, a dead giveaway, sinking into his Guccis whenever he was about to deliver one of his whoppers." While this sums up Mulroney's career and character rather nicely, that's not the point. The point is why do Mr. Sam and Mulroney get it in the neck while Woody Allen gets off easy?

But Richler's real problem with writers writing about other writers may have been that they just didn't make Boswells the way they used to. And there, he had a point. Literary biographers could no longer be expected to be respectful, or to put literature with a capital L first. They also could no longer be trusted to keep their agendas to themselves. The way, say, Richard Ellmann seemed to, writing about James Joyce, or Leon Edel did immortalizing Henry James. *Saul Bellow Drumlin Woodchuck* is as much about Mark Harris's desire to write about Bellow as it is about Bellow's life or work. It's Harris we really get to know, as he chases after Bellow, even stumbling into a not entirely innocent entanglement with Bellow's most recent ex-wife. Harris comes off as an intellectual and driven *shlemiel,* an almost Bellovian character. Bellow, meanwhile, remains a tease. He clearly liked the idea of having a biography written about him, and he was willing to cooperate, but only up to a point. *Sir Vidia's Shadow,* Paul Theroux's kiss-and-tell memoir of his relationship with V.S. Naipaul, is also more revealing of its author than its subject. Theroux is merciless, referring to his one-time mentor as "a crank" and "a blamer."

"I had admired his talent. After a while I admired nothing else," Theroux concludes. "Finally I began to wonder about his talent, seriously to wonder, and doubted it when I found myself skipping pages in his more recent books. In the past I would have said the fault was mine."

Nicholson Baker's *U and I* is kinder to its subject, but it is also, in the end, more about Baker than Updike. Baker admits he's only read a small

Mordecai & Me

portion of Updike's work and declares he won't be bothering to read the rest, despite working on *U and I*. Meanwhile, the real scoop in Ian Hamilton's *In Search of J.D. Salinger* is not in the book, but rather a consequence of it. Hamilton's attempt to record the reclusive author's life succeeds mainly in flushing Salinger out of hiding: Salinger decides to sue Hamilton over "fair use" of a cache of his unpublished letters. In a 1986 deposition intended to block publication of Hamilton's book, Salinger is obliged to admit, under oath, that he is still writing fiction. As a self-congratulatory Hamilton writes, "In the course of this well documented lawsuit, the public is learning more about Salinger than it has in the last 34 years." Coincidentally, Richler reviewed *In Search of J.D. Salinger* for the *New York Times Book Review,* and while he allows that Hamilton has respectable credentials as a poet and a biographer—most notably of Robert Lowell—he still finds the whole literary biography business unseemly, no matter who's doing it. "At the risk of sounding stuffy," Richler writes, "I think it indecently hasty to undertake a biography-cum-critical study of a still-working writer."

"Every writer's life is his own," Saul Bellow tells Mark Harris, his wannabe Boswell. Actually, Bellow tells Harris this through a mutual friend, but Harris gets the message eventually. He's being ditched. Just in time, too, since Harris is gradually arriving at the conclusion that trying to pin Bellow down is futile. Harris's mock biography, *Saul Bellow Drumlin Woodchuck,* takes its title from a poem by Robert Frost in which a woodchuck demonstrates how evasiveness can be an effective survival technique. "I was yet to learn, by my study of Bellow," Harris acknowledges, "that an artist could remain alive only by resisting every effort to make him into a monument."

For James Atlas, Bellow was more white whale than reluctant rodent. Still, when I met Atlas a few years ago, he hardly seemed the Captain Ahab type. There was nothing particularly daunting or driven about him. He looked, instead, like an aging hall monitor, a teacher's pet for whom being clever had always come rather easily. The trajectory of Atlas's career was, indeed, upward and unobstructed. A Harvard man and a Rhodes

An Appreciation of a Kind

scholar, Atlas studied at Oxford with Ellmann, the author of *James Joyce*, the book considered by many to be the best literary biography since James Boswell's *Life of Johnson*. At twenty-eight, Atlas wrote an acclaimed biography of his own, *Delmore Schwartz: The Life of an American Poet*. He also wrote a novel, which fared less well, and he served as an editor at the *New York Times Magazine*. Mainly, though, he made his mark as a literary journalist, a regular contributor to magazines like *Vanity Fair* and *The New Yorker*. Still, it was his biography of Delmore Schwartz that led to Atlas telling Bellow's story. Bellow had been a friend of Schwartz's; in fact, he had made "the dissolute genius poet" the model for the title character in his novel *Humboldt's Gift*. Bellow read Atlas's book and liked it. He also liked the fact that Atlas was, like him, from Chicago and had grown up in a similar world. Once again, Bellow seemed to welcome the idea of a biography. He was also much more cooperative with Atlas than he had been a decade earlier with Harris. He didn't attempt to silence any of the family, friends or colleagues that Atlas intended to contact. He also granted Atlas twelve one-on-one interviews and gave him access to all his letters, papers, and unpublished manuscripts. In the introduction to the biography, Atlas recalls asking Bellow's son why his father let him do the book. His son's reply was, "He realized that you weren't going to go away."

Why he didn't go was the question on Atlas's mind when we met in the fall of 2000 at the end of his publicity tour for *Bellow*. Atlas was wearing a jaunty bow tie to lunch—Bellow-style—but it was the only thing even remotely jaunty about him. Slumped in the last booth in a noisy deli a few blocks from St. Urbain Street, Atlas's expression was glum. His body language was worse, almost dismaying, a perpetual slouch. Even his suit seemed to be shrugging. It was not the posture I was used to seeing from authors on tour. Even if they were fed up with hotel rooms and the same questions over and over again, even if they had developed, during the course of the tour, grave doubts about their work, most put up a front of *bonhomie* and solicitousness. (Except for Richler, who was never solicitous or happy to see you. Or was that just me?)

Atlas should have been on top of the world. He'd just completed an eleven-year project and he had been praised for it on the front page of the *New York Times Book Review*, but instead, he looked like a man with the weight of the world on his shoulders. His biography had proved that there was no way to write a definitive book about Bellow, who defied such a notion by being still around, still writing, and still productive. At eighty-four, he'd fathered a child with his fifth wife.

When we met, Atlas didn't know whether Bellow had read the biography or not, and he was resigning himself to not knowing. He did know that Bellow's wife had announced that she wasn't "very happy about it." He also knew, on the evidence of a review in *The New Republic* he'd seen on the plane on his way to Montreal, that the critic James Wood was not enchanted with his book. Wood sums up Atlas's exhaustive six-hundred-page book as superficial, with no more depth than a celebrity profile in *Vanity Fair*. But Wood's main point was that Atlas was ignoring the big picture in favour of a handful of petty incidents. So what if Bellow behaved badly to a few friends and a few ex-wives? Didn't all his profoundly moving fiction more than make up for that? Shouldn't we cut a great writer a little slack?

I reviewed Atlas's biography a few weeks before I interviewed him and made a similar point. The book was undermined by a tone of disappointment, I said, by Atlas's disappointment that the great man he had chosen to immortalize was not somehow greater. This is a contemporary reflex not to trust greatness, to feel the compulsion to cut it down to size. Still, given that, my own judgement of Atlas's biography was generous. I still considered it a remarkable achievement—most of all because it read like a good long novel, like a Bellow novel, in fact. It showed its subject to be as multilayered and complicated as any of the characters Bellow created. But Atlas, who'd read my review when he arrived in Montreal, was in no mood to let himself off the hook. "So you thought I was too hard on him, too," Atlas said to me almost the moment I sat down. "Well, you weren't alone in your response, and it's made me really think. Every book is flawed, that's for sure. Including mine. But I tried incredibly hard not to write a tear-down book. Obviously, I spent a decade on this, and I revere Bellow's work. He's a genius.

"But did I get sick of Bellow? That's a fair question. I've examined my heart, faulty organ that it is, and, no, I don't think I did. Is it partly my fault if the book came out with this tone? Do I have a secret agenda? I don't think so. If I do, I desperately struggled against it. Was I too tough on Bellow personally? It's hard to say. How much does this bother me? I wrestle with that every day."

Atlas shrugged, and I remembered that shrug a little while later when an even harsher attack on his book than the one by Wood appeared in *Harper's*. For the reviewer, Lee Siegel, the problem with Atlas's biography came down to envy. Atlas wanted to be like Bellow, and when he couldn't be, he set out to make Bellow more like him—small and petty. When Atlas's one and only novel failed, Siegel writes, "a bilious biographer was born."

When I saw that review, I imagined Atlas reading it and slouching even lower at his desk, his posture in free fall. Then I imagined myself in his shoes, which was surprisingly easy, and I felt myself slumping, too.

Chapter 27
Legacy

Our lives are absurd. Hoo boy, are they ever.
—Joshua Then and Now

In Ian Hamilton's biography of J.D. Salinger, Hamilton opens with a statement that was self-serving, self-justifying and, in Mordecai Richler's opinion, "in highly questionable taste." Salinger, Hamilton writes, is "in any real-life sense, invisible, as good as dead." Working on this book in the year or so since Richler's death, I've often had the opposite feeling—that Richler may as well be alive. Everyone I meet has an anecdote they want to share about him. Everyone in Montreal, certainly, seems to be carrying around a piece of him: from an encounter in Wilensky's or from the Baron Byng days, a meeting at a downtown bar, a restaurant in the Eastern Townships, a wedding attended by a friend of a friend, a reading that went memorably wrong. Everyone has an opinion on what made him tick, too. In an appreciation of Richler in *The New Yorker*, former

Legacy

Montrealer Adam Gopnik pointed out that by the end of his life, Richler had "become inseparable from a place, Montreal, and even a country, Canada, without ever flattering or even saying anything particularly nice about either."

At a variety of events honouring him since his death, I've listened to debates over how Jewish he was, how Canadian, how Québécois, what kind of husband he was, what kind of father, how much money he made and whether or not he spoke French. I've overheard people talking about him in the locker room at the gym and while I'm picking up my son at daycare. Our real estate agent called with a story about selling Richler's uncle's house. The uncle told her how his famous nephew showed up with two shopping bags full of booze and drank straight through his father's *shiva* (the traditional seven-day mourning period). He didn't say a word to anyone, but he was listening. Was he ever! Everything the family said showed up in *St. Urbain's Horseman*, the scene in which Jake attends his father's shiva. "All of it in an exaggerated manner, of course. Why? Why else? To make us look bad," the uncle told her. Someone else sent me a short story he'd written, based on his experience driving Richler around town during the shooting of the movie version of *Joshua Then and Now*. The librarian at the Jewish Public Library said, "You have to call my brother. He grew up with Richler." So did the father of a friend. She read *St. Urbain's Horseman* some years back, so she could talk to her father about his childhood, his old neighbourhood. But when she mentioned the novel to her father, he just said, "Richler. Feh!"

In the meantime, the Richler estate, overseen by Michael Levine, is in high gear. Richler-related projects keep getting floated—including a television mini-series based on *St. Urbain's Horseman*, a movie version of *Barney's Version*, an animated children's TV series based on the *Jacob Two-Two* books, even a one-man stage show based on Richler's life and work, with Mordecai as a kind of kosher-style Mark Twain. There was also the nationally televised tribute a year after his death, along with plans for "a major Richler academic symposium" to be held in Montreal some time in the next year or two.

"It's hard to say what Mordecai would have thought about all this," his friend William Weintraub told me. "He might have been a bit embarrassed, but Mordecai was an accessible writer, and he always wanted his books to be read."

An official biography of Richler is not yet in the works, but Michael Levine is talking to lots of candidates for the job, casting a wide net. I know four writers, myself included, who have had preliminary discussions with Levine on the subject. In my case, he called because he had heard about my proposal for *Mordecai & Me* from a Toronto publisher. I said I could send him a sample chapter. A couple of weeks later, Levine sent me an e-mail he'd dictated to his assistant saying that he was "particularly touched" by my proposal. I'm not sure what he meant by that or if he meant anything, but I didn't write back. Neither did he.

I also received a telephone call from Michael Posner, a journalist with the *Globe and Mail*, who is working on an oral biography of Richler, which is to say he is doing the sort of thing I decided not to do. He has permission to talk to Richler's family and closest friends, as well as acquaintances and colleagues, and is asking them to reminisce about Richler. He called because he said he might want to talk to me about Richler. "Same here," I said. But we haven't met. The notion of the two of us sitting across from each other, secretly trying to figure out who has a better fix on Richler, who is doing a better, more definitive job of exploiting his memory, is too unsettling to contemplate. Besides, everyone I have finally got around to talking to about Richler seems to have already talked to Posner. "He's really digging hard," William Weintraub told me.

For instance, Posner talked to Michael Coren before I did. Coren, a columnist with the *Toronto Sun* as well as the author of biographies of G.K. Chesterton, J.R.R. Tolkien and others, received Richler's blessing to work on a biography in the early 1990s. Richler, his family and friends would all cooperate fully. "I knew Daniel Richler," Coren told me, "and I had met Mordecai a few times socially, and he seemed to like me. So I just asked him directly if I could write his biography and he said yes. I was very flattered because I knew he'd turned down a lot of people. But he was keen on the idea. He didn't want an academic to do it, and I guess he saw me as a bit of a rebel. It was a huge undertaking, and I thought I could do it, but I think you have to be from Montreal to do a book like that. I also wasn't a huge fan of his work—I have to be honest. All of this

Montreal-50s-Jewish-thing—I got tired of it. It took me a year and a half to pay back the advance, but when I decided to give the biography up, it was a great weight off my shoulders."

More than a few times over the last year, my wife has also wondered, sometimes aloud, whether I should give up this project. "What purpose would that serve?" I usually snarl, which tends to make her point for her—that writing a book about Richler has not been good for my temperament or our relationship. Her case is getting stronger: the crankiness—me, the walking on eggshells—her, the sleepless nights—both of us. Recently, she also made me a long overdue appointment with a G.P.—without my knowledge or consent—for which I have no choice but to be grateful since he took routine blood tests and diagnosed me with Diabetes Type 2. It may be reversible, he said, though he couldn't promise anything. My wife doesn't blame the book for my condition, but she wonders, also aloud, if it could be a contributing factor. I am, according to my doctor, one of those people you read about in the newspaper every day who drops dead just like that. I thought that was everyone, I considered saying, but didn't. "Don't worry," he added reassuringly, "we're going to make sure you stick around. We need our writers."

There are limits to the negative imagination, Stanley Elkin said. "The head never performs without a safety net and bad news and pain are always surprises. We fantasize upwards." Mordecai Richler expected to write another book. When he returned to Montreal from his home in London a few months before he died, he reassured his daughter Emma that "nothing's imminent," as Emma writes in "Two or Three Things I Know about Grief." A poignant account of her reluctant coming-to-terms with the loss of her father, the piece was published in *Maclean's* a year after Richler's death. It's written in diary form, with Emma filling her father in on "some old news you missed out on," telling him that "Florence is still marking time by you, rushing home to you." She concludes with, "There has been a terrible mistake."

Mordecai Richler knew the situation was grim when he came back to Montreal to find out the cancer was back, but he was being philosophical

Mordecai & Me

about it, according to his drinking buddy John Aylen, and he wasn't throwing in the towel. He made a point of calling Aylen to tell him about a conversation he'd had with his doctor. "Mordecai told me that he had asked the doctor, 'Do you think I have another book in me?' And the doctor said, 'Oh, yes, don't stop writing.' Mordecai was very encouraged by that, encouraged enough to repeat it," Aylen said.

Richler's death felt like "a terrible mistake" for a lot of people when they first heard he'd died, no matter what they may have thought of him. He'd been around so long, and he'd been such a consistent source of amusement and aggravation, that like him or not, he seemed more of a monument than a man. "He had such energy and strength," his New York editor, Robert Gottlieb, told *Maclean's*. "You felt, my God, anyone who can eat as hard and drink as hard, and smoke as hard with apparently no reaction except some excess weight. . . . He seemed indestructible. Florence knew he was not indestructible, but she could only do what she could do. He was not going to change the way he lived."

A couple of months before he died, I'd heard rumours from a newspaper editor who had, in turn, heard from a source close to the Richler family that it was only a matter of time. But Richler hung on and the obit had to wait. In the meantime, I must have forgotten that I knew he was dying—at least I hope I did. Around that same time I was doing one of my speeches at the Montefiore Club. I called it "Confessions of a Book Reviewer: Or Why I'll Never Interview Mordecai Richler Again." Thinking back on the subtitle now, I shudder at how I could have been so tactless, so cold-blooded.

But for a writer, cold-bloodedness goes with the job. At the end of Brian Moore's novel, *Answer from Limbo*, the narrator attends his mother's burial, but instead of mourning her death, a more pressing instinct takes over and he begins to take mental note of the proceedings, filing away everything he sees for later use. He observes "a few clods of earth" on the shovel and the "rumbling sound as they struck the coffin lid." Then he thinks, "Remember, man, that thou art dust. And remember this. Some day you will write it. I was no longer a mourner." At his mother's funeral, Philip Roth had a similar bout of self-awareness and self-loathing. "This profession even fucks up grief," he wrote. "What kind of people are we? We don't even stop taking notes at a funeral."

Legacy

I was taking notes, too, while my mother was dying. I was determined not to forget anything. I was twenty-one and I wanted to be a writer. I thought it was enough to be grief-stricken and angry. I thought it was enough that I had this terrible time in my life to get down on paper. And I was angry with everyone: the nurses, doctors, undertakers, relatives, friends, the rabbi, God. I wanted to know why this had happened. I wanted revenge. I wanted my mother back. And I wrote as if the words on the page could accomplish that. I have never felt more driven, more inspired. But when I reread what I had written, I also realized it wasn't enough. Everyone has a mother, it occurred to me in an instant of cold-blooded writerly detachment, and everyone's mother dies. I have disliked myself often since then, though never as much. Still, like it or not, I wasn't just a mourner anymore. Which is a reason for writing in the first place. Not just to elude death, but to defeat it, somehow to have the last word. Writers may dream about making a splash, but they daydream about their legacy. In Martin Amis's novel *The Information,* two writers compete for fame and fortune. But the real competition, Amis told me when I interviewed him, is for much bigger stakes.

"What all writers should be thinking about is the big prize, the only prize—immortality," Amis said. "No advance or award or rave review makes any difference to the real test. How are you going to do when you are dead? And you'll never know if you pass that test. Still I have to think my books will have a long life. I've always believed in looking at the long view; now I'm clinging to it."

Some of that clinging is discernible in Richler's work, starting with *St. Urbain's Horseman.* His later novels have a great deal in common—they are long, comic, and similarly structured (Richler's then-and-now, back-and-forth style). They are a bit desperate for import and perhaps better for it. All are imbued with the notion, given the increasingly long time Richler was taking between novels, that this may be his last chance to write something that would endure. But his assessment of his own work was never entirely free of doubt. In a 1980 interview with the *New York Times,* Richler was asked, "Which of your novels do you like best?" He replied, "Well, the one I haven't written yet." Immortality was the test you weren't going to be around to take, as Amis put it. As for the results, you could only hope they would be forwarded.

Mordecai & Me

In 1980 David Staines, one of the few academics Mordecai Richler respected (Richler, Staines, and Alice Munro were the jurors for the inaugural Giller Prize in 1994), said that Duddy Kravitz is "the sole name in all of Canadian literature to pass into common usage." More than two decades later, it's still hard to argue the case for anyone else having the same kind of CanLit name recognition. Carol Shields's Daisy Goodwill is close. Margaret Laurence's Hagar Shipley, maybe, but not quite. And can anyone name the protagonists in Robertson Davies' novels? Or Timothy Findley's? Who remembers the name of Michael Ondaatje's English patient or Grace's surname in Margaret Atwood's *Alias Grace*? And can somebody remind me what Pi is short for?

I heard John Metcalf say once that "literature is a relationship, made up of those books a reader takes to his heart." But it's also made up of those books that readers can take for granted—books that are ingrained whether you read them in high school or college or never at all. Richler's *The Apprenticeship of Duddy Kravitz* is the novel, rare in our literature, which falls into that category. Even so, it's starting to lose its hold in one place you wouldn't expect. *Duddy Kravitz* has disappeared from the curriculum of Bialik High School. Bialik is a private Jewish school in "the suburban barrens of Cote St. Luc," as Richler refers to it in *Solomon Gursky Was Here*. It's the place, too, where most of his St. Urbain Street "strivers" ended up. Unlike lower-middle-class Chomedey, where I grew up and where the Jewish population has significantly decreased over the years, middle- and upper-middle-class Cote St. Luc, where my wife is from (yes, it's a mixed marriage) remains steadfastly Jewish. It boasts street names like Einstein, Chagall, and Shalom. And the shopping mall where both high school kids and the elderly hang out is nicknamed, with a mixture of affection and ridicule, the *Shmall*. Bialik is practically across the street from the mall and is distinguished, even for a Jewish parochial school: in addition to instructing its kids in English, French, and Hebrew, Yiddish is also taught. In other words, it's the one place where *Duddy Kravitz* could be taught without resorting to a glossary. But as Linda Gilman Novek told me, "nobody is teaching any Richler at our school." Novek has been an English teacher at Bialik for more than two decades, and she gave up on teaching *Duddy Kravitz* years ago.

"*Duddy* is a *shtetl* story, and the kids here can't relate to that. Their parents can't either. Understand that Duddy's behaviour is linked to his self-esteem and to his wanting to be accepted—by his family as well as the outside world. But we have kids, here, who don't have to strive. When they get their driver's licences their parents get them cars, pretty fancy cars. When you drive a Mercedes at sixteen, there is no hunger anymore. The notion of a man without land being nobody that Duddy's Zaida tries to instill in his surprisingly receptive grandson has no meaning anymore. Today you'd have to say a man without a Benz is nobody.

"And then there's the whole idea in Richler's novel that if Duddy wants sex it has to be with Yvette, a French-Canadian girl. Well, you can forget about that. Jewish girls give blow jobs now."

It was the end of the school year when I talked to Novek and she admitted that she was feeling more cynical than usual. She added, half-jokingly, I think, that she was on her way to becoming a Buddhist. She also suspected her students might still have something to learn from Richler's portrait of working-class aspiration and avarice. "Jews today are still screwing people, of course, but they are carrying water bottles and wearing three-piece suits when they do," Novek said. "These kids I teach are slick on the surface. They are excellent talkers; they all have silver tongues. They can't read or write particularly well, but they can razzle-dazzle you. I've seen them harass teachers for marks, and the thing is now their parents back them up. They are good at looking for every scam and loophole. They're just better at hiding their motives than Duddy is. Duddy is alive and well; he's just dressed better and has nicer props." (In *Barney's Version,* Barney refers to the new generation as no longer Jewish but "of Jewish descent.")

Novek regrets not teaching *Duddy Kravitz* any longer, but she felt she had to stop when she couldn't get a conversation about the book going, when her students stopped making a connection with Richler's characters. "It was a kind of withering away," she explained. "I liked teaching it. I particularly liked teaching it at Bialik because it was a fabulous opportunity to hold a mirror up to these kids. Now the mirror I hold up is Philip Roth's *Goodbye Columbus.*"

Mordecai & Me

Discussing Mordecai Richler's legacy in *Maclean's,* Robert Gottlieb referred to *Duddy Kravitz* as "one of those books that revealed a new world" to an unsuspecting public. But Gottlieb also said that "the later books were more resonant. *Richler* was becoming more of a moralist, and, more important, he was getting better and better. Appropriately, *Barney's Version* is his grandest work."

Grand feels like the wrong word to describe Richler's novels. Inspired, uncompromising, irritating, outrageous come closer to the mark. Charged isn't bad either. If someone asked me now for my favourite Richler novel I suppose I'd say *St. Urbain's Horseman.* I'd add *Atuk* because I liked it more than I expected to, *Solomon Gursky* for its *chutzpah,* and *Son of a Smaller Hero* because, for all its shortcomings, it's so plainly personal. There have been other pleasant surprises—short stories like "Some Grist for Mervyn's Mill" in *The Street* and the uncollected "Mortimer Griffin, Shalinsky, and How They Settled the Jewish Question." The essay collections are flat-out fun, especially the early ones—like *Hunting Tigers under Glass* and *Shovelling Trouble*—with Richler's trips to the Catskills and Israel standing out. Then again, he never wrote anything more moving, more compassionate than his essay "My Father's Life," included in his collection *Home Sweet Home.* The *Jacob Two-Two* stories are, for that matter, inspired.

This impulse to name everything or nearly everything isn't only a matter of caution or hedging my bets; it's also an indication that with a writer like Richler, all his work is of a piece. It's not just that the themes repeat themselves or that the characters and their desires and fears don't change very much or that the story lines resemble each other; it's that his real legacy is not a single work but the way his work blurs together and overlaps. His body of work is more than the sum of its parts; rather, it is the sum of his life.

We remember writers the way we remember people—in fragments. With Richler, it's the mischievousness that's impossible to forget: Eskimos undone by their pious observance of Yom Kippur; Mortimer Griffin finally convinced he's Jewish even though he isn't; Mervyn Kaplansky in "Some Grist for Mervyn's Mill," being advised, with a wink, "You should remember . . . only to write good things about the Jews;" Hyman Kaplansky, a.k.a. Solomon Gursky, preparing an inedible Passover seder for a collection of upper-crust anti-Semites; a softball game in London between aging, ex-pat movie moguls in *St. Urbain's Horseman,* all of them planning their career moves—who to suck up to, who to bully—between strikeouts.

With Richler, it's the straightforward prose, the razor-sharp dialogue you remember. No fancy metaphors for him, no poetic language. In *The Street,* a whole disastrous relationship is condensed to a couple of lines exchanged between a disappointed wife and a put-upon husband. The wife, swooning over Edward VIII's decision to give up the British throne for love, says, "You could tell he was a romantic man. You could see it in his eyes." Her husband replies, "He has two . . . just like me."

With Richler, it's the snottiness, the cleverness, the sanctity of the smart-ass remark, of the perfect dark joke that sticks in your mind. Like Moses Berger at a performance of the play about Anne Frank, enduring an excruciating performance by the actress in the title role, and finally succumbing to his critical judgement, shouting as the Nazis show up, "Look in the attic! She's hiding in the attic!"

With Richler, it's all about getting your own back: on the Bronfmans, for example. Reading in Michael Marrus's biography, *Mr. Sam,* that Sam Bronfman was uncomfortable in the company of the new wave of east European immigrants—poorer, coarser Jews who were noisy and talked with their hands—Richler says that if,

> Sam had ordered his chauffeur to slow down on St. Urbain Street, and had he then eavesdropped on those loud-talking Jews who gestured with their hands, he might have discovered that some were pedlars with an eye on the main chance, others were as obsessed with moneymaking and social position as he was, but that many more were tossing around names and ideas—disputing their merit fiercely—that were now and forever beyond his shallow vision of the bounties the world had on offer.

With Richler, it's all about want. "You couldn't beat Duddy for a dreamer," one of Duddy's detractors has to admit. And even Mordecai Richler's detractors had to admit, to quote Saidye Bronfman, that he came a long way for a kid from St. Urbain Street. Recalling his days in Paris, when he was barely twenty, Richler writes, "All I ever craved for was to be accepted as a serious novelist, seemingly an impossible dream."

Mordecai & Me

And with Richler, it's also about not getting what you want—about that persistent fear that you won't turn out to be what you so badly hoped to be. Duddy Kravitz, Jake Hersh, Joshua Shapiro, Moses Berger, Barney Panofsky are all afflicted. In *St. Urbain's Horseman,* Jake, up in the middle of the night, is tormented by the fact that Orson Welles was famous by the time he was Jake's age, that Dostoyevsky had polished off *Crime and Punishment,* that Shelley was dead.

With Richler, it's all about living according to your own rules, by your own conditions and never relenting. A young Mordecai Richler refusing to speak to his grandfather, recounted in his essay "My Father's Life." Or Barney Panofsky, an atheist, still feeling betrayed enough by his Old Testament deity to complain that the "God we Jews are stuck with is both cruel and vengeful." The precocious description Richler slapped onto the early edition of his first novel, *The Acrobats,* about how the only "thing for a serious writer to write about today" was "man without God," proved indelible. Richler's lifelong search for what he called "a system of values" to replace the values he'd rejected as a child, ends with *Barney's Version,* with Barney honouring his dead father by showing up at the cemetery every year to empty a bottle of Crown Royal rye whisky on the old man's grave and to leave a smoked meat sandwich and a pickle, instead of a pebble, on the gravestone. It's not much, but it's something. Barney's plan for his own end is also, fittingly, personalized: "No rabbi was to speak at his funeral. He was to be buried, as he had already arranged, in the Protestant cemetery ... but there should be a Star of David on his stone, and the adjoining plot had been reserved for Miriam."

In August 2000, eleven months before Mordecai Richler died, I attended the funeral of the novelist and short story writer Hugh Hood at a church near my home. In North America's celebrity culture, most writers slip away without much fanfare. If Richler was the exception, Hood was the rule. Born in 1928, three years before Richler, Hood was not a native Montrealer, but he lived in the city most of his adult life. A curious fellow and an even more curious writer, Hood is nevertheless an important figure in the history and evolution of Canadian literary history. And the ways in which he differs from Richler are instructive. Hood was a devout Catholic, Richler an uneasy Jew. Hood was gregarious and superbly educated. He knew everything about everything. Richler, a notorious hooky player and later a college dropout, knew only what he knew, but *that* he knew tenaciously. Hood, with his Ph.D., taught for many years in the English department of the Université de Montréal. Richler was a freelancer all his working life. Their opposite career paths are also instructive as each other's "road not taken." In 1960, a year after *Duddy Kravitz* was published, Hood's first collection of stories, *Flying a Red Kite,* came out and received, for a Canadian book at the time, considerable international attention and praise. Like Richler, Hood had reached the conclusion that Canadian literature was unworthy of him. Unlike Richler, he was determined to stay, raise it to his level and make it matter by doing battle on the home front. Richler fled first chance he got. Hood was determined—and refreshingly immodest—about becoming the genius Canadian literature was lacking. In the late 1970s, he began an ambitious and quixotic project: a twelve-volume novel called *The New Age,* which would provide a panoramic view of the country's social and political history. *The New Age* was intended to make Hugh Hood, and Canadian literature along with him, famous. As it turned out, CanLit would soon leave him behind. It seemed the more he wrote—and he wrote a great deal—the more obscure he became. He changed publishers several times, and it was increasingly difficult for him to get each new book in the series reviewed or even noticed.

I knew Hood a little. We met in 1986, when I interviewed him at his home in the west end of Montreal. But it was a year earlier that I'd first read *A Scenic Art,* the fifth volume in *The New Age* series. It was about the early days of the Stratford Festival. I was, by turns, enthralled and bored silly. It was a novel suffering from a kind of split personality—ribald and juicy and impossible to put down in parts, dry toast the rest of the time. I backtracked from there, catching up with some of the earlier books in the series, and realized that they were all the same—full of narrative flare as well as what seemed to be a deliberate undermining of that flare. Hood was a magnificent storyteller and an equally magnificent pedant. Side by side with the wonderful stuff in the series, there are great whopping chunks of undigested exposition. If his plan was to merge the two, he never seemed to be working very hard at fulfilling that plan. Hood could write like an angel, but he was also stubborn as the devil. In the end, his stubbornness, to the detriment of his readers, won out.

But I hadn't come to this conclusion when we met. In person, Hood, loquacious and solicitous, couldn't have been less like Richler. When I interviewed him it was about his novel *The Motor Boys in Ottawa*, the halfway point in *The New Age* series. The interview was scheduled to last an hour or so, the usual length for a short profile. Instead, he led me into his basement and kept me there for four hours, long after I'd run out of tape and pertinent questions to ask.

It hardly mattered. He did all the talking. Still, as hostage takings go, it was a pleasure. He entertained himself and me with improvised dissertations on Hegel, Bing Crosby, the *Carry On* movies, classical music, and his immense ambition. His plan was for the twelfth and final volume of *The New Age* to come out at the stroke of midnight of the year 2000. I thought he was kidding; he wasn't. (The final volume, *Near Water*, was off by nine months, and while Hood didn't live to see it published, he did, despite failing health, finish it and the series.) Hood was a curious mix of charm and ego. I'd never met anyone so buoyantly, so unabashedly sure of himself. He started the interview by telling me—before I had the chance to ask—what he was up to. "I might as well say it at the beginning; I think the whole thing is a great work of art," he explained that afternoon. He went on to compare himself and what he was doing to the work of Shakespeare and Beethoven.

In another interview a few years earlier, Hood said, "I think it would be marvellous for Canada if we had one artist who could move easily and in a familiar converse with Joyce and Tolstoy and Proust; and I intend to be that artist if I possibly can; and I am willing to give the rest of my life to it." Which is what he did, but with diminishing returns. Because I liked him and was intrigued by what he was doing, I made an effort to review the next few volumes in the series. But eventually I stopped. Eventually, I also said that I thought his master plan was a mistake, and that his talent as a writer was being overwhelmed by his cockeyed hubris, by his conviction that he was constructing a masterpiece. Over the years, he would

Legacy

call every now and then to talk, but he stopped after that final review ran. I learned later from a mutual acquaintance that he was upset with me, that he felt betrayed.

I went to his funeral in part to do penance and in larger part because he was such an engaging, curious man. Entering the large church where the service was held, I was struck by how few people were there, though maybe I mean how few readers, how few fellow writers. There was an obituary in the newspaper, but I didn't see any significant mention of his career anywhere else. Hood had been a professor for a long time, and at his funeral the tributes came almost entirely from academics. A sad fate for a creative writer.

Mordecai Richler's death—on July 3, 2001—was national news. There were television and radio stories as well as special sections in newspapers and news magazines. In a culture obsessed with Michael Jackson interviews and Celine Dion's baby, Richler was an anomaly, a crossover success. His work was known, even read by some. The outpouring of regard and affection, as well as the amount of media coverage immediately after his death, was remarkable. It's possible that we wanted to show how much we loved him after he died because we had so often disliked him while he was alive. It was possible, too, that Richler had become the one thing he didn't believe writers had any business becoming—a celebrity.

The morning he died I became part of the media machinery, a little too eagerly, I'm embarrassed to admit. A local CBC television producer called to ask me if she could send somebody over to interview me for a segment on the evening news. "What do you want me to say?" I asked. The truth is I was flattered to be called. I knew I may not have been their first choice, but that hardly mattered on television. If Mr. Right is unavailable, Mr. Right Now will do just fine.

The producer wanted what she described as the usual: impressions of Richler, a sense of his place and his importance as a writer, as a political commentator, his legacy, that sort of thing. And maybe I could talk about his influence as well.

"You mean on me?" I asked. No, she said, that wasn't exactly what she meant.

Mordecai & Me

But I did the interview and a few more besides that day, repeating the same true but pedestrian thing about Richler being a CanLit trailblazer. Long before writers like Alice Munro or Robertson Davies or Margaret Atwood arrived on the scene, Richler was the Canadian writer who made a mark internationally. I smirked and added a personal note. I said he was a tough interview, that he could be grumpy and guarded—a strategy, I suspected, to keep strangers at a distance. He was a curmudgeon, our curmudgeon, I added. I made him sound lovable, like the grandfather in *Heidi:* a rough exterior, but a teddy bear underneath. I said he was one of a kind.

But while I was talking in sound bites, I was thinking about that earlier question, the one I had misunderstood about his influence on me. Which is your favourite Richler book? Which one will stand the test of time? I was asked. *Duddy Kravitz,* I said. But I was also thinking, *Is that right? Do I mean that?* At the time, I hadn't read *Duddy Kravitz* in thirty years; the same, more or less, for *St. Urbain's Horseman.* I had reviewed the more recent books, but I couldn't remember that much about them either. It was then that I realized it didn't matter: it was a personality that we were discussing not a writer. I spent that day and the next few infatuated with Richler as a symbol, an advertisement for the writer's life. Reading his work made me want to become a writer, I said, even when I wasn't asked. But that wasn't true. It wasn't his work; it was his example—the story of who he had become and, more important, how he had become it. It wasn't my story, of course, but it was easy to make myself believe, on the day he died, when called upon to sum up his career and his life, that it was close enough.

After doing a live TV interview for an evening news program, I returned home and met a neighbour on the street—a francophone woman, roughly my age, who didn't know much more about me than that I was Jewish and a writer, but that was enough for her to offer her condolences. It seemed like an odd position to be put in, but I nodded and accepted her sympathy. Still, I wondered why she thought this was a personal loss for me and why I let her think that.

I had asked my wife to videotape my last live interview, and I watched it later that night. Then I watched it again. Infatuations don't last long,

Legacy

but obsessions can. That evening I started rereading *The Apprenticeship of Duddy Kravitz,* and the experience would be vaguely disappointing. A month later, I began rereading *St. Urbain's Horseman,* not wanting it to end. And that's how it would go for the next year between Mordecai and me: *Cocksure,* dated the second time around; *Atuk,* the first time around, a pleasant surprise; the essays and reviews, better and more of them than I thought; *Barney's Version,* with a closer look, a braver, richer book. There was much more than I imagined—more to be annoyed by and more to admire.

"It may be lonely at the top," the critic James Woolcott said, "but it's crowded at the bottom." The literary world, Cynthia Ozick said, "operates according to feudal logic: the aristocracy blots out all the rest. . . . Every young writer imagines only the heights; no one aspires to be minor or invisible." Or, as Mordecai Richler would have put it, no one dreams of being justly neglected. Nevertheless, the jockeying for position goes on. One writer rises at another's expense. If they fall, it's because they have become vulnerable to being knocked down a peg; if they don't fall, it's because they are good and because they are lucky, though not necessarily in that order.

On the final page of *Saul Bellow Drumlin Woodchuck,* Mark Harris describes finishing his unauthorized biography of Saul Bellow and then calling Bellow to ask if they can get together to discuss a few final questions. Once the book is finished, Harris tells Bellow, he won't write another word about him. "You sound as if you're about to take a pledge," Bellow says. But he still declines the meeting. Harris shows up at a reading Bellow is giving, and it's then and there that Harris realizes he's done, once and for all, with his elusive subject. After the reading, Harris watches as Bellow "shyly, awkwardly, wordlessly" disappears from the stage. "But I took no notes," Harris writes, "having taken a pledge."

On the final page of *Sir Vidia's Shadow,* Paul Theroux's memoir of the collapse of his friendship with V.S. Naipaul, Theroux runs into Naipaul on a London street. The two have been out of touch. Their last communication was through a third party, Naipaul's wife, who faxed

Mordecai & Me

Theroux afterwards to warn him not to write anything about her husband. This chance meeting in London, Theroux thinks, is a kind of miracle, a last chance to straighten things out. But it's soon clear to him that Naipaul is eager to get away as quickly as possible. Theroux tries to detain him, engage him in small talk, but Naipaul is anxious to go, so Theroux asks, "Do we have something to discuss?" Naipaul says no. "What do we do, then?" Theroux persists. "Take it on the chin and move on," Naipaul says. Then, as Theroux watches his old friend and mentor scuttle away (as Theroux puts it), he thinks, "I was liberated at last. I saw how the end of a friendship was the start of an understanding. He had made me by his choosing me; his rejection of me meant I was on my own, out of his shadow. He had freed me, he had opened my eyes, he had given me a subject." Which is another way of saying Theroux has no intention of taking it on the chin. He will swing back. *Sir Vidia's Shadow* is an insightful, cruel, and compelling record of that punch—a sucker punch.

On the final page of Ian Hamilton's *In Search of J.D. Salinger*, Hamilton explains that his book began with his infatuation with *The Catcher in the Rye*—"an infatuation that bowled me over at the age of seventeen and which it seems I never properly outgrew. Well, I've outgrown it now."

In retrospect, all these fascinating books were doomed to miss their mark. All doomed to end in some kind of Oedipal exasperation. *Writer seeks writer.* It sounds like a creepy personals ad. All these would-be literary biographers arrive at the same conclusion—that it's time to grow up and get on with their own lives and careers.

About halfway through *Mordecai & Me,* at one of the many stages when I felt like throwing in the towel, I got Nicholson Baker's e-mail address through his online fan club. (A writer with a fan club, isn't the Internet grand?) I wrote him a long note in which I introduced myself, explained my project and told him how his book on John Updike influenced me. I was in a mood to confess, so I did. I was fed up with Richler. Had he become fed up with Updike? Was it inevitable? Though I didn't say it in so many words, my message was clear: it was help I was looking for, from someone who had been down this particular path before. A week or so later, Baker replied. His note was brief but gracious, encouraging enough to make me hope he didn't think I was some kind of nut. In answer to my question about his relationship with Updike, Baker said that Updike sent him one of his books after *U and I* came out, with the inscription, "To Nicholson Baker, who made me famous." To my concerns about running out of patience with Richler, Baker said, "Surely your feeling of being fed up with Richler is temporary." And finally, "I hope you find your way to a conclusion."

It was nice of him to write, but his comments didn't help much. If Baker, after his "half-nuts" infatuation with Updike, could put away childish things, it made me wonder why not me? Here's what I've done instead: the copy of *Don't Sweat the Small Stuff* is now officially off my night table, joining Harold Bloom's unread *The Anxiety of Influence* in a pile of books, unauthorized biographies mostly, which I intend to donate to the local library. That way they'll be out of the house, though I'll still know where I can find them, just in case.

"Don't be hasty," my wife says, though she can't keep from smiling when she says it.

"Sorry, from now on, I *am* sweating the small stuff. That's what I do. It's an epiphany, don't you think?"

"Yes, sweetheart. Whatever you say."

"I suppose you'd like that to be the last word."

Maybe, in my own way, I'm still working away at that newspaper photo of Richler I defaced several years ago—the one with the horns and moustache. I can't leave it alone. I imagine myself blackening in the nostrils next. Adding werewolf sideburns. Horn-rimmed glasses. Thickening the eyebrows, Groucho Marx-style. I know it's a game of diminishing returns, bound, finally, to backfire. The more ridiculous I make Richler look, the more ridiculous, the more petty, vindictive, and childish I look. I'm reminded of Nancy Hersh's concern about her husband in *St. Urbain's Horseman*: "If he did not rise as far as he hoped, he might yet diminish into bitterness."

What can I say? I'm also the grudgy type.

Mordecai & Me

"You must be nuts!" The accusation came courtesy of my writer friend in Halifax. I'd e-mailed her to tell her about a private notebook I'd been offered and declined—a notebook that was left behind at Mordecai Richler's funeral. Do I really want to read something like that? I'd written to her. Obviously, she considered the matter urgent enough to call back instead of e-mail. "Do you *want* it?" she said on the phone. "Absolutely. You said no? Well, you call right back and tell that funeral guy, what's his name? Paperback? Paperman? Tell him, yes, you want the notebook, and if you can't go get it yourself or don't want to, then send a courier. Go. Go. Go. If I were there this never would happen. You see why you need me."

Weird things happen when you're working on a book, things you can hardly account for. It's as if a magnetic field develops around you, attracting strange incidents and events. You are granted an inexplicable kind of power. One writer I was interviewing told me how, in his first novel, the mother of his main character gets hit by a car and killed and how the same thing happened to his own mother. "I'm sorry," I said, but then wondered if I'd heard him right. "You mean," I added, "that you wrote about what happened to your mother in your novel." No, he assured me, he wrote about it first, then it happened.

With my novel, something similar occurred, except with a happier outcome. My main character finds himself assuming the role of an expectant father, and while that didn't seem to be at all possible in my own life when I was coming up with the narrative plot twist—I was in my forties, no relationship, no prospect of one—less than a year later I really was about to become a father. I couldn't help experiencing a sort of *déjà vu* or, more accurately, *déjà lu*. It was if I had written the experience into existence. My wife also claims that the night our son was conceived was the night she heard me read from my novel for the first time. "All that stuff about prenatal classes and sympathetic labour pains and delivery rooms—what did you expect?" she says. Here I thought I was writing a novel, admittedly an autobiographical one, but what I was really writing was a memoir before the fact.

In the case of this book, here's what happened: early one Sunday morning, a month or two after I'd begun writing *Mordecai & Me*, just

Legacy

around the first anniversary of Mordecai Richler's death, the phone rang. It was Herb Paperman. The Paperman family are undertakers. For Montreal's Jewish community, they are a tradition, which is another way of saying that they are, when it comes to dying, the only game in town. This explains why you don't want to be getting a telephone call from one of them out of the blue. My first impulse, when the man on the other end of the line introduced himself as a Paperman, was to make sure that I and everyone I cared about was still breathing. But Paperman had been given my name by the rabbi at the Reform synagogue where I had given a lecture on Richler and Philip Roth a month or so earlier. Herb Paperman had come across a notebook in the funeral home's lost and found, with no name on it, just the words: "Re: Mordecai Richler." He assumed it was left behind almost a year ago, when the funeral home had held a private ceremony for the Richler family. The rabbi had suggested it might be mine or, if it wasn't, I might know to whom it belonged. The rabbi told him I was writing a book about Richler and that I might be able to help. Was it mine? Herb Paperman was calling to find out.

For a moment, I considered saying yes, but then changed my mind. Instead, I said I might be able to figure out whose it was by looking at it. What I meant by that I still don't know. Was I trying to pass myself off as some sort of forensic literary critic? We talked some more. He described the contents of the book a little, saying it appeared to belong to someone who had been taking notes at the funeral. That was his best guess in any case. But the more he described the notebook—lime-green, lined, made in Japan—the more I stumbled on my moral bearings. Once I realized what was being suggested—that I take the notebook since no one else had claimed it—I realized I had no business taking it or even looking at it. I said so, thanked Herb Paperman, and forgot about the whole thing. At least I tried to. By the time I hung up the phone, I had changed my mind. My wife was convinced I was doing the right thing by not taking it. "It's too spooky," she said. She also said that she was proud of me for what she thought was my final decision.

My friend, on the phone from Halifax, had a different opinion. She said that this kind of thing didn't fall into your lap for no reason. I know, I told her, which is why I'd already called Herb Paperman back to tell him

I wanted a look at the notebook after all. I lied and said I had thought it over, maybe I could help get it back to its rightful owner. Fine, he said, or words to that effect.

I showed up at the Paperman Funeral Home the next morning. I hadn't been in their office since my uncle died ten years earlier. His funeral had been arranged in the old building on Cote des Neiges, which had been replaced by a state-of-the-art location on Jean Talon. But I remembered the circumstances clearly. After my uncle died, my sister and I had accompanied his widow, our aunt, to her appointment there. I can't remember which Paperman we met, except it wasn't Herb. It was probably one of the kids enlisted into the family business. My aunt was distraught, and we were there to help her cope with death's business side, to sign the appropriate papers, arrange the service and pick out a coffin. Even the softest sell feels like a hard one when you are in a coffin showroom. I didn't envy the young Paperman's job, but that didn't mean I was going to make things easy for him, either. I detested this place and the people who ran it for a lot of clichéd and unfair reasons. They had dealt with my sisters and me when my mother died, and then eighteen months later when my father died, and I had longed then to take out my sorrow and anger on them.

I also seem to remember that whichever Paperman we met with then had been abrupt and insensitive. We had been motherless for less than twenty-four hours, and here he was talking budget and prices. I realize now that no one could have been sensitive enough for me then. No one could have successfully navigated the minefield of bitterness and grief. Almost a decade later, with my aunt, I was still holding a grudge, still looking to get even. So when the Paperman kid—he wasn't really a kid, just a few years younger than I was—told my aunt the prices of the various models, I said, "Can I ask a question?"

He nodded. That's what he was there for—to answer any and all questions.

"What's the difference?" I said. "I mean, really, what's the difference?" He didn't realize this was a rhetorical question and began to explain the particular features, the grain of the wood, the plushness of the satin interior. He also mentioned his own personal preferences, explaining what his choice would be one day and why.

"No, you don't understand. What does it matter?" I said again, then added, "Death is the great leveller; didn't someone say that once?"

He looked puzzled, then put out. Who was I again? A nephew. My aunt looked at me; she was puzzled now, too. My sister, on the other hand, understood. I was settling an old score, never mind that it was an imaginary one. Before he could get back to his sales pitch, I repeated Lou Grant's line from *The Mary Tyler Moore Show*. "When I go," I said, "just put me out in the garbage with my hat on." The young Paperman didn't know what to say to that. Meanwhile, I was having, I realize now, a Mordecai Richler moment—like the time he told off Saidye Bronfman, who was, by all accounts, a sweet, harmless woman. I had slain one of my imaginary dragons. I had proved that there is a point to holding a grudge. Aside from the fact that my uncle was dead and my aunt distraught, I felt swell.

A decade later, waiting for the Paperman's receptionist to fetch the mysterious notebook for me, I felt more like my usual self: ambivalent. As it turned out, no one knew where it was and Herb Paperman had to be paged. It took him a few minutes, but he found it and handed it to me. By then, I knew without a doubt that I had no right to it. I took it anyway rather than explain my predicament. I glanced inside, but the writing, at first glance, was illegible. I didn't want to appear too curious, so I closed it and put it in my pocket. I left my number with Herb Paperman, just in case the person who'd lost it called, which was unlikely after almost a year. When I got home I put the notebook at the bottom of all the file folders and books I had begun to accumulate about Richler, and left it there. I haven't looked at it—until now.

I would like to say it went unread because of my shame at what I had done. But that's not why. The notebook, I came to believe, was a treasure. The sort of thing biographers—real, authorized ones—kill for. If I hadn't looked at it again, it wasn't because I felt I had no right to have it, but because I was keeping it in abeyance as a kind of talisman. Writers are as superstitious as ballplayers, and I was no exception. If, in the course of writing about Mordecai Richler, I didn't discover who he really was or what his work was really about, I always had the notebook.

There are no secrets in it, of course, and the handwriting is harder to decipher than I remembered from my first quick glance. What I can read

Mordecai & Me

of it makes it seem like an early draft for one of the eulogies delivered at the funeral service. The owner of the notebook was not an old friend or a Richler family member; he knew Richler first and foremost as a reader. Richler opened up a world of literature to him and, even though he had come to know Richler later as a colleague and a friend, it's that introduction to his work, to literature, for which he would be forever grateful. Everything you need to know about Mordecai Richler, the unknown owner of the notebook was saying, you can find in his books. He was right, of course: you could always find Richler there. You still can.

Epilogue
Spring 2003

According to Nicholson Baker, your favourite writers have a way of making "you very unhappy when they threaten to be more unlike you as human beings than you had thought." In *U and I,* Baker discovers an opinion of John Updike's he violently disagrees with and, for a moment, the point of his whole book, his "whole imaginary friendship with Updike" is disrupted. Reality kept disrupting my imaginary friendship with Richler. Whenever our paths crossed, it became more and more obvious that a friendship between us, even an imaginary one, was out of the question. It's also true that the more I have read and reread his work this past year, the more I have realized not how much I wanted to be like him, but how much I wanted him to be like me. I realize now that that was an impossible and childish desire. How could he be?

Mordecai & Me

He was nothing like me. Richler was steadfast and uncompromising, even when he acted vindictive and petty. In his work, he was almost never nice, which is a more significant accomplishment than it appears. He was never ingratiating, never, to his everlasting credit, eager to please. Richler had courage and coldness. His toughness was his strength and his weakness.

Writers don't have secrets—not ones they are likely to keep. Readers will uncover them or misinterpret them, so either way, it comes to the same thing: readers will find what they need.

I needed Richler to be more compassionate in his work. And while he tried, in his later novels, to be generous to his characters—most successfully in *Barney's Version*—you could always feel the effort, the strain. What he embraced in his work, he embraced diffidently, as if he were embarrassed to show his soft side. I realize now, having read and reread his work, that the piece I love best is "My Father's Life," the thirteen-page essay he wrote about his relationship with a man he couldn't respect, but couldn't keep from loving. It's full of forgiveness and, more important, full of Richler asking for forgiveness.

Most of the time, though, Richler had an unerring eye for people's petty sins, rationalizations, and pretensions, and for their need to puff themselves up and make excuses. He was hard on the big stuff, but he was harder on the small stuff—on ordinary, everyday human frailty. He couldn't forgive anything, including sins that weren't, in the scheme of things, very important. Richler wrote best about the things he turned his back on. If it was something that was hard to turn his back on—his family, his faith—that just served to make the gesture more heroic. But his hardheartedness often made his readers hardhearted in return.

I needed him to be kinder and not just in his work. I needed him to be kinder to me, which is *my* secret. Is that all this is about—unrequited love? It seems Richler was right: one theme, many variations.

"Did I wake you?" my wife is asking the question this time. We were celebrating this evening (celebrating my arriving at this epilogue), and we ended up having sex, one thing leading to another as it so seldom does in marriage. Before you are married, you plan your seductions meticulously. Before, you strategize and make your moves with the concentrated effort and foresight of a chess master; after, proximity is all that counts. Right place, right time, *right* mood. Sex is one more thing to do, one more thing you *can* do, though that sounds worse than I mean it to. What I mean is that it's precisely this predictability, this accessibility that can be so surprising and thrilling. Small stuff, sure, but hot stuff. Lust with a licence. Who knew? This night, though, the seduction was planned. I'm finished the damn thing, really finished it, I practically shouted after we got home and paid the baby-sitter. My wife fell into my arms, as expected. It was, I figured, time I got lucky. And so now, in the afterglow, or afterword may be more like it, I nuzzle my wife's neck to let her know that I am indeed awake.

"I was thinking," she says. "Can you say, after all of this, that you don't really like his books?"

"But that's not what I'm saying. I'm saying the opposite, that I love his books, but in my own way, with my own biases and idiosyncrasies brought to bear, with my own perverse kind—"

"You mean you love his books, but you're not in love with them?"

"I suppose."

"And him?"

"You mean how do I feel about Richler? Like how I feel doesn't matter. Maybe he was right: nobody really ever understands anybody else. There, that wraps things up neatly, don't you think? Or is that a cop-out? Undefinitive, if that's a word? Unauthorized? Unhinged? Am I being childish? Is that what you think?"

"I'm torn."

"Between?"

"Between you, sweetheart, and the truth."

I switch on the lamp beside my bed, and while my eyes adjust to the light, I fumble around, looking for a pen and paper so I can write down what my wife has said. Just as I have been doing all along.

"Creative nonfiction?" she says.

"You could call it that."

Mordecai & Me

"Sweetheart, I'm only pointing out that at the end of all this, you might say something you don't mean. It's inevitable you'd want to think you're done with Richler, even if you're not, not really, not ever."

"I'd rather you didn't say that right now."

"What is it you want me to say?"

"Sweet dreams."

"All right, then, sweet dreams."

Selected Bibliography

Books by Mordecai Richler

The Acrobats. London: André Deutsch, 1954.
   Richler's first novel remained out of print until a year after his death. In an afterword to the new and the first Canadian edition, Ted Kotcheff sums up his old London flatmate's early style this way: "Hemingway with a soupçon of Camus—not at all bad!"

Son of a Smaller Hero. London: André Deutsch, 1955.

A Choice of Enemies. London: André Deutsch, 1957.

The Apprenticeship of Duddy Kravitz. London: André Deutsch, 1959.

The Incomparable Atuk. Toronto: McClelland and Stewart, 1963.
   A 1989 edition includes an affectionate and gossipy afterword by Peter Gzowski.

Cocksure. Toronto: McClelland and Stewart, 1968.

Hunting Tigers under Glass: Essays and Reports. Toronto: McClelland and Stewart, 1968.
   Richler's first nonfiction collection in which he concludes his foreword by pointing out that while his essays and reviews took time away from his fiction, they were done, unlike his film work, more for pleasure than profit.

The Street. Toronto: McClelland and Stewart, 1969.
   This mix of short stories and childhood memoirs demonstrates just how adept Richler was at blurring fiction and fact.

St. Urbain's Horseman. Toronto: McClelland and Stewart, 1971.

Shovelling Trouble. Toronto: McClelland and Stewart, 1972.

Jacob Two-Two Meets the Hooded Fang. Toronto: McClelland and Stewart, 1975.
   Richler's first children's book was followed by two others, *Jacob Two-Two and the Dinosaur* (1987), and *Jacob Two-Two's First Spy Case* (1995).

Mordecai & Me

Images of Spain. Toronto: McClelland and Stewart, 1977.
    A book of photographs by Peter Christopher with text and an introduction by Mordecai Richler.
Joshua Then and Now. Toronto: McClelland and Stewart, 1980.
Home Sweet Home: My Canadian Album. Toronto: McClelland and Stewart, 1984.
Solomon Gursky Was Here. Toronto: Penguin Books Canada, 1989.
Broadsides: Reviews and Opinions. Toronto: Penguin Books Canada, 1990.
Oh Canada! Oh Quebec! Requiem for a Divided Country. Toronto: Penguin Books Canada, 1992.
This Year in Jerusalem. Toronto: Knopf Canada, 1994.
Barney's Version. Toronto: Knopf Canada, 1997.
Belling the Cat: Essays, Reports and Opinions. Toronto: Knopf Canada, 1998.
    The last nonfiction collection published before Richler's death.
On Snooker: The Game and the Characters Who Play It. Toronto: Knopf Canada, 2001.
    This collection was published a few weeks after Richler's death.
Dispatches from the Sporting Life. Toronto: Knopf Canada, 2002.
    Richler's second posthumous publication features a moving foreword by Richler's son, Noah.

Anthologies

Richler, Mordecai, ed. *Canadian Writing Today.* Toronto: Penguin Books Canada, 1970.
    In an otherwise inclusive anthology, the absence of A.M. Klein seems conspicuous.
Weisstub, David N., ed. *Creativity and the University.* Toronto: York University Press, 1975.
    Richler's astute, scathing, and very funny speech "Playing the Circuit" is published here and, curiously, for an inveterate recycler like Richler, nowhere else.
Richler, Mordecai, ed. *The Best of Modern Humour.* Toronto: McClelland and Stewart, 1983.
    Richler's range of choices—from S.J. Perelman to Philip Roth—is narrow but hard to argue with.
Richler, Mordecai, ed. *Writers on World War II: An Anthology.* Foreword by Mordecai Richler. Toronto: Penguin Books Canada, 1991.

Other Sources

Amis, Martin. *The Information.* Toronto: Knopf Canada, 1995.
    This novel, about writers and envy, singles out book reviewers for special ridicule.
Atlas, James. *Bellow: A Biography.* New York: Random House, 2000.
Atwood, Margaret. *Negotiating with the Dead: A Writer on Writing.* Cambridge: Cambridge University Press, 2002.
    Great title. The best chapters in the book are the most personal ones—Atwood discussing the start of her career.

Bibliography

———*Survival*, Toronto: Anansi, 1972.
>Atwood views *The Apprenticeship of Duddy Kravitz* as more an American than Canadian book, but she does give Richler credit for making the only Canadian character in *Cocksure* impotent.

Baker, Nicholson. *U and I: A True Story*. New York: Random House, 1991.

Bloom, Harold. *The Anxiety of Influence: A Theory of Poetry*. Oxford: Oxford University Press, 1973.

Bruck, Julie. *The End of Travel*. London, Ontario: Brick Books, 1999.
>An undervalued collection of poetry by one of the most appealing poets around.

Cameron, Donald. *Conversations with Canadian Novelists*. Toronto: Macmillan, 1973.
>What is, perhaps, most memorable about Cameron's interview with Richler—"The Reticent Moralist"—is Cameron's odd prefatory note that due to the heat the conversation was conducted with both men "stripped to the waist."

Carlson, Richard Ph.D. *Don't Sweat the Small Stuff . . . and It's All Small Stuff: Simple Ways to Keep the Little Things from Taking Over Your Life*. New York: Hyperion, 1997.
>My wife continues to frequent garage sales, determined to find, among other useful bargains, Carlson's sequel, *What about the Big Stuff? Finding Strength and Moving Forward*. I wish her luck.

Dalfen, Layne. *Dreams Do Come True: Decoding Your Dreams to Discover Your Full Potential*. Avon, Massachusetts: Adams Media Corporation, 2002.
>The book promises to make readers more aware of why they make the choices they do. Unfortunately, it doesn't make the same promise to writers.

Demchinsky, Bryan and Elaine Kalman Naves. *Storied Streets: Montreal in the Literary Imagination*. Toronto: Macfarlane Walter & Ross, 2000.
>A valuable primer to Montreal's literary tradition.

Downton, Dawn Rae. *Diamond: A Memoir of 100 Days*. Toronto: McClelland and Stewart, 2003.
>A wonderful memoir about the courage and the foolhardiness required to do what writers do—commemorate the dead.

Dyer, Geoff. *Out of Sheer Rage: In the Shadow of D.H. Lawrence*. New York: North Point Press, 1998.
>Ostensibly a literary biography of D.H. Lawrence, this hilarious book keeps getting sidetracked by the author's inability to stick with any decision he makes. Dyer's conclusion: "One begins writing a book about something because one is interested in that subject; one finishes writing a book in order to lose interest in that subject: the book itself is a record of this transaction."

Epstein, Joseph. *Partial Payments*. New York: W.W. Norton, 1989.
>In his introduction, Epstein says, "When I write about authors, I am keen to know not only what they have done and how they have done it, but, near as I can discover, what kind of man or woman is behind the work."

Mordecai & Me

Fiedler, Leslie. *Waiting for the End.* New York: Stein and Day, 1964.

Fiorito, Joe. *The Closer We Are to Dying.* Toronto: McClelland and Stewart, 1999.

> A brave memoir about fathers and sons. Richler rarely provided publishers with blurbs, but in this case, he ranked Fiorito's book with Philip Roth's *Patrimony*.

Gallant, Mavis. *The Other Paris.* New York: Houghton Mifflin Company, 1956.

> Gallant's first collection of short stories.

Gibson, Graeme. *Eleven Canadian Novelists.* Toronto: Anansi, 1973.

> Gibson's interview with Richler includes a rare compliment from its subject, who ends by telling Gibson, "Well, thank you. I really never have been interviewed so intelligently before."

Graham, Gwethalyn. *Earth and High Heaven.* Philadelphia: J.B. Lippincott Company, 1944.

Goncharov, Ivan. *Oblomov.* Translated from the Russian by Nathalie Duddington. New York: Everyman's Library, 1992.

> *Oblomov* was first published in 1859.

Hamilton, Ian. *In Search of J.D. Salinger.* New York: Random House, 1988.

> What I liked about this unauthorized biography is precisely what Richler didn't: Hamilton's confession that his book "would also be a semispoof in which the biographer would play a leading, sometimes comic, role."

Harris, Mark. *Saul Bellow Drumlin Woodchuck.* Athens, Georgia: University of Georgia Press, 1980.

Hemingway, Ernest. *A Moveable Feast.* New York: Scribner, 1964.

Hobson, Laura Z. *Gentleman's Agreement.* New York: Simon & Schuster, 1947.

Hood, Hugh. *Near Water.* Toronto: Anansi Press, 2000.

> The twelfth and final volume in Hood's ambitious and quixotic New Age series. *Near Water* was published posthumously.

Kaplan, Justin, ed. *The Best American Essays 1990.* Boston: Ticknor & Fields, 1990.

> This volume—part of a wonderful series of personal essays edited by Robert Atwan—includes novelist Jay McInerney's moving tribute to his teacher and mentor Raymond Carver.

Klein, A.M. *The Second Scroll.* New York: Alfred A. Knopf, 1951.

Lerner, Betsy. *The Forest for the Trees: An Editor's Advice to Readers.* New York: Riverhead Books, 2000.

> Lerner, who's worked as both a writer and an editor, offers revealing insights into what makes writers tick: "It is my educated guess that every time a writer gets a big advance, a big feature story, or a big movie deal, or climbs onto the bestseller list, other writers wonder, *Why isn't that me?*"

Lopate, Phillip. *Portrait of My Body.* New York: Anchor Books, 1996.

> Lopate's essay "The Dead Father: A Remembrance of Donald Barthelme" is memorable for Lopate's candid expression of his mixed feeling about his older colleague. He didn't care much for Barthelme's work; nevertheless he longed for Barthelme to befriend him, which he never really did.

Bibliography

Mailer, Norman. *The Spooky Art: Some Thoughts on Writing.* New York: Random House, 2003.

> This book is notable for Mailer's confrontational attitude toward his reviewers, in particular his assault on Philip Rahv, a critic who dared give him a bad review. "I was perfectly pleasant and everything seemed all right," Mailer writes, "except we were both tilted alarmingly.... He was in an absolute panic, waiting for me to strike.... He was a heavy man, and the two of us probably looked like two doughnuts crushed together at one end of the box."

Mallon, Thomas. *In Fact: Essays on Writers and Writing.* New York: Pantheon Books, 2001.

> Mallon, who is best known in this country for an uncompromisingly harsh review of Margaret Atwood in the *New York Times,* succeeded Richler as *GQ*'s book columnist.

Marrus, Michael. *Mr. Sam: The Life and Times of Samuel Bronfman.* New York: Viking, 1991.

Martel, Yann. *The Life of Pi.* Toronto: Knopf Canada, 2001.

> I promise to finish this novel eventually. I'm told, by the many people who like it and wonder why I don't, that it has a very satisfying ending.

Moore, Brian. *Judith Hearne.* London: André Deutsch, 1955.

> Richler first brought Moore's manuscript to the attention of his own British publisher André Deutsch. Moore's first novel was later published under the title *The Lonely Passion of Judith Hearne.*

Orwell, George. *England Your England and Other Essays.* London: Secker and Warburg, 1953.

> This collection includes Orwell's essay "Why I Write," a title Richler used for his own declaration of his literary principles.

Ozick, Cynthia. *Fame & Folly.* New York: Alfred A. Knopf, 1996.

> Of particular interest is Ozick's essay "Alfred Chester's Wig," a moving reminiscence of a literary rivalry. Chester, who is mainly forgotten now, was a big deal in the 1950s and was in Paris around the same time as Richler.

Richler, Daniel. *Kicking Tomorrow.* Toronto: McClelland and Stewart, 1991.

Richler, Emma. *Sister Crazy.* Toronto: Knopf Canada, 2001.

Rosenberg, Leah. *The Errand Runner: Reflections of a Rabbi's Daughter.* Toronto: J. Wiley & Sons, 1981.

Roth, Philip. *Patrimony: A True Story.* New York: Simon & Schuster, 1991.

> For my money, this is the best memoir around.

——*Reading Myself and Others.* New York: Farrar, Strauss and Giroux, 1975.

> Richler never apologized and never explained, but Roth, in this book, does a lot of both. Still, self-justification is seldom this engaging.

Schiff, Stacey. *Véra (Mrs. Vladimir Nabokov).* New York: Random House, 1999.

Schulberg, Budd. *What Makes Sammy Run?* New York: Vintage, 1993.

Shapiro, Lionel. *The Sixth of June.* New York:Doubleday, 1955.

Southern, Terry and Mason Hoffenberg. *Candy.* New York: G.P. Putnam's Sons, 1958.

Symons, A.J.A. *The Quest for Corvo: An Experiment in Biography.* New York: New York Review of Books, 2001.

> First published in 1934, this oddball quest for an obscure writer by an obsessed biographer was a favourite of Richler's. Symons believed that "biographers choose their subjects because they find some image of themselves there."

Theroux, Paul. *Sir Vidia's Shadow: A Friendship Across Five Continents.* Toronto: McClelland and Stewart, 1998.

> Nasty but compelling.

Updike, John. *More Matter: Essays and Criticism.* New York: Alfred A. Knopf, 1999.

> This collection includes Updike's *New Yorker* review of *Barney's Version,* which praises Richler for pioneering "the geriatric novel." Updike seems to be coming to Richler late. He also writes, "Not since the late Stanley Elkin and the early Philip Roth have I seen a writer take such uninhibited delight in caricaturing Jewish types."

——*Self-Consciousness: Memoirs.* New York: Alfred A. Knopf, 1989.

Weaver, Robert, ed. *The First Five Years: A Selection from The Tamarack Review.* Oxford: Oxford University Press, 1962.

> This retrospective includes Richler's 1957 interview with Nathan Cohen as well as Richler's short story "Mortimer Griffin, Shalinsky, and How They Settled the Jewish Question."

Weintraub, William. *Getting Started: A Memoir of the 1950s.* Toronto: McClelland and Stewart, 2001.

> An invaluable look at young writers starting out, it includes the early correspondence between the author and Richler, Mavis Gallant, and Brian Moore.

Wilson, Edmund. *O Canada: An American's Notes on Canadian Culture.* New York: Farrar, Strauss and Giroux, 1965.

Wisse, Ruth R. *The Modern Jewish Canon: A Journey Through Language and Culture.* New York: The Free Press, 2000.